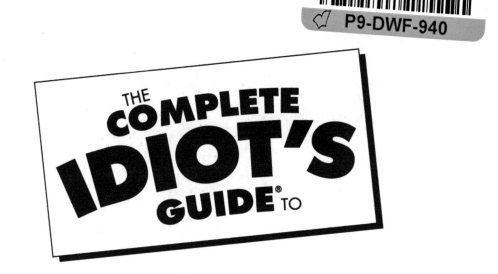

THE COMPLETE **IDIOT'S** GUIDE® TO

Long-Term Care Planning

by Marilee Driscoll

ALPHA

A member of Penguin Group (USA) Inc.

I dedicate this book to my grandmother, Josepha Schreiner.

Copyright © 2003 by Marilee Driscoll

International Standard Book Number: 0-02-864380-1
Library of Congress Catalog Card Number: 2002110186

06   05   8   7   6   5   4   3

Interpretation of the printing code: The rightmost number of the first series of numbers is the year of the book's printing; the rightmost number of the second series of numbers is the number of the book's printing. For example, a printing code of 02-1 shows that the first printing occurred in 2002.

Printed in the United States of America

Note: This publication contains the opinions and ideas of its author. It is intended to provide helpful and informative material on the subject matter covered. It is sold with the understanding that the author and publisher are not engaged in rendering professional services in the book. If the reader requires personal assistance or advice, a competent professional should be consulted.

Publisher: *Marie Butler-Knight*
Product Manager: *Phil Kitchel*
Managing Editor: *Jennifer Chisholm*
Acquisitions Editor: *Mike Sanders*
Development Editor: *Michael Koch*
Production Editor: *Billy Fields*
Copy Editor: *Amy Borrelli*
Illustrator: *Chris Eliopoulos*
Cover/Book Designer: *Trina Wurst*
Indexer: *Julie Bess*
Layout/Proofreading: *John Etchison, Brad Lenser*

Contents at a Glance

Contents

Foreword

Like everyone, our readers are concerned about investing wisely, saving for retirement, and reaching their financial goals. But one major issue could upset all of these plans: What will happen to their money if they end up needing long-term care?

It's a legitimate concern: The average cost of a private room in a nursing home now tops $61,000 per year—and round-the-clock care in your home tends to be even pricier. Either you've seen your parents struggle with these costs or you're concerned about them yourself. And the numbers aren't getting any easier to swallow: If the price continues to rise by 5 percent annually, 1 year of care could cost more than $160,000 in 20 years—just in time for most Baby Boomers to reach the age when they're likely to need assistance. At that price, even a short need for care could quickly destroy the retirement nest egg that you've carefully built over several decades.

The good news is that there are plenty of strategies to help you plan for long-term care expenses. Whether you're in your 40s or your 80s, you can take steps now to lessen the financial blow. The more planning you do in advance, the more options you'll have when you finally need care—whether you end up getting it in a nursing home, in your own home, or in an assisted-living facility.

That's why this book is so helpful. It's the only guide that explains the entire range of options for funding long-term care, and it's presented objectively by an expert who knows the issues.

Marilee Driscoll has been educating people about long-term care funding options for years and is known for her ability to translate complex issues into understandable terms. She's dealt with the subject from all sides—she speaks to consumer groups and reporters throughout the country and she teaches CPAs, insurance agents, and other specialists about the issues. She's a key resource who is good at explaining not only the pros and cons of long-term care insurance, but also how to get the best deals and how government incentives can help. And she reveals some secrets of the industry— like how two policies can look similar but end up being very different at payout time. In this *Complete Idiot's Guide*, you'll learn about all the details that will help you make smart buying decisions.

But this book stands out because it also explains alternatives to long-term care insurance. It's a much-needed reference for everyone—even people who don't qualify for or can't afford the insurance option. Marilee shows everyone how to make the most of government programs, the truth about Medicaid, and she'll help you find many other places where you can uncover money to pay for care.

Long-term care planning is a giant issue that everyone should be concerned about. You can always hope that you won't become one of the millions of Americans who end up needing this type of care, but the best strategy is to plan for the possibility now so you won't have to be anxious about it in the future. After reading this book, you'll understand all of your choices and be able to take action—which should take a giant worry off your shoulders.

—Kimberly Lankford, contributing editor, *Kiplinger's Personal Finance Magazine*

Introduction

The statistics are bad news for people planning on secure retirement. More than 50 percent of people age 65 today will need long-term care before they pass away. This care, which can be given in your own home, an assisted living facility, or in another facility like a nursing home, can cost $50,000 per year and more.

Much of this care is provided for free by unpaid family members and friends. Of all paid care, 23 percent is paid for out of pocket, by personal checks drawn against retirement income and life savings. Medicare pays only another 14 percent of the total bill for paid care services. Medicaid is the biggest payer of long-term care, paying 45 percent of the bill—but you must be poor to qualify. Long-term care insurance will pay for this expense, but this relatively new type of insurance is not for everyone.

Employers such as the federal government are rolling out payroll-deduction long-term care insurance. Should you buy? You want to leave money to your kids; should you do Medicaid planning?

Objective information on long-term care planning is extremely hard to access. But that's no excuse for not planning. The less planning that we do, the more that we rely on luck. And that's not a plan most people are comfortable with.

What's *your* best choice? *The Complete Idiot's Guide to Long-Term Care Planning* presents the raw facts, the pluses—and minuses—of long-term care insurance, Medicaid planning, and other ways to pay for long-term care. The information in this book, combined with legal and financial advice on options available in your state, will help you pull together a plan that you understand, and can live with.

Who Should Read This Book

This book is chockfull of information for people who want to take care of their retirement planning; anyone who is thinking of buying long-term care insurance; people who are thinking of doing Medicaid planning; consumers who fear losing their life savings to long-term care costs; sons or daughters who may become responsible for their aging parents; financial and legal advisors who help people do retirement planning; and people who has already bought long-term care insurance but aren't sure that they did the right thing—or that they have the right policy.

How to Use This Book

The Complete Idiot's Guide to Long-Term Care Planning is divided into six parts.

Part 1, "The Truth About LTC," introduces you to long-term care choices, and how your method of payment can influence your choices when you need care and how to put together a game plan for doing long-term care planning.

Part 2, "Paying with Your Own Money," explains what assets you can use to pay long-term care, including some assets that you never thought could be used in this way. Should you use your own money to pay for long-term care, purchase an insurance policy instead, or a little of both?

Part 3, "Government Programs," introduces government programs such as the Veteran's Administration and Medicare that pay for some long-term care for some people. Find out if you should plan on these programs, and also how state and federal governments are encouraging you to buy insurance.

Part 4, "The Truth About LTC Insurance," helps you find the long-term care insurance that's right for you. Can you even qualify for it if you want it—from a health point of view? Where should you buy it—at your workplace or through an insurance agent? And since every strategy has pluses and minuses—what are the top five problems with this insurance?

Part 5, "A Buyer's Guide to LTC Insurance," explains what you need to know to choose a good policy that is properly designed.

Part 6, "The Truth About Medicaid," covers the limitations of the system. Medicaid planning could be a great move for you, or the biggest mistake that you'll make for the rest of your life.

Finally, the appendixes provide resources for you to supplement the information in this book. From your state's Division of Insurance, Medicaid Department, to helpful websites, they're all here!

If you have a question about only one particular aspect of LTC planning, you can target the respective chapter for answers. However, you should read Chapters 1, 2, and 3 to truly understand what you are planning for. In these chapters, you'll read about the housing choices and other decisions made by people and their loved ones when long-term care is needed. Almost everyone will want to read Chapter 4.

Extras

Throughout the book, you will also encounter many more tidbits of information that have been highlighted by friendly icons. Here's what to expect:

Wisdom of the Aged

This box offers ideas and tidbits that I think are interesting, but they're not vital to your long-term planning process. If you're in a hurry, you may want to skip over them.

LTC Lowdown

This box captures advice and tips that I would tell you if we were meeting in person.

Truth & Consequences

This box provides information that you might not think of, unless, of course, you've been studying long-term care planning for a few years. Check these boxes to make sure you avoid planning mistakes.

Marilee's Memo

This box features definitions for terms that you may not be very familiar with. Long-term care planning includes words from the legal, medical, and financial world, so I've tried to translate them into words you know.

Acknowledgments

No author is an island, and my insights into and knowledge of long-term care planning were enriched by a number of people, including Aaron Amarnick, Cynthia A. Bascetta, Peter H. Bell, Alexander A. Bove Jr. Esq., Meredith Brown, Steve Cohen Esq., Gary Corliss, Guy Cumbie, John Cutler, Bill Driscoll, Corrine Duncan, Steve Ellis, Paul Forte, Jolene D. Fullerton, Ed Jette, Samuel X. Kaplan, Lindy Keay, Ruthann Lacey Esq., Ralph Leisle, Harry Margolis Esq., Kathryn Melendy, Jessica Miller, Paul Moe, Steve Moses, Eric R. Oalican Esq., Ted Pass, Mike Pinkans, Kate Salmon Robinson, Victoria Ross, Ronnie Smith, Sharon Spoon, Claude Thau, Sandra Timmermann, and Jane Washburn. Many thanks also to the dozens of people over the years who have given me the gift of sharing their personal long-term care stories.

This book wouldn't have been possible without the guidance of Beth Chapman, Dee Lee, and Nancy Michaels, the assistance of Eileen Fortunato and Eileen Lutz, and the loving support of my family.

Thank you all.

Trademarks

Part 1

The Truth About LTC

Long-term care. Home health care. Rest homes. Nursing homes. Why should you worry about these topics now? You may be working hard, with obligations and bills up to here. Maybe you're retired, comfortably; you're "all set."

In this part I'll explore why each one of us should consider long-term care planning—and what we're planning for. I'll take a look at how your financial situation can directly impact where you live when you need care. And, in Chapter 4, I'll direct you to the chapters in this book that will be most helpful to your situation. Everyone, no matter their health or their money situation, can benefit from planning now. Let's start!

Chapter 1

Why You Should Care About LTC Planning

In This Chapter

- ◆ The perfect retirement plan—NOT!
- ◆ The mistake to avoid at all costs
- ◆ As options grow, funding is scarce
- ◆ It's only natural to need help

Are you planning on living a long time? Have you noticed the television commercials showing silver-haired seniors whooping it up in convertibles and on dance floors? The good news is that we are living longer. And at any given age, many of us are more active than our parents were at that age. Chalk it up to knowledge of nutrition, better medical care, and those hours working out at the gym. Even so, we don't tango endlessly into the sunset. At some point, most of us will experience either a physical loss or mental loss that leaves us dependent on others for help. At some point, it is likely we will need long-term care.

Marilee's Memo

Longer lifespans make LTC almost inevitable. In the early 1900s the average life expectancy was 46; that figure has nearly doubled. Life expectancies are now 74 for men and 80 for women. The fastest-growing segment of our population (according to the U.S. Census Bureau) is age 85+. Eighty percent of people age 85+ need assistance. More than one in two Americans age 65 now will need long-term care before they pass away.

Long-term care can cost $50,000 per year and up. It is not covered by health insurance or any government program except Medicaid. There are two huge problems with relying on Medicaid for LTC: It requires that recipients be poor to qualify, and it has what policymakers and lawyers call "an institutional bias." In other words, in most states Medicaid will pay for care only in the last place on earth you want to be: the nursing home.

Longer lifespans have placed stress on the two big government programs that most Americans count on for security in retirement: Medicare and Social Security. Americans who want to stay in their own home as they age, and who don't want to rely on government programs, have no choice: They must plan how they will pay privately for their own long-term care. This book gives you the information you need to make an educated decision about the best way for you to do that.

Long-Term Care and Your Retirement Plan

We've all seen the face of long-term care. Some have witnessed firsthand the financial, physical, and emotional challenges of long-term care with a relative or friend. Regardless of our personal experiences, we've heard of the challenges faced by Ronald Reagan, Christopher Reeve, Michael J. Fox, Janet Reno, Muhammad Ali, and others. Mitch Albom's book, *Tuesdays with Morrie: An Old Man, a Young Man, and Life's Greatest Lesson*, on the best-seller list for what seems like an eternity, has further raised the country's awareness of debilitating, chronic disease and long-term care.

As some of the examples just mentioned show, the need for long-term care doesn't always hit during retirement years. As we plan for retirement, we must plan for the possibility that we may not be healthy until age 65. If it makes sense to buy life and disability insurance during our working years, then it must make sense to buy long-term care insurance. After all, the life insurance provides our family money when we're no longer able to. But what if, instead of dying, we live and need long-term care? The financial impact on our family is even worse—we are no longer earning money, and someone needs to take care of us. Disability insurance will replace our paycheck, but neither disability nor health insurance will pay for someone to provide our long-term care.

And, if the need for long-term care strikes after age 65, Medicare, like the health insurance we have under age 65, won't cover this expense over the long run. Just as disability is the greatest threat to our financial security during our working years, long-term care is the greatest threat to financial security in retirement. And woe to the working-age adult whose disability requires long-term care. No disability-insurance plan or retirement-savings plan is complete without long-term care planning.

How Long Does LTC Last?

OK, say we know what long-term care costs annually. But when we need long-term care, how long do we need it for? It seems like a really easy question, but it's actually a tough one to get our arms around. Here's why: We could look at the average length of nursing home stays, but that is misleading, because many people are in a nursing home for only a few days or week to recover from a hospital stay. So the average nursing home stay, which is between 2.5 and 3.0 years, is deceptively short.

We could look at the claims experience of insurance companies selling LTC insurance. But that would underreport the actual time that people need long-term care—once they've reached their policy maximum benefit, the claim is closed and future care isn't tracked. So, for example, someone with a three-year benefit-period policy who has collected benefits for three years is no longer tracked by the insurer—even though the person may receive many more years of care.

There's another problem: It is estimated that 80 percent of the long-term care in this country is provided by family and friends. This unpaid care is called informal caregiving. No organization tracks this care. So imagine the months or even years of informal care someone receives at home before he or she enters a nursing home. That isn't captured anywhere. Only paid professional care is captured in home health care statistics. I think that it's smart to realize that most statistics that you see are underreporting the length of LTC received—that the problem is even worse and more daunting than is being reported.

There are studies right now, commissioned by both government entities and the insurance industry, to get better data on the real length of time that people need long-term care. Stay tuned.

LTC Lowdown

A decline in health that results in a need for long-term care attacks and depletes the best retirement plans. Not many individuals and couples have planned for an extra $50,000 or more per year built into their retirement planning ... and that figure is *per person*!

What Are the Causes of LTC?

What causes the need for long-term care? The answer very much depends on the age group in question. AUL LTC Solutions, Inc., in Avon, Connecticut, works with well over a dozen long-term care insurance companies and has compiled the following information.

The leading causes of long-term care claims under age 65 (in alphabetical order) are as follows:

◆ Arthritis

◆ Cancer

◆ Injury

◆ Malfunctions of the nervous system

◆ Stroke

The leading causes of long-term care claims over age 65 (in alphabetical order) are as follows:

◆ Alzheimer's

◆ Cancer

◆ Diabetes

◆ Injury

◆ Malfunctions of the nervous system

LTC and the Middle Class

Long-term care planning is a dilemma unique to the middle class. The rich have always had the option of private paying for any care they desire, either in their home or the facility of their choice. The poor have always had government-funded welfare options to rely on: namely, Medicaid (the government welfare program that is the biggest payer of long-term care in this country).

The federal government's General Accounting Office reports that 23 percent of the nation's long-term care bill is paid for out of pocket. That means people writing personal checks, against their life savings and their retirement income. These checks are primarily written by the middle class, I believe, in an effort to avoid having to go to a Medicaid nursing home bed.

The dilemma of the middle class and long-term care has never been as eloquently portrayed as in the 1989 PBS documentary featuring Walter Cronkite, *Can't Afford to Grow Old*. In this documentary, we see family after family exhausting their life savings to keep loved ones out of nursing homes. We see the tragic plight of an older, single woman who has run out of money for the home care that she needs. She must face the reality of a move to a nursing home, since the government programs in her area won't pay for the small amount of home care she needs

Marilee's Memo

Private-paying for long-term care means paying with either your own money or long-term care insurance. Publicly funded long-term care, in contrast, would be paid by government programs such as Medicare or Medicaid. Generally, people who pay for their care with their own money have more choices than those on publicly funded programs.

each day. We hear the heartbreak as she discussed what to do with her closest friends—her pets that aren't allowed in the nursing home. The result of not having enough money to private pay for extended LTC can be gut-wrenchingly painful.

Unless you have enough money to private pay for extended LTC (check out Appendix E for average costs in your state), you must plan for long-term care. The price of not planning can be much too high.

Forever Young in America

I'm not sure what the root of it is, but most Americans have a fear of growing old and of the elderly. Perhaps it's our history of fighting tooth and nail for independence—and elders remind us that, as we age, we are interdependent or even fully dependent on others. Maybe it's in our blood—as many of our ancestors came over on boats to the New World, and only the heartiest survived. The settlers who crossed America in wagon trains buried along their journey all but the strongest. Maybe, in our mind's eye, we still see ourselves as robust trailblazers, with no use for the weaker ones among us.

We all know that famous line from a Who song, "Hope I die before I get old." Here's another song lyric, sung by the group Blondie: "Die young, stay pretty."

If you are lucky, when you were young you experienced a close friendship with at least one senior citizen. You needed to slow down your quick walking pace so that the two of you could enjoy a stroll. You listened as your friend reminiscenced of a time before you were alive. He was your friend, and you weren't focused on the age difference.

One day, you noticed that your friend was old. Perhaps it was a jar he couldn't open, or the slope of his back that you hadn't noticed before. You noticed he was becoming dependent … dependent on the kindness of friends like you and relatives who lived nearby. You worried about him being alone. One day, you will be like he was, and your friends and loved ones will worry about you.

Slowing down and needing help is a normal part of aging. For all the hoopla about active retirements and whiz-bang miracle medical devices, it's almost inevitable that most of us will need help as we age. As the saying goes, "Something's got to get you!" Perhaps this help will be a few days at the end of our lives. Perhaps we will need years of help, as the average life span of someone diagnosed with Alzheimer's disease is nine years.

The need for long-term care is not necessarily tied into great physical or mental decrepitude and despair. Perhaps our need for care will be similar to my grandma's. She was healthy as a horse and sharp as a tack until age 99, but her hands were crippled and frozen by arthritis. She did exercises every morning until age 93, and had taken such good care of herself that she remained active and alert while needing more than 10 years of long-term care assistance.

Although the odds of needing long-term care increase as we get older, the need for long-term care can hit us at any age. Forty-three percent of people in this country receiving long-term care are under age 65. This statistic sounds like it can't be right, doesn't it? Here's what's behind it: Only 12 percent of the total population of the United States is under age 65 (source: 2000 Census). So because those under age 65 make up the vast majority of people living in our country (88 percent), they weigh in at 43 percent of those requiring long-term care. Put another way, although the age 65+ population makes up only 12 percent of the total population, they account for 57 percent of those receiving long-term care. So if you are over age 65, your odds of needing long-term care is almost ten times more than someone under age 65.

By the way, don't think that the United States is unique in floundering about trying to figure out how to finance care for its aging population. Many, many countries, such as Japan and Germany to name only two, are grappling with the same challenge.

The Old Woman and the System

Like most people, I became familiar with the problem of long-term care financing only when a family member had a crisis. My beloved grandmother, who I called Nanny, passed away at age 99 after spending 10 years in a nursing home. Years earlier, I spent every Saturday night at her house. She cut lilacs for the vase next to my bed, so that their fragrance would fill the room. She made me ice cream sodas as a special treat, and curled my hair using an old-fashioned curling iron that she heated in the flame of her gas stove. When she needed the kind of long-term care that we could no longer provide her in our home, she went to the facility that she proudly referred to as where "the rich people go to." She had two things going for her—her doctor was on the nursing facility's board of directors, and she was private-pay—she had a pile of money from the sale of her house. She spent this money on her care and eventually ended up on Medicaid. I remember her tears when she explained to me that she couldn't buy me a wedding present—she had no money. She had said for years, "I want to live to see you get married," and she was devastated that, when the day came, she wasn't able to give me a special gift. Did it matter to me? Of course not—the greatest gift my grandmother gave me was herself—but this proud woman's dignity was robbed by the crazy system that we have in this country to pay for long-term care.

Young-Old and Old-Old Planning

The concept of retirement is now being redefined, as we live longer and our society changes. One the one hand, some people are taking early retirement, stopping work in their early 50s. Planning for how to get traditional health-care coverage for a young retiree until Medicare starts at 65 can be a formidable problem. And, of course, the early retiree also has to plan for future long-term care.

Wisdom of the Aged

"Although 'elder care' is a new phrase and a new concept, over 20 percent of today's workforce, about 120 million strong, expects to assume elder-care responsibility for parents or other seniors over the next three or four years. By 2005, 37 percent of U.S. workers will be ages 40 to 54, the prime years for caring for elderly parents. Conservatively, one in three of us will care for an elder by the year 2020."

—From the book *Don't Put Me in a Nursing Home*, by Claude Amarnick, D.O.

The concept of retirement—a time in your life where you either do not work or work less—is a relatively new one. The life expectancy at birth for a male born in 1950 was only 65 years. Now we know that we are living many, many years in retirement.

Geriatricians have started recognizing two phases of retirement: "young-old" and "old-old." Young-old is the early years of retirement, when an individual now has the time and the health to pursue the activities that we normally associate with retirement. That phase may last for a few months, or many years.

Normally a decline in health marks that beginning of our old-old retirement. Sometimes old-old is used to describe people older than 85. Very few old-old people escape the need for long-term care. In fact, the need for LTC grows dramatically in the years after age 65. From ages 65 to 74, 12.1 percent of people need long-term care. From ages 75 to 84, 27.2 percent need long-term care. For people over age 85, 69.8 percent need long-term care. It's estimated that more than 90 percent of the old-old population needs some kind of assistance.

As a society, if we plan at all for retirement, we plan for funding the activities and travel of young-old retirement. The financial burden of long-term care for the old-old is often neglected. By the time the retiree realizes this gap in his or her retirement plan, it is often too late to avoid exhausting assets or having to rely on government programs for the poor.

Your Mission

In addition to figuring out how to cover your living expenses in retirement, you also need to give some thought to how to cover the increased living expenses associated with needing long-term care. Am I Chicken Little? A visit to your local nursing home will prove I'm not. There you will find dozens of older *people* (primarily women—women outlive their husbands after having provided their husbands care at home) who never planned on spending their final years in a nursing home. Many of them could be receiving their care somewhere else, but they're not, for one reason—they don't have the money to private pay for care anywhere else, and the government's Medicaid program is paying their bill. As I mentioned before, in most states Medicaid funds nursing home care, not home care. Money talks, and people on Medicaid are relatively voiceless.

The Government's Solution

One of the major reasons that many consumers decide *not* to plan for long-term care is this: They are waiting for a new federal program that will cover long-term care, like Medicare pays for their health care.

When President Clinton proposed massive health insurance reform in 1993, many people thought the plan would cover long-term care. There were provisions for long-term care in the proposed program, but the long-term care benefits were based on financial need, and were therefore not available to many Americans. As you know, the proposed health care reform didn't pass. Proposed legislation since then has revolved around modest tax credits for family caregivers and incentives to purchase private long-term care insurance.

However, there persists even to this day a perception among many Americans that the limited long-term care coverage available through Medicare and Medicaid will some-day be enhanced through a new government plan. "Take a look at the statistics," they argue. "Americans are getting older, they need long-term care. They want to receive care in their own home, not in Medicaid nursing home beds. Hard-working Americans shouldn't have to bankrupt themselves paying for long-term care. The current system doesn't make sense, and the federal government will have to respond with new programs." All these statements make sense; however, in my opinion and the opinion of many others, it's not going to happen.

There are a number of reasons that a sweeping new federal program to pay for long-term care reform is unlikely to happen. The most important is economic. Our legislators are struggling to find ways to keep Medicare, Social Security, and Medicaid funded. Talking with members of Congress, it is clear that they are looking toward private solutions to pay for long-term care. That means private-pay—your wallet paying dollar-for-dollar for LTC services or you wallet having bought long-term care insurance—and paying pennies for dollars of benefits. Medicaid will remain the program of last resort—for those who are poor and cannot afford private insurance.

There is a lot of evidence that the federal government will not be enhancing its long-term care benefits for citizens. Back in the summer of 1996, the Health Insurance Portability and Accountability Act (HIPAA) gave us a tax deduction for qualified long-term care insurance policies (in effect since January 1, 1997).

HIPAA was the first act of Congress to encourage Americans to do private long-term care planning. A second bill, the Long-Term Care Security Act, was passed unanimously by Congress and signed into law in the fall of 2000. This law instructed the U.S. Office of Personnel Management (OPM) to make long-term care insurance available to the federal employees, retirees, and eligible family members and eligible others, and to what is referred to as the "federal family." That payroll-deduction plan was rolled out in early 2002.

As this book goes to press, the U.S. Congress is considering other bills to encourage Americans to plan to pay for long-term care privately. One bill would make it easier for taxpayers with LTC insurance policies to qualify for the federal tax deduction for this coverage. Currently, individuals need to itemize and have high medical expenses to take this deduction. Other plans being considered on Capitol Hill have favorable implications for citizens doing long-term care planning. They include bills which would make the tax treatment of life settlements (the sale of a life insurance policy by a senior—discussed in Chapter 7) as favorable as that of viatical settlements (the tax-favored sale of life insurance by someone of any age who is terminally ill), and also new tax breaks for taxpayers who buy annuities. Annuities are a type of tax-favored accumulation investment vehicle designed for retirement savings, which can be turned into an income that you can't outlive. They can be used to pay for long-term care, or to fund the purchase of long-term care insurance (see Chapter 6).

HIPAA, the federal employee long-term care insurance program, and pending legislation are all programs that show the government's intention: to provide taxpayers with incentives to do their own long-term care planning. The messages from Washington are consistent and clear: The chance of a new government program to pay for long-term care is not only remote—it's not even being discussed.

State governments are encouraging residents to plan for their future long-term costs, too. Approximately half of the 50 states have either tax credits or tax deductions for long-term care insurance. Some states have other incentives, such as partnership programs, for people to purchase long-term care insurance. (For more details on government incentives and partnership programs, refer to Chapter 12.)

The Least You Need to Know

♦ The need for long-term care can strike at any age. Many people need long-term care before age 65.

♦ Long-term care consists of help with everyday activities, such as getting dressed and taking a bath.

♦ Medicare and health insurance do not pay for or provide long-term care.

♦ Medicaid, the government program for the poor, is the biggest payer of LTC in the country. It will not pay for home care in most states.

♦ The federal government and many state governments are promoting private paying for long-term care by offering tax and other incentives.

Where Do You Want to Live When You Grow Up?

In This Chapter

- ◆ Why home may not be as sweet as they say it is
- ◆ A primer on home health-care services
- ◆ The ABC of CCRCs and other care options
- ◆ A closer look at assisted living

Where do you want to live as you age? If your health declines? If your spouse passes away? Your finances can make these housing choices a reality—or a pipe dream. If you don't know what your housing options and desires are, it's tougher to do long-term care planning.

The best time to look into housing options is definitely before you need to, and probably before you want to. After all, who wants to consider the fact that one day keeping up a house and a yard may become too much? That climbing the stairs to a second-floor bedroom may become impossible? That to remain at home you may need to bring in home health care? Here's the reward for being practical: Any legwork and planning that you do today is likely to increase your choice of housing options in the future.

Let's take a look at what housing choices are out there, and what they cost. There are many options in between staying in the home where you've lived the last few years (or decades) and moving to a nursing home—and they grow more plentiful each year.

> **CAUTION**
>
> **Truth & Consequences** _____
>
> Have you seen the bumper sticker "Be nice to your kids. They choose your nursing home"? The truth is that by refusing to consider long-term care or "what-if" planning scenarios, many people sign themselves up for nursing home living (described in detail in Chapter 3), if they want to or not. By planning where and how you'd like to live as you grow old, and lining up the means to pay for it, you shift the burden off the shoulders of your children and other family members, and assert your right to control your own life. Make your plans. Share the plans with your family and your advisors. Fund the plans. I hope you never need them, but doesn't it feel great to be prepared?

Growin' Old in Your Own Home Sweet Home

When I talk to a roomful of people and ask where they'd like to live as they age, the resounding answer is almost always "Home!" Sometimes a troublemaker in the crowd will yell out, "Nursing home!" Most of us, however, plan on staying at home. Whether we are able to do so or not is a different matter.

When I write about the ability to stay at home, I mean the ability to stay home safely and happily. Unfortunately, there are many seniors who live in misery in their homes, unable to cook and care for themselves and their surroundings. They don't have money to hire help, and don't have friends and family who care. None of us plan for that kind of existence. So how can we stay in our own home as we age, to do what these days is commonly called "aging in place"?

One of the things that you can do right now, regardless of your age, is to plan ahead. There are some homes in which you are more likely to be able to "age in place" than others. I'm talking about homes that have been designed or updated with senior-friendly touches. If you are renovating or decorating a room or house, think long-term. Replace old doorknobs with attractive door levers (easier for arthritic hands to use); widen doorways (for wheelchair access); add grab bars. These kinds of renovations can be difficult to accomplish when the long-term care crisis hits.

Senior-friendly house planning can save you from injury and/or future expense as you age. More and more builders and renovators are sensitive to these issues; some are even specializing in senior-friendly work. When buying a house that you may want to stay in as you age, look for the following advantages: one level living; no steep or long driveways; location within walking distance of stores and doctors, or on a bus line. More and more seniors are moving into a senior-friendly environment while they are still healthy, to make their lives easier when they age and their health changes.

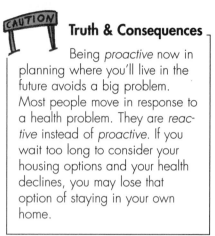

Truth & Consequences

Being *proactive* now in planning where you'll live in the future avoids a big problem. Most people move in response to a health problem. They are *reactive* instead of *proactive*. If you wait too long to consider your housing options and your health declines, you may lose that option of staying in your own home.

Home and Not Alone: Spouse

One of the biggest factors that determines if someone ages in his or her own home is the presence of a healthy spouse. The first member of the couple to need long-term care almost always receives this care at home. The healthy spouse usually does everything he or she can to keep up the household and keep the ailing husband or wife at home.

When a couple says that they are planning to live in their house for the rest of their lives, it's important that they plan for a reality they'd rather not think about: how the spouse who will be left alone after the first spouse dies will live. Who will be the surviving spouse's caregiver? Is the house senior-friendly? Does it have room for a live-in caregiver? Is there money to bring in home care?

When it comes to long-term care planning, women are often more practical than men. Women are the traditional caregivers (although this is changing). The average married woman knows that she is likely to be alone at the end of her life, and she is motivated to plan for this. When married couples do long-term care planning, this planning is, effectively, a gift for the wife. If they have planned for private long-term care funding, the funds allow her to bring help into the home when her husband needs long-term care. Part-time professional home health care lifts some of the burden of caregiving off her shoulders. If the couple has done Medicaid planning, her finances are protected as she seeks out Medicaid coverage for her spouse. There are few things sadder than the widow of a man who refused to plan for long-term care, whose health and finances have been ruined by her spouse's long-term care needs.

The Quiet Man and His Wife

Talking about caregiving, I am reminded of an elderly gentleman I see several times a week on my neighborhood running route (OK, most days I walk it!).

He lives with his wife in Plymouth, Mass., in a single-story, small house, with a driveway just big enough to hold two cars. I see him because he sits all day in a lounge chair at the picture window. When I walk by, we wave at each other. His view is of the lake across the dirt road where I walk. This is his entire view of the world, as his health doesn't allow him much mobility. He sees the leaves change color in autumn, the snow fly in winter, the return of the birds to the birdfeeder by his window in the spring, and the kids who walk to the lake's beach to swim in the summer.

I can't help but compare his view to the view shared by a woman I knew in a Boston nursing home. She shared a room with three roommates. Instead of having a picture-perfect window view, they looked at walls of painted cinder block. Two of the four were bedridden; the other two sat in padded chairs next to their beds. They were barely aware of the seasons changing outside, and only the coats on the visitors betrayed the weather. You see, the windows in the room they shared were higher than eye level. They couldn't see outside at all. Imagine the difference in quality of life between the elderly man and this woman. They were both physically limited to living their lives in a chair—but what a difference the surroundings make.

I wonder what living choices the wife of the man in Plymouth will have when she is no longer able to be out and about ….

Home and Not Alone: Informal Caregivers

A healthy spouse is not the only person who can help you stay in your own home. A child, friend, or anyone else who can be with you when you need long-term care can increase your likelihood of being able to enjoy your familiar surroundings at home.

If your designated caregiver needs to work to support herself, plan now for how you will pay her for the care she provides. If she quits a full-time job to be your caregiver, keep in mind that employee benefits such as health and disability insurance may not be replaceable, and that benefits often cost 30 percent of someone's salary. Consult with an accountant, lawyer, and your property and casualty insurance agency (where you insure your residence and car) for more information on how to legally hire and pay an employee.

As you look into how to pay for informal, unlicensed caregivers, be aware that the vast majority of long-term care insurance doesn't cover unlicensed caregivers, and won't pay family members even if they are licensed. Some policies will cover both unlicensed and family caregivers, as discussed in Chapter 17.

The Medicaid program, discussed in Part 6, never pays for unlicensed or family care-givers. In most states, Medicaid pays for very little home.

LTC Lowdown

There have been reports of a new, exciting alternative to professional caregivers. *Caregiving circles* consist of a group of people who agree to take care of each other in the future. This works really well when most members are in their 50s and 60s, and only one or two members need ongoing care. But I think it must fall apart when the friends are in their 70s and 80s, and there are not enough able-bodied caregivers who can drive to and care for their disabled friends.

An Adult Child's Home

Many people plan to move in with a child when they need long-term care. If this is your plan, discuss all the details ahead of time, and have them worked out. The best time for this discussion is before your health fails. What bedroom will you inhabit, and is it easily accessible? Will an in-law suite (sometimes called an accessory apart-ment) be built for you, and who will pay for it?

From a planning point of view, discuss who will provide for care that you may need. You may want to plan on the ability to hire a home-health aide privately so that the burden of caregiving does not fall squarely on the shoulders of your loved ones.

There is an interesting housing option for seniors who want their own living space, attached to someone's (usually an adult child's) home. The Elder Cottage Housing Opportunity (ECHO) manufactures a modular home designed to be temporarily added to a single family home. When it is no longer needed, the unit can be taken off. Check with your local zoning laws to see if zoning or variances for ECHO homes are a possibility.

Independent Living—with Some Twists

Home doesn't have to be a single family house, condo, or apartment. There are other kinds of homes available that may make it easier to age in place gracefully and with dignity.

◆ **Adult communities:** This is an age-restricted development where all residents need to meet a minimum age. Normally outside home and yard maintenance is built into the fee structure. When you require long-term care, you make your own arrangements just as you would living in a house in any neighborhood, or you move to another setting.

♦ **Manufactured-home communities:** Many seniors choose to retire in retiree manufactured-home communities. They are similar to adult communities, though the homes are normally less expensive to own or rent, as they are pre-fabricated/manufactured or, in some cases, mobile homes. Some residents live in a primary residence in one place, then winter in a manufactured-home community in a warmer place.

♦ **Naturally occurring retirement communities:** This is any area where the residents have aged together. It may be a suburban residential neighborhood, where everyone bought new houses 40 years ago when they were young families, or a rent-controlled apartment building in a big city. Like other older adult communities, they often have built-in support systems, as residents who know each other check out for each other. A risk in a naturally occurring retirement community is that if residents are all frail, the value of the support system erodes. Also, the resident mix can change at any time, since there are no age restrictions in place.

♦ **Shared housing:** Remember the television sitcom *The Golden Girls*," in which four older women shared a suburban house? Some retirees choose to live with a roommate or roommates, who may or may not be relatives. Costs vary tremendously, depending on the property and the number of adults.

Weighing the Cost of Staying at Home

Besides the presence of a healthy spouse, one of the biggest factors in whether a senior in need of care can stay in his or her home is finances. The ability to pay privately for care and other services such as home maintenance and housekeeping can allow someone who otherwise would need to move to a facility to stay at home.

This is evidenced by the fact that most wealthy people do not receive their long-term care in a facility. Around-the-clock care can be outrageously expensive, easily topping $100,000 per year. Before you dismiss around-the-clock home care as something that only celebrities and members of prominent families have, consider this—I the training that I do for CPAs, most accountants in the class report having prepared a return for a client spending $100,000+ on home health care. Many of our friends and neighbors are exhausting their life savings for this type of care. Prominent examples include Katherine Hepburn, who lives in her home in Old Saybrook, Connecticut, with an army of attendants! If you are planning on remaining at home even if your health is very bad, investigate what private-duty nursing shifts and around-the-clock home health aide costs in your area.

The Blessings of Home Health-Care Services ...

Although most people say they want to stay in their home forever, not everyone can. Often, the ability to stay in your own home depends on the availability of local help and services.

These services vary dramatically state to state and even town to town. Some require payment (sometimes on a sliding scale), while others are free. Researching whether your town has the kind of services you'd need if you required home-based long-term care could be as important as planning how to pay for this care.

If you are planning on subsidized community services, be aware that you may not be able to get the services when you need them. Some communities have a one-year wait for minimal services; others have an abundance of services immediately available. Don't count on a service until you've verified that it is available locally. Also, be aware that funding for these services is often reliant on charities or state and local taxes. As such, the funding, and the program can change at any time.

The only way to get this information is to be a gumshoe; like Peter Falk in the old *Columbo* TV series, you need to do some detective work. Ask a lot of questions. There could be programs that any one source may not know about. Good sources of information on home health-care services include the following:

◆ Your personal doctor

◆ The local council on aging or senior center

◆ Home health-care agencies

◆ State executive office of elder affairs

◆ An adult child's employer's employee-assistance program

◆ Medicare supplement or HMO community liaison or claims person

◆ Charities (such as Alzheimer's Association, American Parkinson Disease Association, and so on)

◆ Meals-on-Wheels

◆ Town hall

◆ Hospitals

◆ YWCA and YMCA

◆ Places of worship

- ◆ Fraternal organizations and clubs

- ◆ Veteran's programs

- ◆ Financial and legal advisors

- ◆ Admissions directors of senior housing

- ◆ A professional geriatric-care manager

- ◆ Local librarian (sometimes a librarian is designated for senior services)

Not only do services vary by location; sometimes they vary depending on your diagnosis! Some charities, for example, offer home support services for specific diseases, such as Alzheimer's or Lou Gehrig's, only.

... And the Chances of Getting Them

You can have all the money in the world, yet if your area doesn't have the kind of services you need to stay in your own home safely, you could be forced to move to a facility—even though you could afford round-the-clock care.

As you'll learn when reading this book, money doesn't solve all the problems of long-term care. But it sure does solve a lot of them! If you live in an area that has a large population of older people, you are likely to have access to more age-related services. Both government and private businesses target these areas when deciding where to locate services. As the U.S. Census Bureau states in their report "The 65 Years and Over Population: 2000," issued October 2001, "Many government agencies use data on the older population to implement and evaluate programs and policies."

As the American population ages, without increases in funding, services will continue to be strained. This is an important reality when planning for future long-term care. The system of care delivery and financing is already not working in many areas. The need for services, driven by an aging population, is being met by fewer available governmental resources. Forward-thinking, practical people with the ability and means to plan can see that it is in their best interest do so.

Any new services will be brought, I would imagine, to those locations where the elderly population can be most efficiently served. Rural areas, where houses are miles and miles away from each other, are already feeling the pinch of scarcity of professional home-health services. The travel time between homes makes this a less practical area to serve—either by companies looking to make a profit or government entities looking to use tax dollars efficiently.

According to the U.S. Census Bureau, Clearwater, Florida, leads the list of cities with a population of 100,000 or more that have the highest proportion of people age 65 and older. In Clearwater, 21.5 percent of the residents are age 65+. Altogether, six Florida towns are listed in the top 10 of places with the highest proportion of population age 65 and older. The other four cities are Honolulu (17.8 percent), Warren, Michigan (17.3 percent), Livonia, Michigan (16.9 percent), and Scottsdale, Arizona (16.7 percent). In the year 2000 census, Florida led the country with 17.6 percent of its population age 65 and older. However, there are many counties that exceeded Florida's statewide average "seniors population rate."

When It's Time to Move

The time may come when you have to move out of your home, and being aware of this fact will help you make better decisions for your long-term care planning. According to Judie Rappaport, co-author of *Eldercare 911: The Caregiver's Complete Handbook for Making Decisions*, the top six reasons why a senior may no longer be able to live in his or her own home are …

- ◆ **Lack of transportation.** It's difficult to exist without the ability to shop for food, keep doctors appointments, or provide for other needs. When the senior can no longer drive, alternative transportation may not be available, affordable, or manageable.

- ◆ **Excessive frailness.** When 24-hour supervision is needed to help avoid falls, evacuate in a fire, prepare meals, or provide assistance with some of the activities of daily living, the cost of home care may be prohibitive or there may not be a family member or advocate available to monitor the services.

- ◆ **Severe dementia.** Aggressive or uncontrolled behavior may make it unsafe for the senior to remain at home without supervision, or may make supervision in a controlled environment necessary for the safety of all and quality of life for other family members.

- ◆ **Lack of community services.** The type, quantity, or quality of services seniors need to remain safe at home—such as no-charge or sliding-scale home care, day care, transportation, and monitoring—may not be available or the senior may not qualify for admission to the program.

- ◆ **Lack of family or advocate.** It's easier for seniors to age in their own homes with a family member or professional advocate to help look after details such as medical needs, home repair, and insurance. Frail, confused seniors who remain alone in their own homes may become easy targets for scams.

◆ **Severe illness.** When around-the-clock treatment or care with specialized medical professionals and equipment is required, a nursing home may be the most effective choice for many people. Seniors with a high net worth may have the option of bringing extensive care into their homes; for others the cost is too prohibitive.

Reading through the list of the top six reasons that seniors must enter an institution, did you notice that four of the six are, at some level, financial? The ability to afford transportation, to overcome the lack of community home care services by hiring private-pay home care, and to be able to hire 24-hour help (needed due to excessive frailness or severe illness) can save the senior from having to go to the nursing home. Seniors who plan ahead of time how to pay these expenses privately dramatically increase the odds that they can remain in their homes.

Adult Day-Care Centers

Adult day-care centers (ADCC) offer an incredibly valuable service. They provide companionship, food, and care for a loved one while the caregiver works or takes a break. Many ADCC are nonprofit, though some are for-profit. Seniors can attend from one day a week to five days a week. Typically, round-trip transportation is covered.

CAUTION

Truth & Consequences

One limitation of adult day care centers is that they may limit their program to a six-hour day. This may not be long enough for a caregiver to continue working full-time while their loved one is in the program.

These programs can allow seniors to remain living at home with a spouse or someone else who needs to work during the day. Special programs for cognitive impairment/dementia can provide a daily respite to avoid caregiver burnout.

Costs are usually very reasonable, and may include up to three meals a day. Some programs are covered by Medicaid. Most modern LTC insurance policies pay for licensed adult day-care center programs.

Continuing Care Retirement Communities (CCRCs)

A CCRC is a combination of many different senior housing options. Most CCRCs include an independent living component that is similar to an apartment or townhouse, an assisted living facility, and a skilled-nursing unit (or nursing home). Many people choose to move to a CCRC because it provides "soup-to-nuts" housing and services; the intent of most residents is to live the rest of their lives at the CCRC.

CCRCs are regulated in most, though not all, states. Terms of the written contract signed by the resident vary dramatically. Some CCRCs are pure rentals; however, most involve a buy-in with a refundable entrance fee. When a CCRC involves a buy-in, a large, up-front entrance fee, typically ranging from $75,000 to $350,000, is made. In most cases, proceeds for the sale of the resident's former primary residence are used to pay the entrance fee.

In addition to this payment, there is a monthly service fee. This monthly service fee may be level for all residents, or it may increase as the resident transitions from independent living to assisted living, then to nursing home care. In exchange for these monthly payments, the resident is promised that he or she will receive a lifetime of care.

Even under the model where residents pay the same monthly fee regardless of their level of care, the monthly fee normally increases over time, as costs rise. A uniform fee regardless of care level can be very attractive to those people who want to keep their monthly expenditure manageable, no matter what the future may hold. In many cases, long-term care insurance is bundled into the monthly fee. This takes some financial pressure off the CCRC, since it collects a benefit to provide LTC to the resident.

With many CCRCs you must be relatively healthy in order to enter. The CCRC owner is planning on residents not needing care for a certain amount of time, in order to keep the fees reasonable.

The contract specifies what percentage of the entrance fee will be reimbursed to the residents or their estates when they move or die. Typical "refund" rates would be 70 to 90 percent. The interest earned on the entrance fee is not paid to the resident, though the resident may be responsible for paying income tax liability on the inputed interest income.

What recourse do you have if the CCRC goes bankrupt? This isn't a concern with a rental CCRC—you'd just move. But if your property is not a rental, your big entrance fee could be lost in a bankruptcy, leaving you financially vulnerable, perhaps when you need long-term care. Your state's executive office of elder affairs (Appendix C) and your lawyer can help you understand any risks involved before you invest in senior housing.

Truth & Consequences

Before you sign on the CCRC contract's dotted line, ask about the history of rate increases in the monthly service fee. Does the CCRC limit the amount of increases contractually? If you already own LTC insurance, can you get a reduced monthly fee?

Some CCRCs follow a true real estate model. Units are bought and sold like single-family homes when residents move or die. Residents can make a profit on their unit if it becomes more desirable, or they can be "stuck," owning a property that they cannot sell when they want or need to.

An Assisted Living Facility by Any Other Name ...

It wasn't that long ago that there was no such thing as an assisted living facility (ALF). In the "good old days," facilities other than nursing homes had many names:

- Board-and-care homes
- Rest homes
- Personal-care homes
- Homes for the aged
- Residential-care homes
- Domiciliary-care homes

More than 500,000 people live in these licensed facilities. It is estimated that there are as many unlicensed facilities as there are licensed ones. There are many types of board-and-care homes, from homes that have two beds, to institutions with more than 1,400 beds. A variety of different services are offered, and prices vary from $400 to $4,000 per month. In some states the words "assisted living facilities" and "board-and-care home" are used interchangeably.

These facilities provide room and board for the poor, infirm, and elderly. In the 1980s, many housed chronically mentally ill individuals who had just been deinstitutionalized moved to these homes. Now, most people who live in room-and-board facilities are the frail elderly.

The smaller facilities are often in private homes, and run by a live-in operator. Traditionally, board-and-care facilities or homes have offered and continue to offer the lowest-cost option for facility care.

The Pros and Cons of Assisted Living

The assisted living industry has been described as "board and care for the rich." Most residents of assisted living are not rich, but they are predominantly upper-middle class or wealthy.

Many seniors who look into assisted living suffer sticker shock when they see the base monthly payment, which is typically $2,000 to $5,000. Most seniors have no mortgage payments, and when they do their payments typically are in the hundreds, not thousands, of dollars. A monthly payment of $2,000 or more seems outrageous to them. In the case of ALFs, however, this monthly payment usually includes meals (maybe two or three a day) and weekly housekeeping, and may include laundry and even daily care assistance. In any event, assisted living is both less expensive and more desirable than nursing home care.

Although some ALFs are too expensive for most seniors, the industry has responded in recent years with much more affordable facilities. If you looked at assisted living in the 1990s but balked due to the high cost, take another look. A lot has changed.

There are some aspects of ALFs that are not usually offered in board-and-care settings, including the ability to lock doors, have a private bathroom, live in a private apartment setting instead of only a bedroom, and "order up" care help and perhaps nursing services.

ALFs offer peace of mind for the resident and his or her family. The facility is designed to maximize the independence, safety, and quality of life for the senior.

More and more people are planning on spending their senior years in an ALF. The reasons are obvious to anyone who has been to visit one of these attractive facilities. They offer apartment-style living, with community dining rooms that resemble restaurants. The housekeeping, laundry service, help with bathing and other activities of daily living, and medication reminders add up to a very attractive package for most seniors.

In some states, ALFs provide health care and nursing care; regulations in other states prohibit ALFs from offering those services. Many ALFs offer a busy activity schedule, shuttle service, and sometimes on-site amenities such as health clubs and hair salons. Most ALFs are rentals, with the monthly rental cost usually much less expensive than living in a nursing home. Some ALFs follow a true real estate model. Units are bought and sold like single-family homes.

There is currently no federal oversight of ALFs. Compare this to nursing home care, where most facilities are subject to federal oversight, because Medicare and Medicaid pay for so many residents. ALFs are regulated in most states, but not all states regulate ALFs. This lack of uniformity and regulation places a tremendous burden on the consumer. Ask to see a contract in advance, and review it closely.

ALFs offer the best of both worlds: the privacy and independence of apartment living with the services most needed by seniors. An apartment in an ALF looks much like any other apartment, with one exception: There is no stove. Many units do have a microwave, kitchen sink, and refrigerator. Most meals are eaten in a community dining room.

The Best-Selling Author

My mother was a best-selling author. I am an insurance agent who also happens to have published a master's thesis on gerontology. My mother's story may be helpful to others doing long-term care planning.

We were lucky in that while she was still active, my mother wanted to plan for her future care needs. Mom had money, but she knew how expensive care could be. She wanted money specifically allocated for long-term care, so she bought long-term care insurance. Because of her planning, there was no conflict among her children with how her money should be spent.

When Mom first needed long-term care, we started out with home health care. She had been diagnosed with Parkinson's disease, and her health was failing. Home care didn't work for us. Mom lived alone in Nebraska, and I lived in California. The care was too hard to coordinate.

From home she moved to a nursing home. I started to visit once a month to watch out for her. The place looked great on paper. It didn't have a bad smell like a lot of nursing homes, but there was very little consideration for her dignity. We decided to move mom to an assisted living facility that everyone thought great, except for Mom. She called it a prison. On one visit, I found her passed out on the floor. She had hit her head again. I wasn't happy with the facility anymore, either. When I flew out to visit, I couldn't eat meals with Mom, because they required that you buy the meal ticket ahead of time.

The second assisted living facility was ideal. It was much more like a home. They had a room for me to stay there when I visited, so that I could spend more time with Mom on my trips. They took great care of Mom. She died there in early 2002.

The ability to make decisions about where Mom should live without have to worry about the money was wonderful. Besides the cost of long-term care, there are many expenses you don't necessarily think of, such as plane trips, rental cars, and hotel rooms when visiting a loved one. There were also some expenses that were not covered in the basic monthly charge at the assisted living facility. We were on firm financial footing; we didn't have to think "Boy, we have to pay for this, *too*?" One day, I saw my mom was struggling with putting on her stockings. All she had to do was ring a bell to get assistance, but Mom wouldn't do that. Trying to convince Mom to call for help whenever she needed it, I asked one of her friends if she used the available help. The woman said, "I don't ring for more help than's absolutely necessary, because I have to pay every time I do that." I felt so bad for this woman, who said she never wore stockings anymore because she couldn't put them on by herself. I wondered what else she was sacrificing. Later, I explained to Mom that she should call for help, saying "Remember, we have a policy that pays for it." Mom replied, "Oh, that was a really good idea."

I remembered what a patient in the nursing home had said to me years ago, describing another resident: "It's so horrible that she's hanging on so long, it's so expensive." Long-term care planning frees our elders from feeling like financial burdens. It gives them choices they wouldn't otherwise have.

Planning can't take away all the problems of a loved one needing long-term care, but it can take away some of the biggest ones.

CAUTION

Truth & Consequences _____

Let's say that you have an LTC insurance policy that covers assisted living facilities. However, if you move to an ALF before you need care or supervision, your policy may not pay the bill. That's because your policy benefits must be triggered in order for a claim to be paid (most are triggered by either a loss of two activities of daily living—also known as ADLs—or a cognitive impairment). If you move to an ALF because you don't feel like cooking and housekeeping anymore but you have no ADL loss or cognitive impairment, your claim will not be paid.

Living It Up or Down

It is estimated that anywhere from 15 to 70 percent of the nursing home population could live in residential-care ALFs instead. One survey reported that there is little nursing care in nursing homes. Thirty-nine percent of residents received no care by an R.N. in 24 hours. Of those who did, they received an average of 7.9 minutes.

Assisted Living facilities vary dramatically in the services provided, the type of residents that they attract, and in the "poshness" of the surroundings. Some resemble high-end private country clubs. Others are converted strip motels! As the president of a big chain of facilities once told me, "If you've seen one assisted living facility, you've seen one assisted living facility."

Shared units are inhabited either by married couples or by roommates. These units are often called companion units.

Wisdom of the Aged

An often-cited benefit of assisted living facilities is the social aspect of the move. Prior to moving, residents are usually in their own home. As one resident reported to me, "I didn't know how lonely I was in my house until I moved here."

Often when we think about needing long-term care, we think of the physical limitations. Or we think about a cognitive impairment, or a dementia, like Alzheimer's. Elders who have no cognitive problems often report that although their physical ability is limited, it is the lack of social and emotional connection that they find depressing. Depression is a big problem among the elderly. Did you know that the suicide rate for elderly men is the highest of any population group, including teenage boys?

A setting that gives us private space combined with the easy ability to connect with others is probably a great goal as we consider long-term care planning.

Evaluating the Cost of Assisted Living

If you may want to include an ALF in your LTC planning, get your arms around the cost of the facility you desire. The cost of assisted living facilities varies dramatically dependent on location, just like the cost of nursing homes. In addition, there are three typical variables that determine your cost:

◆ The size and type of apartment

◆ The amount and type of services received

◆ The living situation (is the apartment shared?)

When considering the cost of assisted living, be sure to include the total cost of incidentals. The base monthly cost of a unit may seem affordable, but additional charges can add up quickly. Become familiar with what is, and isn't, included.

Some facilities include in their base price 45 minutes of care a day per resident. For the spouse of a frail resident who needs no care herself, she'd be paying for 45 minutes of unused care. The healthy older person who moves in primarily for the social setting, the food preparation, and the housekeeping would also be paying for care that would not be used. Other facilities offer care on a purely à la carte basis.

Some facilities require that certain purchases be made in the facility (for incontinence supplies, for example). These requirements can raise the out-of-pocket cost to a resident who may be prohibited from pursuing lower-cost supply options.

When evaluating the cost of an ALF, make sure that you understand what exactly is included in the base price, and what is extra.

In most states, ALFs are primarily private-pay facilities. Some state welfare programs include ALF under their group adult foster-care programs. Check with the marketing director of the ALF or your state Medicaid office. (For an office in your area, check the list in Appendix B.)

If a resident wants to terminate his or her contract with the assisted living facility, most facilities require 30 days notice and payment. Some require 60 days, and require the notification to be on the first day of the month. This can be an expensive problem for the family members of the resident who decides to move to a nursing home (or who passes away) on the fifth of the month. They (or their heirs) must pay for the remainder of that month, give notice on the first, then pay for 60 more days! Contracts should be easy to read and reasonable. I believe that fairness of contracts give a potential resident insight on how much residents and their family are valued.

What are typical reasons that someone must leave an assisted living facility? In some ALFs, chronic incontinence can force a move. Other facilities have special incontinence programs. In some ALFs, a dementia such as Alzheimer's would force a move.

Others have special programs just for residents with Alzheimer's disease. By the way, the most expensive type of assisted living facility care is cognitive impairment or Alzheimer's care. The cost for care in the special programs is often close to the cost of living in a nursing home. This is because this care is so labor-intensive.

CAUTION

Truth & Consequences

Many people who move into an ALF do not live there for the rest of their lives. Once their health declines, they move to a nursing home. According to a recent AARP study, 78 percent of residents who left assisted living for another setting did so because they needed more care. When visiting an ALF, ask at what point that a resident must move. The answer varies widely. Most people are shocked to learn that the average length of stay in an assisted living facility is only about two years. An ALF is not an environment where those who experience significant functional declines can "age in place."

The Least You Need to Know

♦ Your finances can make your retirement housing choices a reality—or a pipe dream; the best time to look into housing options is definitely before you need to, and probably before you want to.

♦ If you plan on moving in with adult children, discuss your plans in detail with them, before your health fails.

♦ Two of the most important factors that determine whether someone ages in his or her own home or not is the presence of a healthy spouse or an involved child within a short drive.

♦ There are many options in between staying in the home where you've lived the last few years (or decades) and moving to a nursing home, and these options grow more plentiful each year.

♦ You can have all the money in the world, yet if your area doesn't have the kind of services you need to stay in your own home safely, you could be forced to move to a facility—even if though you could afford around-the-clock care.

♦ When considering the cost of assisted living or nursing home care, be sure to include the total cost of incidentals.

♦ Most people who move into an ALF do not live there for the rest of their lives; the average length of stay in an assisted living facility is about two years.

What You Must Know About Nursing Homes

In This Chapter

- ◆ Nursing homes in a nutshell
- ◆ The nursing home population
- ◆ The nursing home crisis
- ◆ The cost of going to a nursing home

Why should you read this chapter, when you are absolutely certain that you will never go to a nursing home? Have you ever heard the saying, "There are no guilty men in jail"? Every inmate will tell you that he is innocent. Well, just as there are no guilty men in jail, there are no people living in nursing homes who planned on going there.

I think we can agree that we'd find it odd if someone told us that she'd planned during her working life to enter a nursing home. To paraphrase another sentiment, "Nursing homes are what happens when you have other plans."

If your long-term care planning includes making sure that you never need to go to a nursing home, you still need to read this chapter. Read about how other people, who, like you, never wanted to go to a nursing home, but ended up there. Learn from their stories, and learn how the system works. Ignorance isn't bliss when it comes to long-term care planning.

What Are Nursing Homes?

Nursing homes (sometimes called skilled-nursing facilities) provide both long-term and short-term care. Many residents enter a nursing home for what is called skilled or rehabilitative care after first being hospitalized. Those stays are usually short, and in 1997, 30 percent of residents left the nursing home because they had either stabilized or recovered. The average duration of their stay was 45 days.

When we talk about long-term care, most people agree that we are talking about care that lasts more than 90 days. This care can extend to many months and even years. Long-term care is needed by frail elders, the chronically ill, and the disabled of any age.

Long-term care is received in many settings. However, when we talk about nursing homes, we are not talking about the young disabled. Only 9 percent of nursing home residents are under age 65.

There are 17,000 nursing homes in the United States, serving 1.6 million residents. Eighty-six percent of nursing home facilities were certified by both Medicare and Medicaid in 1997, the most recent year for which data is available. Three percent are certified by Medicare only (that means they don't accept Medicaid); and 9 percent are certified by Medicaid only (they don't accept Medicare). Slightly over 2 percent are private pay only; they don't accept Medicare or Medicaid.

Truth & Consequences

People do not move into a nursing home the first day that they need long-term care. Many people do not go to the nursing home until they have already received care in their own home or an assisted living facility for quite a while. That's why statistics on average nursing home stays may not be much help in figuring out the amount of money you may need for future long-term care.

Nursing homes provide 24-hour nursing care, skilled care, and personal care. Skilled care is given under a doctor's orders by licensed medical personnel. An example of skilled care would be physical, occupational, and speech therapy, such as the care someone would receive after a stroke. Personal care, often called custodial care, is help with functions such as eating, dressing, and bathing. These functions are referred to by members of the medical community as activities of daily living (abbreviated as ADLs). In addition to eating, dressing, and bathing, ADLs also include toileting, continence, and transferring. An example of transferring would be helping someone move from a bed over to a chair.

Who Goes to Nursing Homes?

Although 40 percent of people receiving long-term care are adults under age 65 and 3 percent are children, the majority of people needing long-term care are seniors. Many people who need long-term care at younger ages are cared for in a family home. As we said earlier, only 9 percent of nursing home residents are under age 65.

Our odds of needing long-term care in a nursing home increase as we age. According to the 2000 census, less than 2 percent of all people ages 65 to 74 live in nursing homes. From ages 75 to 84 the number jumps to 5 percent. At age 85 and older, more than 18 percent of us live in a nursing home.

Compared to the 1990 census, where 25 percent of people age 85 and older lived in a nursing home, the figure for the 2000 census showed a big drop. Here's what I think is behind it: The age 85+ group is the group most likely to be a nursing home for extended long-term care. Since 1990, many new alternatives to nursing home care have sprung in most areas, most notably assisted living facilities. These new facilities are an attractive option for a nursing home resident with fewer health problems who has the ability to private pay. These new options are "skimming the cream," taking the healthiest and wealthiest people out of nursing homes. What's happening to nursing homes is that their occupants are much older, much frailer, and more likely to be on public assistance than in prior years.

LTC Lowdown _____

Find out information, including the latest inspection reports, for nursing homes across the country at the Medicare website: www.medicare.gov. Medicare refers to nursing homes as SNFs (skilled-nursing facilities).

Nursing Homes Are a Female Problem

The nursing home population is predominantly female. Visit any nursing home and you will notice that the vast majority of the population is female. The Center for Disease Control (CDC) reports that there are about three elderly women for every elderly man. However, some of the men are there for *post-hospital*, short-term rehabilitation stays. The long-term occupants of the nursing home are primarily women.

Marilee's Memo _____

Post-hospital, subacute care is skilled care that is given after a hospital stay. Often this care is rehabilitative, as in the case of a patient who suffered a stroke and is receiving occupational and physical therapy. Post-hospital, subacute care is given under a doctor's orders by licensed medical people, and is normally covered by Medicare or by health insurance. It is not long term, and usually lasts less than eight weeks.

Why does the nursing home seem to be a feminine fate? It's quite obvious, when you think about it. With any couple, the first member of the couple who has failing health is normally taken care of by the healthy spouse.

Consider a typical couple. He is a couple of years older than she is, and he needs long-term care first. She takes care of him in their home, often ruining her own health in the process. If he does have to go to a nursing home, it is normally at the end of his life, and for a very short time. Only when there is no other choice will the healthy spouse put the sick spouse in a nursing home.

So the husband passes away first, and his wife is left in the house by herself. When she eventually needs long-term care, who is her caregiver? If she has children nearby, perhaps they can help out. If the woman needs 24-hour supervision, families are often stretched to the breaking point. Without a healthy spouse to oversee upkeep and maintenance of the house, it often becomes no longer practical for her to keep the house. That's why many women receive their care in a facility, often a nursing home.

Wisdom of the Aged

Long-term care insurance companies report that facility long-term care claims spike in January. They speculate two reasons: The prospect of another season of snow removal (in those areas of the country affected by snow), while coping with health problems causes seniors to choose to move. Another suspected reason is that family members traditionally gather together for Thanksgiving and winter holidays. Siblings who may not meet except for once a year are able to see how well (or poorly) Mom or Dad is doing. Problems which are not apparent over the phone are obvious in person. Often the difficult decision to move a loved one into a facility is the result of a family holiday pow-wow. Many seniors who plan on staying in their own homes forever find that this desire is undermined by the difficult realities of maintaining a household by themselves.

Only 17 percent of nursing home occupants are married. The message is loud and clear: The first person in a couple to need long-term care may likely receive most of his or her care at home. After he or she passes away, the spouse who is left will likely receive his or her care in a facility like a nursing home. Staying in your home, an ideal which is often described as "aging in place," is often unattainable for those who are widowed, divorced, or never married.

Avoiding Poverty in Widowhood

There's a second reason that many women are destined to knock on the nursing home's front door. Almost 17 percent of widows age 65+ live in poverty. Overall, women have a poverty rate of almost double the male poverty rate at age 65 and over. The biggest payer of nursing homes is Medicaid. According to the American Health Care Association (www.ahca.org/secure/cost1.htm), Medicaid pays for 69 percent of the nations' nursing home patients. However, Medicaid will pay for your care only if you are poor. In many areas of the country, the only full-time, around-the-clock type of long-term care that someone on Medicaid can get is in the nursing home. If a woman is poor, she won't have the option of other places to receive care in these areas.

Surprised that so many older women live in poverty? There are many reasons. Women tend to have lower pensions, since on average they are paid less then men. They also tend to have intermittent work histories because of child raising, which hurts pensions and Social Security.

The other reason that many older women live in poverty or just barely above it is a real tragedy, since it is totally avoidable in many cases. Many widows are impoverished because they and their husbands didn't do proper life insurance planning. When a spouse dies, the pension he earned is normally cut in half, and Social Security may be reduced. Because two can live as cheaply as one, the surviving spouse's expenses often don't drop much. (According to the U.S. Congressional Committee on Ways and Means, in 1998, 60.4 percent of women age 75 and older were widows.)

Truth & Consequences

Since many widows become impoverished as a result of their husbands' death, every couple (even seniors) should do special planning. Take a look at what the household income would be if either you or your spouse were to die. If the surviving spouse in either case does not have enough money to live comfortably, the couple should purchase life insurance. Yes, sometimes life insurance is needed in retirement years.

Signs of Our Changing Times

Nursing homes are a modern invention. In the old days, medicine was more of an art than a science. Before antibiotics and more modern advances, families did what they could to keep elderly relatives comfortable until they passed away. In the 1700s, they would stay in what the *Boston Globe* called the "borning room," a room in the middle of the house that was the warmest room ("Green Acres," March 17, 2002).

It seems to me that the building of nursing homes was a direct response to many economic realities. Over the last hundred years, America moved from an agriculturally based to a heavy-industry-based to a service-based economy. When people lived on farms, women kept the house and contributed to the economic strength of the family by gardening, milking, and cooking for the family and workers. These functions tied her to the home, so caring for an elderly relative in the same home was logistically possible.

As people migrated away from farm work and automobiles became widely available, it became economically possible to live further away from both the workplace and family members. Women started working outside the home, so taking care of a relative needing long-term care might mean quitting a paying job. This was the beginning of families suffering financially when it became necessary to care for an elderly loved one.

In 1965, the introduction of long-term care funding through Medicaid allowed families to transfer the burden of caring for poor family members to the government. The idea of paid, professional long-term care given by someone other than a family member is a relatively new one.

 **LTC Lowdown**

Besides money, what can account for the fact that one senior lives in a nursing home and another senior needing the same level of care is able to stay in his own home? Having family nearby makes it more likely for people to continue to live in their own home as they age. Most people who pay for professional home care have this care supplemented by unpaid care given by family. Thirty-one percent of *informal caregivers* work.

The World War II generation was the first to have employer-paid health insurance and pensions. Some say that perhaps they are both the first generation and the last.

Even though their parents rarely lived long beyond age 65, the WWII generation ushered in the health insurance safety net that provides health insurance for most people age 65 and older in the United States—Medicare. In the same year (1965), Medicaid was also added under the Social Security Act.

Medicare and Medicaid accomplished much good, but they also helped foster a mentality of entitlement. Although Medicaid was initiated to pay for health care for the poor, it quickly became a way for middle-class families to pay for long-term care. Reliance on government replaced the understood agreement between the generations within a family: that the able-bodied cared for the old and infirm.

With no such thing as *assisted living facilities* or *continuing care retirement communities*, there was, until recently, little incentive to plan personally for how to pay for long-term care. The only option to home care was Medicaid, and the government paid that bill for most.

 Marilee's Memo _____

A **continuing care retirement community** (CCRC) is a facility which provides for care in a variety of settings. These communities are set up to provide a continuum of care, and encourage "aging in place." CCRCs provide independent living, assisted living, and nursing home care, all in the same location. Residents in facilities pay a large up-front fee, which is partially refunded to their heirs when they leave. An additional monthly fee is required; in some CCRCs this fee remains the same no matter what level of care they are receiving.

In addition to finances, there are many other factors that conspire to make nursing homes or other facilities a logical choice for care:

- ◆ Elders are living longer with complicated medical conditions. They are frail and need medical treatment and care well beyond the ability of what many families can provide.

- ◆ Medical advances have lengthened the duration of long-term caregiving in many cases, and family caregivers can burn out.

- ◆ The increasing prevalence of single-parent households and dual wage-earning households means that many adult children have little time to be caregivers.

- ◆ Divorce and remarriage have fractured families and fostered, in some cases, a lack of familial obligation.

- ◆ Our mobile society with smaller families means there are fewer groupings of siblings and other family members living close by to share the caregiving load.

- ◆ Lack of community support for people who choose to become a caregiver.

In summary, today's families use professional long-term care for a variety of reasons: complex medical needs of patient, economics, changed family structure, response to societal pressure, and lack of caregiver support.

How Long Do People Stay in Nursing Homes?

You may have heard that the average length of stay in a nursing home is down. That's true, but unless you understand what's behind the drop, you may jump to the conclusion that the importance of long-term care planning is declining, since we need less nursing home care. The trend toward shorter stays is seen in the last two National Nursing Home Studies, conducted by The National Center for Health Stats. In 1985, the average stay was 2.8 years; in 1997 (the lastest statistics), the average stay was 2.5 years.

The likeliest reason for the shorter average stay is simply the increasing number of beds in nursing homes which are used for rehabilitation after a short hospitalization. As hospital stays become shorter, people age 65+ are increasingly likely to be released to a nursing home to recover. These beds are used by people an average of only 45 days. These short stays make average stay numbers almost misleading.

 Marilee's Memo _____

Although the average stay in a nursing home is two years and six months, do not think that you don't have to worry about your nursing home stay lasting three years or more. Most people who enter a nursing home are there for very short-term care after a hospital stay. If one person is in the nursing home one month and one is there five years, the average length of stay for these two people is two and a half years!

Imagine a nursing home room with four beds over the course of a year. There are three elderly women who have each been in the nursing home for seven years, in three of the beds. The fourth bed had a series of short-term, rehabilitative patients. Using the average stay of 45 days for the short-termers, that adds up to eight women who stay in the fourth bed over the course of the same year. From this data, the average nursing home stay is two years. But three of the residents were there for seven years each! That's the problem with reporting averages—they may or may not reflect what's actually happening.

The short-term nursing home stays after hospitalization end because the patients stabilize and are released. Long-term residents leave the nursing home for two primary reasons: hospitalization or death.

If you ask the admissions directors of nursing homes, they will probably tell you the same thing they told me. The people in their nursing homes, in general, stay either less than one year or more than three years. They'll explain that some residents have been there for more than 10 years (those residents are usually women).

Why We Don't Want to Go to Nursing Homes

Americans are weaned on the idea of self-sufficiency and self-determination. Those who immigrate to America often feel even more strongly about the importance of independence and control. When we enter a nursing home, there is a loss of control over our lives. We lose privacy, because most nursing homes do not have private rooms. For most of us, we have never shared a bedroom with anyone except our spouse, with the possible exception of a college roommate.

When we enter the nursing home we suffer from a lack of control around our surroundings. We become subject to a schedule: Meals are served at the same time each day, and lights out are at the same time each day. If we used to enjoy a glass of wine with meals, that is not allowed. We may not even have our own phone. If we do, conversations aren't private.

It's hard for a healthy, independent person to imagine moving to a nursing home to live. But when we consider the apparent negatives of nursing home living, we are wise to also consider the option of living at home with the kinds of physical and mental limitations many nursing home residents have. People who suffer from conditions such as cognitive impairment or depression, or who are wheelchair-bound with complex health problems, sometimes cannot live safely by themselves. Even seniors without these problems can become isolated and lonely living in their home on their own.

Wisdom of the Aged

Many health-care professionals feel that there are many people in nursing homes only because they failed to plan for a disabling illness. They maintain these people could instead receive their care at home. As part of your long-term care planning, investigate the services (paid and free) that are available to you from the government, as well as programs offered by private, fraternal, or religious organizations. If you need help finding these, or you are trying to get information remotely, you may want to hire an independent *geriatric-care manager* (*GCM*). A GCM is a person who consults with individuals and families about their options concerning long-term care. These are the people who know what is available and how much it costs. Fees vary, so ask that up front. The most objective advice will come from a GCM whom you pay, not one who is paid by an organization.

Depending on the nature of the need for care and the support (paid and unpaid) available, staying home can be even worse than living in a nursing home from both a safety point of view and a social point of view.

Why People End Up in Nursing Homes

Today's nursing home population is older and sicker than ever. In 1997, 51 percent of residents were age 85+.

Taking a look at the reasons people were admitted, cognitive impairment, incontinence, and functional decline were leading factors. More than half of nursing home residents are cognitively impaired. When cognitive disorders progress, patients can exhibit behaviors such as hitting, wandering, and the inability to keep themselves safe. Often at this point, families who have been able to keep a loved one at home must resort to institutional care.

Almost all nursing home residents had more than one diagnosis when admitted. The most common diagnoses did not change from 1975 to 1997. The top conditions were cardiovascular disease (including hypertension and stroke), mental and cognitive disorders (including depression, anxiety, and Alzheimer's), type II (adult onset) diabetes, hypothyroidism, and other disorders of the endocrine system.

Ninety-six percent of nursing home residents need help with bathing. Sixty-two percent are using a wheelchair; another 24 percent use a walker. Forty-four percent of nursing home residents have difficulty controlling both the bowel and the bladder. It's easy to understand how even a Herculean effort among a family to keep an elder at home can sometimes not be enough.

What Do Nursing Homes Cost?

Nursing homes vary dramatically in cost. These variances are obvious on a state-by-state basis, but even nursing homes in the same town can have significantly different costs. In determining what your cost of care would be if you needed nursing home care, it helps to know where you are likely to receive care. Do you see yourself staying in the same area that you are now, or are you planning on relocating?

Let's say that you own a vacation property in a different area, and that you have designated that house as your retirement house. Check with the Office of Aging in the state where you plan on living (for contact information see Appendix B), or ask your financial advisor for information on the cost of nursing home care in that state.

Many planners like to consider the worst-case scenario in terms of the amount of money needed to pay for long-term care. For most of us, worst case is the nursing home. However, I need to point out that round-the-clock professional care in your own home can cost more than living in a nursing home (see Chapter 2).

CAUTION

Truth & Consequences

Many people think that they will relocate long distances when they retire. Reality contradicts this. Although 39 percent of people age 60 and older do move, a 2000 study cited by the AARP has shown that 80 percent of those moves are local.

Let's consider what nursing homes cost. Unless indicated, most nursing home surveys are based on semiprivate (two people to a room) costs. Most nursing homes do not have private rooms. Many have rooms for three to four people in addition to semiprivate rooms. The quoted charge normally includes room and board, but does not include charges for any skilled care that may be required. MetLife's Mature Market Institute survey released in 2002 lists the high, low, and average private and semiprivate rates per day of nursing homes in selected geographic areas in all 50 states. The average cost nationwide for a private room is $167.82 per day; for a semiprivate room, it's $142.56 per day. (Please see Appendix D for the costs in your area.)

All right. The nursing home is expensive, and we don't want to go there anyway. What can we do today to make sure we retain our health as we age? Most people would say that walking an hour a day would keep the doctor away. If you believe the true story about Alois, a strong man who lived until age 93 (see box on next page), there appears to be more than a kernel of truth to that.

The nursing home industry has dramatically changed over the last few years. Every day nursing homes are going out of business, closing their doors because they are bankrupt. They can't find and keep staff. Reports of nursing home abuse are rampant. Nursing home litigation (suing nursing homes) is a fast-growing area of the law. Judgments and payments to settle lawsuits are making the nursing homes' financial situation even worse.

Families don't understand how nursing homes can be losing money when they are paying an average of about $4,300 a month for care (if they are paying out of pocket).

Why should we care that nursing homes are in crisis? Whether we have a loved one in a nursing home, are a taxpayer, or may enter a nursing home ourselves, we all have a vested interest in making sure the industry is adequately funded and providing quality care.

The Old Tailor: Alois's Story

Grandpa came to the United States from Germany. He was a tailor, and wore a fine suit to work every day. He said that you could judge a man by his suit, hat, and shoes. (This was well before casual Friday!) He used to walk back and forth to work; a car was a luxury back then. When he retired, he walked even more. At a minimum, he would walk back and forth to the German men's club, logging about three miles a day. Just as he was starting to have occasional trouble with balance, he was saved by his new grandchildren. He would lean on the old-fashioned stroller, so he never needed a cane or walker. His children had to bring the stroller in for new wheels, because he wore them out! Most days he went out twice a day, pushing his granddaughters up Main Street to the cemetery, to the park to feed the pigeons, and to the old men's club where he'd have a beer and they'd get a soda.

Grandpa had a pacemaker put in at age 84 because his heart wasn't pumping properly. Imagine having a pacemaker put in before 1970—they were new back then! It caused quite a stir when he started chasing Grandma around the house. He was a new man.

He didn't slow down until age 88. His daughter remembers, "He had lung problems, and a circulatory condition. He started falling. The blood would drain out of his head and he would look ashen. He fell down on the street. A couple of times he ended up in the emergency room. His wife couldn't lift him anymore. They'd call us to drive over and lift Grandpa up. We had kids of our own, and it was hard to juggle taking care of everyone."

This robust man who exercised every day needed the kind of care that only a nursing home could provide. After awhile he couldn't walk anymore, and was wheelchair-bound. He died at age 93 of heart problems after living in the nursing home for three years. The nursing home was paid for out of the tailor's life savings. As his wife, a retired seamstress, said, "Why would we ask for help when we have the money?"

 **LTC Lowdown**

Nursing home costs vary dramatically region to region. The 2002 daily rate for a nursing home in Montana was reported to be only $52 a day; a facility located on an island in Alaska cost $704 a day (*Business Wire*, March 4, 2002). Take into account the costs where you are likely to be when you need long-term care. Some states are notoriously expensive for nursing home care. These include Alaska, New York, Connecticut, District of Columbia, Hawaii, Massachusetts, New Jersey, and Pennsylvania.

Nursing Homes and Your Wallet

There have always been more desirable and less desirable nursing homes. Ask any group of seniors and they can quickly tell you the best nursing home in town—and the name of the one they'd never want to go to. When my grandmother needed nursing home care, she was able to go to the facility most people agreed was the best one. The best facilities often have the biggest waiting lists. She had two distinct advantages on her application for admission—her doctor was on the board of directors, and she was a private payer. Grandma (I called her Nanny) described the Jerome Home as where "the rich people go."

CAUTION

Truth & Consequences

Does it make a difference if you are private pay? In some ways. Here's why: It's not that the nursing home people are mean and uncaring, it's that they have to have a certain number of private payers to stay afloat. That's right. In many states, Medicaid, which pays the bill for about 70 percent of the nursing home residents in the country, reimburses the nursing homes at less than their actual cost of care, according to the Center for Long-Term Care Financing. That's why private-paying patients, whether they are paying with life savings, reverse mortgage proceeds, or any other method, find it easier to get into the more desirable nursing homes.

The nursing homes' hands are tied. They want to give great care, and they are mandated to provide a certain level of staffing and care. Good care costs money. But the government Medicaid program, which is the nursing homes' biggest source of payment, is not paying enough to cover their costs. According to the national accounting firm BDO Siedman, Medicaid is underfunding nursing homes by more than $3 billion a year. In Vermont, for example, nursing homes are reimbursed $19.95 less per day than the cost to care for a patient. In Florida, the daily shortfall is $12.10.

How did that come about? Once Medicaid started paying for nursing homes, the nursing home industry responded with a building boom. The Medicaid program was overwhelmed by the resulting costs, and instituted a program designed to control construction of new beds. This program was called the Certificate of Need (CON) program. By the mid-1970s, construction had slowed. The smaller supply of beds raised rates; Medicaid responded by capping its reimbursement rates.

The nursing home industry fought the federal government, which mandated high levels of quality care, but whose funding wasn't sufficient to consistently provide the required care. The Boren Amendment was a federal law that required Medicaid to reimburse at reasonable rates. Here's what happened: The Balanced Budget Act of 1997 repealed the Boren Amendment!

The policy of inadequate Medicaid reimbursements means that nursing homes must charge private payers a rate that effectively makes up for the shortfall of each

Medicaid bed. Think about it. A nursing home admits an 80-year-old woman today, who private pays her bill for one year before going onto Medicaid. From that point on, in many areas of the country, the nursing home is losing money every day on that resident. Unfortunately, low Medicaid reimbursements have forced most facilities to staff at minimum requirements. That's not only a problem for the nursing home owner or the nonprofit that runs it, it's a problem for all the staff and residents.

And the news is just getting worse. Likely future cuts in Medicaid could be catastrophic for the nursing home industry and its residents. Medicaid is funded by both federal and state governments. In early 2002 at an annual meeting, "the nation's governors were unanimous in declaring Medicaid's cost the most urgent crisis they face" (*Los Angeles Times*, March 5, 2002).

Wisdom of the Aged

By the way, pay no attention to stories that lead you to believe that Medicaid recipients get worse treatment than private-pay residents. I have heard some people insinuate that Medicaid recipients get worse food and are even beaten by abusive workers, while private-pay patients are spared. This simply isn't true. Most workers in a nursing home have no idea which occupants are private pay and which are not. The problem of bad food and abusive care is a problem for residents regardless of how they pay their bill. Unfortunately, elder abuse is not limited to nursing homes or facilities. A frail elder living alone at home may be at even greater risk of abuse from home-care workers than someone living in a nursing home.

More than 77 percent of people entering a nursing home are eligible for Medicaid on day one. Of the remaining 23 percent, many people are there for short-term rehabilitative services, with Medicare paying the bill. The reality for nursing homes today is that there are not many private-pay long-term residents to subsidize the Medicaid recipients.

For many nursing homes, Medicare has become the cash cow, throwing off enough profit to keep the doors open. Have you noticed that, in the last few years, your local nursing home has changed its name? Perhaps it used to be called Main Street Nursing Home, and now it's called Main Street Skilled and Rehabilitative Facility. That's because the facility is positioning itself to attract the short-term Medicare patients, not the long-term Medicaid patients.

When not enough money is coming in, cuts must be made. Perhaps there are no raises not given to critical staff members, perhaps meals are less palatable, or maybe the 25-year-old drapes can't be replaced.

Here's what's starting to happen. Some nursing homes are quitting the government programs, and turning strictly private pay. There have been occasional very high-end nursing homes that have done this for years, but in general, people on Medicaid have been in the same nursing home as their private-pay neighbors.

Private-Pay Nursing Homes

A nursing home in my hometown has turned exclusively private pay. Guess what? Its daily rate is less than all of its local competitors—because there is no need to subsidize Medicaid recipients. It is generally considered to be the best nursing home in town.

During a trip to London, a local man pointed out to me the "private hospital." He explained that, although England had free national health care for everyone, the rich people went to the private-pay hospital that wasn't supported by the government. If you weren't rich, you could gain access to the private-pay hospital by purchasing private insurance.

If I were to take out my crystal ball, I would say that we may be headed that way when it comes to nursing homes. The providers will seek out private payers, where they can cover their expenses, make a profit, and not be subject to the extra layers of government supervision and paperwork (this can be good and bad!). Private payers, I believe, will continue to have the most attractive options.

> **CAUTION** **Truth & Consequences** _____
>
> Private-pay nursing home residents can usually get a private or semiprivate room. Many Medicaid-paid residents find themselves with two or even three roommates. If they are admitted to the hospital, their room will not be held indefinitely awaiting their return. A private-pay person has the option of simply packing up and moving to another facility if he or she is not happy with where he or she is living. The growing number of exclusively private-pay options is never an option for someone relying on Medicaid.

If you are a baby boomer, you may recall watching the '60s cartoon *The Jetsons*. Viewers were treated to a futuristic world where personal flying vehicles replaced cars. Where will the Jetsons receive their long-term care? No one knows for sure, but I believe the future will be a two-tier system, where people whose care is funded by government dollars will go to certain facilities, and private payers will go to more attractive private facilities.

It's starting to happen already.

The Least You Need to Know

- No one plans on entering a nursing home ... but many do.

- If you are widowed, never married, or divorced, and need long-term care as a senior, you may need to go to a nursing home; 83 percent of nursing home residents do not have a spouse.

- Since nursing homes lose money on many Medicaid beneficiaries, private payers usually have an easier time entering more desirable facilities.

- Nursing homes are expensive; the average cost nationwide for a semiprivate room is $142.56 a day.

- The nation's nursing homes are in a crisis; losses and bankruptcies are common.

- Likely future cuts in Medicaid could be catastrophic for the nursing home industry and its residents.

Chapter 4

Putting Together an LTC Game Plan

In This Chapter

- ◆ Six steps toward a winning LTC game plan
- ◆ When's the best time to plan
- ◆ LTC waits for no one

Throughout this book, we look at a variety of ways to pay for long-term care. It's never too early to look into long-term care planning for yourself or for a loved one. The younger you are, the more planning choices you are likely to have. For example, if long-term care insurance is part of your plan, approximately 7 percent of people under age 60 who apply are declined; of those who wait until age 70 to apply, approximately 25 percent have their application declined. But even people over age 80 and in bad health have planning options. Whatever age you are now is the right age to start.

Contrary to popular belief, a long-term plan does not need to be set in stone. Someone who puts in place a plan at age 45 will hopefully revisit that plan several times. Government and social programs may change, which may affect a plan; as an elder law attorney said to me recently, "In 20 years, there may be no Medicaid program." As investments are accumulated and home equity grows, long-term care insurance may become less important in someone's long-term plan.

Your Six-Step Action Plan

The nature of planning involves taking the information that's available and then making informed decisions. Some people do long-term care planning to protect their life savings. Other people have few assets and do long-term care planning so that they will the same care choices as people with more money. Some children help their parents with long-term care planning out of love and a sense of obligation. They want to help their parents maintain dignity and independence as they age. Some parents do the sort of long-term care planning designed to maximize the inheritance left to their children, even though it is not in the parents' best interest to do so. Read on for how to approach putting together your own personal LTC plan.

Marilee's Memo _____

Your personal action plan:

Step 1: Set yourself a deadline.

Step 2: Research local care options and costs.

Step 3: Access your financial situation.

Step 4: Access your health situation.

Step 5: Meet with an advisor.

Step 6: Implement!

Step 1: Set Yourself a Deadline

One of the best things that you can do in regards to long-term care planning is to set a deadline. The task of researching and implementing a long-term care plan can seem so daunting, that I have seen people drag it out over a couple of years! Here are some of the reasons that even smart people dillydally:

♦ **Smart person's excuse #1: I'm afraid to make the wrong decision.**

Let's say, for example, that you've determined that you should buy LTC insurance, but you're afraid. Afraid that you'll buy the wrong policy, so you keep putting off doing anything about it. The biggest mistake that you can make in long-term care planning is waiting too long and analyzing too much. For example, if you know that you want LTC insurance, purchase a policy now. But keep researching, and set a deadline for either keeping the same policy or applying for a better policy that you found and that you expect to keep. Maybe your deadline is just before your next birthday (when the insurance price jumps a little bit), or maybe you set your deadline for two months from now. As long as you are healthy, you have all the options in the world. The biggest risk you run is that your health changes before you've made a decision.

Marilee's Memo

A limited-pay policy is an insurance policy for which, although you pay premiums for a limited number of years, the insurance continues for the rest of your life. You are essentially pre-paying for your insurance. Don't buy a limited-pay policy until you know the policy is a "keeper."

◆ **Smart person's excuse #2: I'm afraid the company that I'm relying on (the reverse mortgage company, the insurance company, or another company) will go out of business.**

Protect yourself to the greatest extent possible by discussing the health of any company with the advisor who is recommending it. Check with your state's attorney general's office about companies offering programs such as continuing care retirement communities or discounted home health-care plans. Check with the insurance department of your state government (Appendix A) about life-settlement companies, viatical companies, annuities, and long-term care insurance companies.

Independent ratings companies such as A.M. Best, Moody's, and Standard & Poor's offer their opinion on the financial strength of insurance companies. If an advisor recommends a company that has ratings that are not in the top tier, ask why. Appendix E lists various resources where you can find ratings information. In addition, if buying long-term care insurance, you should ask for information on any premium increases that the company has had over the last 10 years.

By the way, every state has a guarantee fund that is a safety net to help policy-holders of insolvent companies. It's not the FDIC, but there is a high level of comfort for any individual policyholder in the fact that insurance is highly regulated. It is common practice when an insurance company falters, that regulators step in and strongly encourage other insurance companies to take over the policies. Sometimes payments are made to the acquiring insurance company to compensate them for taking on the policies. Be practical. Which is the greater risk: that a highly rated insurance company goes out of business and no company takes over the policies, or the risk that you'll need long-term care?

◆ **Smart person's excuse #3: LTC is not something that I can plan for. I'll have to do the best when (if) it happens.**

For most people, the need for long-term care hits when they are least likely to be able to handle it themselves. They are usually in their late 70s or 80s. In many cases, they are suffering from a decreased mental capacity. If you think it's difficult to plan now, imagine how difficult it will be years in the future when you can no longer balance a checkbook! It's been said that "aging isn't for sissies." Any planning that you do now will likely make your life much easier and more satisfying in the future.

> **Truth & Consequences** _____
>
> In this book, I focus on helping people decide how to pay for long-term care. When we need long-term care, some of us will be incapacitated; we may be unable to communicate our wishes. In that case, legal documents called health-care proxies and durable powers of attorney can be very helpful. The health-care proxy allows someone you have designated to make medical decisions on your behalf, under certain conditions. Health-care proxies are often available, at no charge, at hospitals. The durable power of attorney (POA) gives someone else the ability to execute legal transactions on your behalf. A POA could be used to sell property or liquidate a bank account. Ask your lawyer for more information on these.

Step 2: Do Your Research

Research the local cost of care and what subsidized and free care may be available. Tour local facilities and call home health care agencies to inquire about the costs for care by the hour and for an eight hour shift.

If you plan on retiring in a different area than where you live now, you should look into the care there. Note that in some areas, such as New York City and Cape Cod, Massachusetts, local costs are much higher than the state average. The resources listed at the back of this book, and/or your financial advisor, can help you with this step. (For more information, see Chapters 2 and 3.)

Step 3: Access Your Financial Situation

How would you categorize yourself: wealthy, middle class/upper-middle class, or poor?

If you consider yourself wealthy, do you have enough income and/or liquid assets to pay for long-term care? (The four chapters in Part 2 have more information on this.) If you can self-pay, are you comfortable paying this expense yourself, or would you like to transfer the risk to an insurance company? Read Chapter 8 for a discussion of self-funding. The chapters in Parts 4 and 5 will help you if you decide to purchase LTC insurance. If you are considering Medicaid Planning, be sure to read chapters 21—24. Medicaid planning is usually not recommended for the wealthy, for reasons described in Chapters 22 and 24.

If you classify yourself as middle class or upper-middle class, you are probably doing everything right—saving for retirement and such— but you don't have enough cash to easily pay for extended long-term care. You have a lot of options (as discussed in Parts 2, 4, and 5). For reasons that should be obvious when you read the chapters, I do not recommend that you rely on the government programs described in Parts 3 and 5. The options under government programs are usually biased toward institutional care, such as nursing homes. The funding for these programs is precarious, and the mood in Washington is to beef up these long-term care benefits for the poorest of the poor only. Most middle-class and upper-middle-class people will want to private pay, using the options described in Part 2 and/or purchase long-term care insurance to pay. Long-term care is so expensive, and government programs so limited, that *most* middle-class people who can afford and qualify for LTC insurance are smart to purchase this protection.

Finally, if you have low income and low assets, but you own your own house, you may want to consider a reverse mortgage (read Chapter 5). If you have low income, low assets, and no house, you probably don't financially qualify for private-pay options. If you can't comfortably afford the average LTC insurance premium ($150 per month), or you have less than $50,000 in assets, you financially are not a good candidate for long-term care insurance. If this is the case, you should read the four chapters on Medicaid in Part 6, as well as Chapters 9, 10, and 11; you may qualify for other government programs, too!

Step 4: Access Your Health Situation

This is an important step for a couple of reasons. If you already need long-term care (or the need for care is imminent), you may not have much time to plan, and you definitely have fewer options. Poor health (as defined in Chapter 13) means that buying long-term care insurance is not an option for you, though reverse mortgages, medically underwritten annuities, and life insurance policies might all be funding possibilities. If these are not options for you, you may choose (or have to) rely on the government Medicaid program (discussed in Chapters 21–24). If you need long-term now (or soon), and are low-income and have few assets, be sure to check out the government programs described in Part 3 to see if you qualify.

If your health allows you to buy long-term care insurance, you can consider this option. The chapters in Part 4 will help you figure out if you are a good candidate for this coverage.

Step 5: Meet with an Advisor

See a financial advisor, such as an insurance agent and/or a legal advisor, such as an elder law attorney, to get customized advice on how your long-term care plan might look and what it would cost. Chapter 21 will help you choose an elder law attorney; for your best choices in insurance agents, look to Chapter 16. Be sure to ask the advisors about alternatives to their recommendations, and also what the downside is. Every plan that has an upside also has a downside!

Step 6: Implement!

Here's the part of the plan that a lot of people never do. Planning that isn't implemented is like an engaged couple that never marries ... the intention is nice, but there's something wrong. If you are serious about planning how to pay for your long-term care, learn about your options, select good advisors, and then do the planning that makes sense for you. You (and your family) will be glad you did.

Marilee's Memo

Are you financially vulnerable, but your kids are doing well financially? More and more adult children are buying long-term care insurance for their parents. They want their parents to have the same care choices as people with more money. The insurance lifts some of the burden off the children, who no longer have to worry about whether Mom (or Dad) will be able to afford the care they want.

Is LTC Insurance Financially Appropriate for Me?

Long-term care policies are evolving; companies are consolidating. It's tough to know what long-term care facilities and home care will be like in 10, let alone 20, years. Does that mean that you shouldn't buy this insurance until the "last minute"—until you are about to retire? *No!*

What about the risk that there will be a new government program implemented to pay for long-term care, so that you didn't need to buy long-term care insurance? One prominent financial planner calls this "sucker risk," as in you were a sucker to buy something that the government now covers. Is the government going to put in place a comprehensive new program to pay for the baby boomers' long-term care? In my opinion, *No!*

Why do I feel so strongly about this? I've seen enough and read enough to know that long-term care planning is a critical part of planning for health-care expenses. And the young—those under age 60 or so, those who have not yet built up a pension or paid off a mortgage—are in many cases the most vulnerable.

Life itself is risky. Anything can happen to us at almost any time. In thinking about long-term care, and, in fact, your whole financial situation, it's important to try to figure out what risks you can afford to take. What risks can you not afford to take? Could you afford to have your house burn to the ground, uninsured? If not, you'd better pay your homeowner's insurance bill. I remember reading the words of a financial guru (I wish I could remember his name) who said that a big part of financial success is not necessarily making the best decision all the time. Instead, it's in not making mistakes you can't recover from.

How Young Is Too Young?

In fact, you could say that no disability insurance program is complete without long-term care insurance. That's because disability insurance replaces your earned income (pay or salary) that is lost when you're sick or hurt and can't work. But if you have the "wrong kind of disability" and also need long-term care, you're in trouble. Your disability insurance will replace your earned income, but there's nothing that's designed to pay for the long-term custodial care that you might need; your health insurance certainly won't cover it. Well, nothing except Medicaid, which, as you'll read in Part 6, first requires that you be poor, and then will not usually pay for care anywhere except a nursing home.

How young is too young to do long-term care planning or buy LTC insurance? Ask Mickey Dee, who was featured on the front page of the *Boston Globe* (May 2, 2001). He was a music promoter, journalist, and radio-show host before suffering a major stroke during routine surgery at age 36. The story reported that he was kept on his employer's payroll until the health insurer paid out the maximum allowed under the policy. Since then, he has been reliant on friends who help in his rehabilitation, and have helped him apply for Medicaid. One hundred forty local musicians were playing to raise money for a benefit fund to contribute to the cost of Dee's long-term care. The year before, they raised more than $60,000. Dee suffers from locked-in syndrome, in which he is conscious and has cognitive function but cannot speak or move.

Ask my relative, who in 1999 announced that she had M.S. and had to resign from her full-time job (with two children in college). She was 46 years old. One day the phone rang. It was my relative, who asked me how she could buy that insurance that I

LTC Lowdown _____

None of us know when our health will take a turn for the worse. We don't get to pick the illness or the accident, or even the age the problem happens. It's hard for us to realize that we have no control over this. People who plan for the worst and hope for the best are never in the situation of saying, "If only I had …."

talked about, because she knew she was going to need it. I had to fight back the tears as I told her it was too late—she couldn't buy the insurance now, because she was already diagnosed. I knew this meant that, as her disease progressed, she and her husband would likely be faced with horrible choices: exhausting their life savings to keep her at home, or signing her up for Medicaid—essentially handing her over to the system that only pays for nursing home care in her state. After that telephone call, as someone who had always planned to buy long-term care insurance in my 50s, I bought a policy at age 39.

Time Waits for No One

Here's a true story. When I train insurance agents and CPAs, I hear stories like this at every class. A man met with his insurance agent to check in before he and his wife flew to Florida for the winter. The insurance agent recommended that they finally apply for the long-term care insurance that had been recommended in the past: "Before you go to Florida, let's do the LTC insurance." Both husband and wife applied, and they left. Their first week in Florida, the wife had a heart attack on the golf course. Her sister called the insurance agent back in their home state, asking, "Did the LTC insurance go through?" She was able to tell her sister, who was in intensive care after a quadruple bypass, the good news: Her policy was in force. Are you waiting for a better time to sit down with an attorney and update your documents, or to buy long-term care insurance? I've never heard of anyone getting healthier. Don't wait. Be brave. Do the planning. Then, go on living!

The Waiting Game

Are you one of those people who likes to beat the system? Want to apply for long-term care insurance at the optimal moment, so that you give the insurance company the least amount of premiums for the maximum benefit? Then apply for a policy with a lifetime benefit immediately before your claim. What, you say, you don't know when that is? Well, that's the rub.

You can take quite a bit of consolation in the fact that you won't actually be paying in less premiums if you wait a few years. The cost of purchasing long-term care insurance creeps up every year that you delay. Premiums for a new policy almost double every 10 years that you wait to buy over age 55. So if you wait to apply, though you will be paying for far fewer years, you will be paying higher annual premiums.

The insurance companies have figured it all out. The professionals who figure out the pricing of insurance policies are called actuaries. They usually have math degrees and have passed a series of ten grueling examinations. Thinking that you can beat them at their pricing strategies is like thinking you can consistently beat the house at a casino. When you do a sophisticated type of financial analysis called a Net Present Value, which takes into account the return on your investment options, and the time value of money, you will find that the pricing on a long-term care insurance policy from any one insurance company is effectively age-neutral.

Let's take a look at the premium costs at different ages for long-term care insurance. The prices stated represent the average annual premium from four different insurance companies. All quotes reflect a daily benefit of $100, with a 90-day elimination period, 100 percent coverage for home health care, and 5 percent compound inflation protection. Remember, the premium shown are averages—a quote that you receive will likely be higher, or lower.

The three-year benefit (period) means that the policy pays a maximum benefit of three years. For the policies shown, they pay up to $100 per day × 365 days per year × 3 years, for a benefit of $109,500 (this benefit grows by 5 percent compound a year, due to the inflation protection).

The lifetime benefit means that the policy pays a maximum daily benefit (before inflation increases are added) until the insured recovers, dies, or is no longer receiving care covered by the policy. For the policy design shown below, the benefit of $100 is multiplied by 365 days a year, for a yearly benefit of $36,500 (before inflation is added). Because of the unlimited benefit period, there is no limit to the amount that the policy will pay over the insured's lifetime.

Age 40

	3-year benefit	$562
	Lifetime benefit	$1,019

Age 50

	3-year benefit	$733
	Lifetime benefit	$1,362

Age 60

	3-year benefit	$1,120
	Lifetime benefit	$2,016

Age 70

	3-year benefit	$2,193
	Lifetime benefit	$3,782

(Source: StrateCision, Inc., Needham, Massachusetts, www.ltca.com)

But, wait, what this analysis hasn't taken into account is something very important: the effect of the built-in inflation protection. So if I'm 40 and wait 10 years to purchase a $100 daily benefit (DB), I can't just buy $100 daily benefit. At 50, I would need to buy a $155 daily benefit, to have the same daily benefit that I would have had if I had bought the policy (with 5 percent compound inflation protection) at age 40. At age 50, the same policy with a 3-year benefit that would have cost $562 at age 40 ($100 DB) would cost $1,100 at age 50 ($155 DB).

Then, there's the other problem with this financial analysis. It assumes that the consumer maintains his or her health, and can apply for insurance at any age and be approved.

Truth & Consequences

Waiting to apply for long-term care insurance exposes you to the risk of developing a medical condition that makes coverage unavailable or more expensive. In some cases, you may already have a condition that you are simply not yet aware of! And what if you have not only a decline in health, but actually need long-term care before you got around to applying? By applying for long-term care insurance, you shift these risks from your shoulders and your bankbook to the insurance company.

The Least You Need to Know

◆ Health-care proxies and durable powers of attorney can be important legal documents in the case of incapacity.

◆ Postponing the decision to apply for long-term care insurance makes no sense economically, or from a health point-of-view.

◆ Set yourself a game plan with a deadline, so that your long-term care planning doesn't get derailed.

◆ There are three primary things to consider when doing long-term care planning: your health, your financial situation, and your desire to control where you receive care.

◆ Long-term care insurance completes a health and disability insurance plan.

◆ Many people put off doing long-term care planning until their health changes and their options become greatly limited.

Part 2

Paying with Your Own Money

Many people think that long-term care planning means either buying a long-term care insurance policy or doing Medicaid planning. There are many other private-pay options, which I explore in Part 2. If you're already retired, you may plan to pay for your long-term care by tapping into the value of your home, and/or selling your life insurance policy. Instead of purchasing a traditional, stand-alone long-term care policy, you may chose to buy a combo life insurance and long-term care policy (or an annuity with an LTC benefit) to pay for your care.

Finally, I take a look at paying for long-term care with your own money. Be sure to read Chapter 8 if you are planning on paying for care this way. Like every other option, paying with your own money has pluses and minuses. By examining all the options that are available to you, an informed decision can be made.

Home Equity Conversion/ Reverse Mortgages

In This Chapter

- ◆ When your house becomes a bank
- ◆ The three types of reverse mortgages
- ◆ Why you should consider a reverse mortgage

Most of us do not have high enough income to pay for long-term care out of our monthly budget. If our income is not enough to cover our care costs, we must turn to our savings. A quick look at our savings, which may be in stocks or bank accounts, may quickly show that our life savings would eventually run out if we liquidated them to pay for extended long-term care. Whether we run out of money quickly or slowly depends on the cost of our care, but most importantly on how much money we have.

However, many seniors don't consider that they have access to a huge asset which can be a significant source of funding for long-term care—their home, or primary residence. For many seniors, this is their biggest asset. You may be thinking, seniors couldn't sell their house to pay for long-term care—where would they live? You may also be thinking that most seniors want to stay in their own home, and have long-term care services come to them.

But let's imagine this: What if a senior could liquidate the value of her house, while living in that same house until he or she died? The money could be used to pay for actual long-term care services or long-term care insurance, and no payments need to be made by the senior or any other co-owner of the property. That's the beauty of a home-equity conversion, or reverse mortgage.

Reverse Mortgage? What's That?

Most of us are familiar with mortgages. We pay a monthly check to the bank or mortgage company for years, while building home equity. Eventually, we own our home free and clear. A reverse mortgage is the reverse! As the homeowner taking out a reverse mortgage, you are tapping into your home's equity through either a lump sum or a series of payments. But these payments are made from the reverse-mortgage company, into your pocket. Reverse mortgages are sometimes called *home-equity* conversions.

Although the amount that you can get from a reverse mortgage is based in large part on the equity in your home, a reverse mortgage is very different than a home-equity loan. A home-equity loan requires that you show the ability to pay back the loan from your income. A reverse-mortgage lender expects the loan to be paid back from the sale of the house, so your income is not important. Reverse-mortgage lenders do not consider your ability to pay back the loan from your income or other assets beyond your home. They do require, in most cases, that you live in the home as your primary residence.

Marilee's Memo

Home equity is the value of your house that is truly yours. Take the amount that your house could be sold for and subtract the amount of any mortgages or loans against the house. In the early years of a mortgage, the home equity can be very low. Most seniors have no mortgage and their homes have appreciated, giving them a lot of home equity.

With a reverse mortgage, the reverse-mortgage company is the only company with rights against the title of your home. If you have a first mortgage loan, you will be required to pay this off. Most people do this with the partial proceeds of the reverse mortgage at closing, although you could pay off any existing mortgage with personal funds ahead of time.

Reverse mortgages can put money in your pocket to pay for long-term care, purchase long-term care insurance, or pay for anything else you desire.

Like other home-based loans, there are many costs involved with reverse mortgages. If the reverse mortgage is held for many years, these costs are spread out, and become more economical. Like a home-equity loan or the refinancing of a mortgage, a reverse mortgage does not normally make sense over the short term. For example, you would not take out a reverse mortgage if you were planning on selling the house in the next year.

The application fee of a reverse mortgage is likely to include an appraisal fee and a credit report. The loan-origination fee, closing costs, insurance, and a monthly servicing fee are added. These fees can all be added to your loan balance. These costs may make other sources of funding more attractive, if the senior has other assets to use. Reverse mortgages are generally not recommended for seniors who have other assets that can be used first.

Truth & Consequences

To compare the costs of reverse mortgages, get the total annual loan cost (TALC). This number combines all of the costs into one rate. The lender must provide this number; it's required by federal law. The TALC rate for any reverse mortgage falls over time as your loan balance grows, and the up-front costs are a smaller percentage of the total loan balance. That's why the longer you live in your home, the more attractive a reverse mortgage becomes.

If your strategy is to use your resources to pay privately for your long-term care, and you are not worried about what you leave after you die, a reverse mortgage can make a lot of sense. Here's an important point: Most people who own their own home and few other assets will end up quickly on Medicaid, which will usually put them in a nursing home and place a lien against their house. So they are not able to pass the home along to heirs anyway.

Aren't seniors better off using the equity in their home to give them a pile of money for private-pay care choices? Seniors have worked hard their whole lives to buy their homes, and they should feel comfortable using this asset to improve their quality of life.

LTC Lowdown

How much can you get from a reverse mortgage? The amount available to you depends on your age (the minimum age is 62 for most programs), the home's value and location, the cost of the loan, and the interest rate. The available amount can vary dramatically from one program to another, and from lender to lender. For example, the amount available on federally insured HECM (Home Equity Conversion Mortgage) loans is capped by limits that vary by county—based on the county's median home value. Other loans do not have this restriction.

What Properties Are Eligible for Reverse Mortgages?

If you own a single-family home, the property qualifies for a reverse mortgage. If your property is part of a multiple-unit owner-occupied building with four units or less, a condo, or a manufactured home, you may be able to qualify for some reverse mortgage loan programs, but not all. However, if your property is a mobile home or a co-op, your chances of getting the loan are slim (although pending legislation would make co-ops eligible).

How Is the Mortgage Paid Back?

Of course, like every other way to finance long-term care, there is no free lunch. Eventually, by the time of your death or when the loan comes due, the loan balance (the amount you received plus interest and some other miscellaneous charges) must be paid. If you are considering a reverse mortgage to pay for long-term care, in most cases you are planning to stay in your home forever, so the loan would not be due until you died. At that point, your house would be sold by your heirs and the loan balance paid. Instead, your heirs may instead choose to keep the house by paying off the loan themselves.

Interest rates on reverse mortgages are almost always variable. The HECM program regulations limit its lenders' ability to change or increase your rate. HECM lenders can change your interest rates once a year or once a month, depending on the option you have. With a HECM loan, if your interest rate has been raised to five points above your initial rate, it is capped. For example, if your original interest rate on your reverse mortgage was 5 percent, you would know that the interest rate could never be more than 10 percent.

As you remember from earlier in the chapter, the lender requires that you live in the home with the reverse mortgage as your primary residence. What if you needed to leave your house to receive your care in a nursing home? Let's say that you took out a reverse mortgage at age 75, planning to stay in your house forever. You were receiving long-term care in your home, and had almost run out of life savings to pay for the care. You used the proceeds from the reverse mortgage to pay for your care. After many years, at age 87, your health declines sharply, and you need 24-hour care. The burden of managing a home becomes too much and you enter a nursing home. You are expected to spend the rest of your life in the nursing home. Most reverse mortgages would become due once your house was no longer your primary residence. Since the loan would be due, you would sell your house and pay back the reverse lender any money owed. Any excess would go to you.

The vast majority of reverse-mortgage loans are what are called *nonrecourse*. This means that the lender can only look to the home for repayment of your loan. The lender cannot look to your other assets or income, or to your heirs. If you live an unexpectedly long time, and the lender pays you much more than the value of your home, the lender has no recourse beyond your home. And, as long as you are living in the home and maintaining your obligations under the loan agreement, you cannot be kicked out.

Truth & Consequences

If you are considering a reverse mortgage, first check with your financial and/or legal advisor. Before making any decision, review all the tax consequences, consequences to your heirs, and also any impact on federal and state assistance programs.

When you have a reverse mortgage, you are still the owner of your home. You still must pay for all the normal expenses of home ownership, such as maintenance, property taxes, and repairs. If you are considering a reverse mortgage to pay for those types of home expenses, look into whether your local, county, or state government has special loans for this purpose. They are often bargains, and do not have to repaid until you move or sell the house.

This financial instrument (a reverse mortgage) can be a lifesaver for seniors whose homes have significantly appreciated through the years. It can provide cash to pay for in-home care, delaying or even eliminating the need to move to a nursing home. Many seniors are cash poor and "house rich"; a reverse mortgage can give them the money they need.

Who Offers Reverse Mortgages?

There are three basic types of reverse-mortgage loans:

♦ **Federally insured Home Equity Conversion Mortgage.** The HECM is administered by the FHA (Federal Housing Administration). These loans are offered by banks, mortgage companies, and other private-sector lenders. Since they are federally insured, the U.S. government is on the hook to make payments if the lender goes out of business. If a mortgage is not backed by FHA, it is backed by the issuing private company. Federally insured loans may be offered by any lender approved by the FHA. These lenders require potential clients to attend a seminar on reverse mortgages put on by someone that is not connected with the sale. All current products require a counseling session.

- **Proprietary reverse mortgages.** Proprietary reverse mortgages are backed by private companies. They are offered by banks, mortgage companies, and other private lenders. They may offer the highest loan-advance amounts on a home if its value exceeds the average home value within the county where it is located.

- **Public-sector loans.** Sometimes called single-purpose reverse mortgages or deferred-payment loans, these are loans offered by local and state governments specifically for a certain purpose. Some programs require the proceeds be used to repair or improve your home, others are to pay property taxes. Under a property-tax-deferral program (PTD), the taxes are not paid until the house is sold. These types of loans make it easier financially for seniors to remain in their own home, and to maintain that home. Some programs are limited to low-income seniors. These loans do not have to be repaid until the house is sold.

Wisdom of the Aged

The HECM program tends to have the lowest cost loans. HECM tells lenders the loan limits. HECM also collects a mortgage insurance premium on any HECM loan. A law passed in December 2000 allows the mortgage insurance premium to be waived if the borrower is using the loan proceeds to purchase a tax-qualified long-term care insurance policy. As of spring 2002, this law had not yet been implemented.

What Are My Payment Options?

Reverse-mortgage companies offer a variety of ways that the equity in your house can be paid back to you. Some companies offer lump-sum payments, lines of credit, or periodic payments (such as monthly). Other companies allow the homeowner to take a combination of payment options; perhaps a lump sum for most of the equity, with the balance available as a credit line.

Let's say that a senior needs long-term care, but does not have a life-threatening problem. Her monthly income isn't high enough to cover her cost of care and her other living expenses. She has very few assets except for her house. This senior takes out a reverse mortgage because she wants the money to pay for her long-term care. She chooses monthly advances of her reverse-mortgage loan amount.

What if you would prefer a different payout schedule? Just because the lender you are talking to doesn't offer a certain kind of payout, don't make the assumption that the payout isn't available through another lender.

Can They Kick Me Out If I Live Too Long?

The first reverse mortgages required that the money be repaid after a certain number of years. These mortgages (called "fixed term") are no longer available.

Fixed-term loans paid out a higher monthly payment, since the payout was limited to a certain number of years and not tied into the homeowner's lifetime. This often led to a big problem. Consumers who wanted to stay in the home when the loan came due were sometimes unable to repay the loan, and had to sell their house to meet their obligation.

Most modern reverse-mortgage loans are not due for repayment as long the person is living in their home. This fact is very important: A senior whose home is being reverse mortgaged does not have to worry about living too long, "using up" his or her home's equity, and being kicked out in the cold.

Reverse mortgages are similar to annuities in one important way: They can both be structured to offer an income that you can't outlive. With an annuity, the *risk* of the consumer living too long is transferred to the insurance company; with a reverse mortgage, the risk of someone living too long is transferred to the financial institution. On average, some consumers will die sooner, and some will die later. Since they deal with extraordinarily large numbers of people, insurance companies and other financial institutions can take risks that individuals would never consider.

 Marilee's Memo _____

Risk is uncertainty about the possibility of a loss. If we knew for sure that we would not need long-term care, we would not spend a moment thinking about how to pay for it. Most of us do not know if we will need care, and how long the care will last. We run a risk of needing care. When we decide to protect ourselves financially against a risk we are practicing risk management. Risk management is the basis of modern financial planning.

That's also why only relatively healthy people should consider a reverse mortgage that provides for a lifetime payout only. If you are already ill and have a shorter-than-average life expectancy, you will not receive the full benefit that a healthy person with the same house would experience. If your health is not good, you may want to look into the fixed-term reverse mortgage that we talked about earlier.

Oops, It's Due and I'm Still Here!

There are some circumstances that can force seniors with a reverse mortgage to repay their loan before they die. These circumstances vary lender to lender. Make sure that you are aware of your lender's requirements, and that you are comfortable with them. Here are some typical conditions that may mean you have to repay your loan. Your specific loan agreement may have these conditions, or others.

Your loan may require repayment under either an acceleration clause or a condition of default if you (or the last surviving borrower) …

- Are absent from the home for a certain length of time, such as 12 months.

- Fail to maintain your homeowner's insurance.

- Change the use of the premises.

- Donate or abandon the house.

- Perpetrate fraud or misrepresentation.

- Incur eminent domain or condemnation proceedings.

- Declare bankruptcy.

- Rent part of your home on more than a month-to-month basis.

- Are deemed by a member of the medical community as unable to return to your home.

Wisdom of the Aged

What if you want a guaranteed monthly income that lasts as long as you live—even if you move out of your home? Consider taking out a reverse-mortgage amount in a lump sum, then purchasing a lifelong annuity with the proceeds. Keep in mind that annuity payouts vary between insurance companies, and that your privately purchased annuity is an obligation of the insurance company you buy it from, not the reverse-mortgage company or the FHA. The combos can be expensive, since your loan value is growing due to interest payable on the lump sum. Some people minimize the loan balance by splitting their reverse mortgage in two. They take a lump sum, which they use to buy a deferred annuity, with the plan of making it an annuity that pays regular income in the future. The balance of the loan they take as a limited-term monthly advance.

The income from either an annuity and/or a reverse-mortgage combo may jeopardize your eligibility for low-income programs. If you are on this type of program (such as Medicaid or supplemental security insurance) or may want these programs in the future, before you enter into one of these contracts, look into how the income might impact your eligibility.

If the senior is healthy enough to buy long-term care insurance but it is unaffordable, the proceeds of a reverse mortgage can be used to purchase long-term care insurance. Here's how it might work. A 70-year-old widow wants to stay in her house until she dies. She has gotten a quote for long-term care insurance, but she cannot afford the hefty premium on her fixed income. So she takes out a reverse mortgage in the form of a credit line. When premium payments are due, she writes the check against her reverse-mortgage loan account to pay for her long-term care insurance.

What Happens If I Want to Sell My Home?

If the balance due on the loan is less than the value of your home, you repay the loan and pocket the difference. If you die before repayment, your heirs do the same. Your heirs have the choice of keeping the house and repaying the loan out of other funds. If your home appreciates at a very high rate, your equity could grow, even though the interest charged to the loan increases the balance.

CAUTION

Truth & Consequences

Although most seniors want to live in their own home until they die, if they are living alone when they need long-term care, in many cases they are not able to do so. Here's one reason: A single/widowed senior can often find the burden of maintaining a house with compromised health quickly becomes overwhelming. There are two major exceptions to this: those who have strong local support groups of family and/or friends (informal caregivers), and those who are living in a house that is well suited for long-term care needs.

What Happens If I Change My Mind?

What if you sign up for a reverse mortgage and then, for whatever reason, you change your mind? After closing, you have up to three business days to cancel the reverse mortgage. Within that time frame, you must do what's called exercising the "right of recession" in writing. Keep in mind that Saturdays count as business days for this purpose; Sundays do not. It's a better idea not to sign anything at the closing unless you are absolutely, positively sure a reverse mortgage makes sense for you.

LTC Lowdown

How are reverse-mortgage proceeds taxed? Since the check you receive against a reverse mortgage is transferring your equity into cash (as a refinancing), it is not subject to income taxes.

The decision to enter into a reverse-mortgage agreement can be difficult for many seniors. Most Americans have a strong attachment to their homes. It may be the place where they raised a family. Through good times and bad, the home was the backdrop to their lives.

People keep large, difficult-to-maintain homes in some cases because they cannot bear to sell them. Memories tie us to homes, and increase our desire to pass along our homes to our children. Many seniors are reluctant to enter any agreement which may make it difficult for their children to inherit their home.

But at what cost? Practical people know that, in many cases, after they die their children will not move back to into their home. The cost to carry the house is prohibitive, and often the child ends up selling the home anyway.

Think about your options:

♦ Continuing to live in your home as your financial situation is now.

♦ Selling your home and moving.

♦ Continuing to live in your own home with a reverse mortgage.

When considering a reverse mortgage, I encourage seniors to "look out for number one" and make the decision that is in their personal best interest.

Special Programs for Taxes or Home Maintenance/Improvement

Before you look into a reverse mortgage to help pay your property taxes or for home maintenance or improvement, first look into local, regional, and state programs that may be available. Property-tax breaks for seniors and for veterans are common, as are programs that allow you to defer your property tax until you move out of your home. Some, though not all, programs require applicants to qualify as low income. Check with your town government, your area council on aging, and your state's Executive Office of Elder Affairs/Aging (see Appendix C) to find out about available programs.

An Ideal Candidate

Years ago, when I was a financial advisor, I met with an 82-year-old widow in her large, beautiful home in one of the most expensive neighborhoods in the Boston area. The home had a market value of well in excess of $1 million; it had been purchased 50 years earlier for a heck of a lot less! The woman wanted to meet about long-term care insurance. Her daughter explained that maintaining the house and paying the property taxes consumed almost all her mother's income; she had no money to pay for long-term care insurance. I suggested they look into a reverse mortgage.

Truth & Consequences

If you think that you may someday want to qualify for Medicaid, depending on your timing and overall goals, a reverse mortgage may or may not make sense. You would want to make sure the income from the reverse mortgage is structured favorably for Medicaid purposes. This usually means setting up the reverse mortgage as a line of credit as opposed to other payment options.

Like many people, this woman didn't want to consider taking a loan against her home. I suppose that she wanted to leave it free and clear to her children. But many seniors would be well served to consider using the value that has built up over the years in their homes.

The Least You Need to Know

- Reverse mortgages can be used by cash-strapped seniors who otherwise couldn't afford to pay for long-term care (or long-term care insurance) and stay in their own home.

- If you are on Medicaid, SSI, or other programs for low-income seniors, or may want these programs in the future, look into how reverse-mortgage proceeds might impact your eligibility.

- Reverse-mortgage programs vary dramatically in their costs, payouts, and guarantees.

- You can choose to take your reverse-mortgage money in a regular monthly loan advance, or a credit line that you can use at any time.

- The lowest-cost reverse mortgages are offered by state and local governments for home repairs and maintenance, and to pay property taxes.

- The reverse-mortgage loan, plus interest, must be paid back under certain conditions, including when you move out of the house, sell the house, or pass away.

Annuities for the Sick and Healthy

In This Chapter

- ◆ An investment that lasts as long as you do
- ◆ Annuities that pay more if you're sick
- ◆ Combo annuities or life insurance with a long-term care benefit

What are your choices if you've decided that you want long-term care insurance, but your health doesn't allow you to buy the insurance? You may be happy to learn that there are some insurance products that don't care about your health. There are other insurance products that actually favor those in bad health!

Before you consider these insurance products, make sure that you truly do not qualify for traditional long-term care insurance. Many people who thought that their health problems would mean they couldn't get LTC insurance have been pleasantly surprised. The health considerations to qualify for life insurance are very different than those to qualify for long-term care insurance. For more information on medical underwriting, please refer to Chapter 13.

Annuities in a Nutshell

An annuity contract is a special type of investment contract issued by an insurance company. The term *annuity* is used to describe two very different types of financial instruments. An annuity can be either an asset or it can be income.

Deferred (Asset) Annuities

When someone is saving for the future with an annuity, or has purchased an annuity to be used in the future, that annuity is an asset. It has a stated value, just like a bank account or a mutual fund statement. This type of annuity is called a deferred annuity because the decision to annuitize (turn it into a regular income) has been deferred. Any interest that is credited as time goes by is calculated on the value of the annuity asset. The annuity owner could cash in that annuity and receive a check for the surrender value of the contract.

Annuities are sometimes described as a tax-advantaged wrapper that holds an investment(s). Traditional fixed annuities pay an interest rate determined by the insurance company. Another type of annuity, a variable annuity, can hold investments such as stocks or mutual funds.

An annuity's surrender value is the amount of the check that you would be sent if you cashed in your annuity. Most annuities have surrender charges that apply to cashing in the contract and either taking the money yourself or reinvesting it into another annuity with another insurance company. These surrender charges can be very high, though most of them drop off after a certain number of years, such as 7 or 10 years.

Make sure that you are familiar with the annuity's surrender charges before you buy. Surrender charges are a double-edged sword for the consumer: They allow insurance companies to pay higher rates of interest, since they essentially "lock" you into keeping the money with that company by penalizing early withdrawals. Some annuities waive surrender charges after a certain age, or if you are taking out money to pay for long-term care. Many contracts allow you to take out 10 percent a year with no surrender charges.

Annuities have some distinctive characteristics that make them especially attractive to retirees and those who are saving for retirement. The earnings on the money held in an annuity grows tax deferred. This means that, until the money is taken out, the annuity owner pays no income tax on the earnings. By contrast, earnings on money held in a savings account or in a mutual fund, for example, is taxable income to the account owner that same year.

CAUTION

Truth & Consequences

Before you consider either cashing in an annuity or rolling it over into another contract, check out all the costs involved. In addition to possible surrender charges, there may be other penalties or taxes imposed when you move annuity money. Make sure that you understand the positive and negatives involved any time that you touch annuity money. Sometimes waiting for your next birthday could save you hundreds or thousands in federally imposed penalty taxes if you are liquidating annuity money, or waiting for the end of the next contract year could save you avoidable surrender fees. If an annuity move will cost you fees or penalties, make sure that you clearly understand why it is in your best interest to go ahead.

An annuity, like life insurance, does not go through probate when the account owner dies. Instead, the proceeds pass directly to the beneficiary named in the contract. Many seniors like this aspect of annuities, because it minimizes the expense of probating an estate. Also, since annuities pass to the beneficiary under contract law and are not governed by any will, they are not as likely to be disputed as a will could be by disgruntled relatives and friends.

Marilee's Memo

Assets are property of value. An asset may be tangible—which means that is has a physical form, such as a home—or an asset may be intangible, such as an annuity contract or a savings account. In order to qualify for many government-provided long-term care services, you must have very few assets.

Meanwhile, the interest that is credited to your annuity, is earning interest also. This tax deferred compounding effect is also a feature of cash value life insurance. The contributions into tax-qualified plans, such as 401(k)s and IRAs, also grow tax-deferred, but the amount that can be paid into these contracts is restricted. Sometimes people who have "maxed out" their qualified plan contributions purchase annuities to supplement their retirement plan with a tax-advantaged investment.

Immediate (Income) Annuities

An immediate annuity is a monthly (or other regular interval) series of income payments that someone buys with a lump sum. The lump sum may be in a deferred annuity with the same insurance company, or it may be from other personal funds. This kind of annuity is called an immediate annuity in the lingo of insurance agents. When people buy a stream of income by purchasing an annuity, they are purchasing the promise of an insurance company to make future payments by paying a lump sum of money today.

Some people purchase an immediate annuity to pay for their long-term care insurance. They may have a rainy-day fund, that they have set aside to pay for long-term care services. But that money will be wiped out quickly if long-term care is needed. By purchasing a lifetime annuity with a portion of the rainly-day fund, which then pays the long-term care insurance, they now have much more money to pay for long-term care, and they don't have to pay for the long-term care insurance premium out of their monthly budget. This works well if the amount the annuity pays is equal to the long-term care insurance premium. Make sure that you've looked into the taxes due on the annuity payments, and realize that if the insurance has a premium increase, you will have a shortfall.

LTC Lowdown

In the financial-services business, the type of annuity that I'm calling an income annuity is often called a single-premium immediate annuity (SPIA). Even though most of us consider this type of product an investment, the insurance word *premium* creeps in, because annuities are always issued by insurance companies.

As you know, a premium is money that you pay in exchange for an insurance policy, such as life insurance, long-term care insurance, or an annuity. But how about the annuities that you might buy from a brokerage house or a bank? Those institutions have either set up their own insurance company or they have an agreement to sell the annuities that are issued by an insurance company.

Why would someone trade any amount of money that they had in their hand today for a promise of a bunch of smaller payments in the future? It's simple: Most annuities are lifetime annuities, which means that the insurance company promises to make these payments for the rest of the persons' life—no matter what happens to interest rates, no matter how the stock market performs, and no matter how long they live.

Now you may be thinking, "What if I die the month after giving the insurance company a big check? Do they keep the money as profit?" Usually, the answer is no. That kind of annuity would be called a life-certain or life-only annuity. If you bought this type of SPIA annuity, the insurance company promises to pay you a certain amount periodically (monthly, for example), as long as you are alive. When you die, the payments stop—even if you die shortly after signing the contract and paying the insurance company.

Most annuity contracts today have a minimum payment or survivor provision. For example, an annuity may be described as a "10-year-certain." Payments would continue for the lifetime of the annuity owner, but the insurance company guarantees at least 10 years of payments. If the annuity owner has died, the payments would be made to the *beneficiary* named in the contract.

Marilee's Memo _____

A **beneficiary** is the person, persons, or legal entity (like a charity or a business entity) that is named to receive money in a financial contract in the event of the death of a named person. When more than one person is named to share the proceeds, they are called co-beneficiaries. It makes good sense to name a second beneficiary in case the first beneficiary dies before proceeds are paid. That person is called a secondary beneficiary. The third beneficiary in line is called the tertiary beneficiary.

The promise to make payments as long as someone lives is an important promise. Social Security and certain types of pensions aside, there is no other financial product that you can purchase that offers to last as long as you do … "through good times and bad, as long as you shall live." What if you live to the ripe old age of 107? No problem. What if interest rates fall and the insurance company, which has promised you a check for a certain amount each month, is actually losing money on the annuity you bought? It's not your problem.

Medically Underwritten Annuities

Traditionally, an immediate annuity that pays an income (a SPIA—single premium immediate annuity) is purchased only by people who think they are healthy, who figure that they are likely to live longer than the average person. They figure that they can beat the insurance company at their own game. Payouts for traditional SPIAs are calculated based on the assumption that those people who buy annuities are projected to live quite awhile. That meant that people who weren't healthy as horses got the short end of the stick if they bought an annuity. Even though their health was compromised, they weren't paid more to compensate for their expected shorter lifetime. Until now.

Let's say that a certain senior needs long-term care. Maybe it's in his own home, or in a facility like an assisted living facility. His income isn't high enough to pay for the care, and he has some assets. But he's afraid that the assets may run out while he is still alive. If he were healthy, he would consider an annuity, which would pay as long as he were alive. But if, in addition to needing long-term care, he suffers from a medical condition that shortens life spans, he can get a bigger annuity-income payout with a medically underwritten annuity.

When you purchase this kind of annuity, the shorter your projected lifespan, the larger your payout. These annuities are taking into account that your medical condition makes it likely that you will pass away earlier than if you were still healthy.

Wisdom of the Aged
Could you do better by investing the amount of money that you are considering putting into an annuity, then paying yourself the same monthly payout the annuity company would have paid you? Maybe yes, maybe no. It depends on how long you live and where you've invested your money. Do you take into consideration the time that you are spending managing the account or accounts yourself? Have you made a plan for the day that you are perhaps too sick to continue to manage the account yourself? How much is not having to worry about outliving your money worth to you? There are many reasons that smart people decide to buy a life annuity.

Let's look at a few examples. The following table shows how someone with health problems can purchase a specific lifetime income stream for much less money than someone who is healthy. For example, for a monthly income of $4,000, an 86-year-old man who is healthy would need to pay $288,440. This same insurance company charged only $145,500 for the same annuity amount, based on the man's diagnosis of Alzheimer's. Perhaps the man wants to pay for private assisted living facility care, and is buying the annuity to make sure he will always have income to pay for his care.

Note that annuities can be structured to increase each year, or to provide for a refund at death. Of course, these options increase the cost of the annuity. Each case and payout is different, depending on the health of the person and what they are looking to accomplish. In addition, like any insurance product, premiums vary between insurance companies.

In the following chart, the monthly income is the amount that the individual wants the insurance company to pay them. The next column is the amount of money that they would pay to buy that annuity, taking into account their health problem. The traditional SPIA column is the much higher amount that someone who purchased a traditional annuity, with no medical questions, would have to pay to get the same monthly annuity income. A medically underwritten annuity charges less for the same lifetime income stream, since your health is taken into consideration.

Medically underwritten annuities are relative newcomers to the United States, and they are not available in every state. Like any other kind of annuity, they are regulated by the insurance department in each state. If you are calling your insurance department to ask about the availability of medically underwritten annuities, you would want to speak with someone in the life insurance section. If these annuities are approved for sale in your state, the insurance department can tell you which insurance companies are offering them.

Sample Annuities: Traditional and Medically Underwrittern

Gender	Age	Prominent Health Conditions	Monthly Income	Traditional Annuity Single Premium	Medically Underwritten Annuity Single Premium
Male	84	Stroke/diabetes	$4,500	$356,080	$168,000
Female	86	Alzheimer's	$2,400	$183,560	$99,500
Male	82	Parkinson's	$3,500	$303,050	$134,000

Sample premiums provided courtesy of Golden Rule Financial Services, a division of Golden Rule Insurance Company, Indianapolis, Indiana

LTC Lowdown

When planning on buying an immediate annuity (an income stream of payments) with a lump sum of money to pay for a lifetime of long-term care, consider that the cost of care is likely to go up each year. If your income remains flat, you could be stuck. Take into account that Social Security income goes up with inflation each year, as do some pensions. There are a few options. One is to buy an annuity with an increasing payment. Another is to keep some money aside as an asset annuity, with a plan to liquidate it in the future to cover likely higher costs.

Deferred Annuities for the Sick

What if you are not healthy enough to get traditional long-term care insurance? When you consider your long-term care financing options, you may come across products that will give you a long-term care benefit—no matter what your health is today!

Some people purchase annuities to save for retirement, because of the income-tax deferral on the earnings. Other people purchase annuities because they are the only investment vehicle that guarantees a lifetime income stream.

A new reason for many to consider annuities is the fact that some companies are offering even uninsurable people a limited long-term care benefit as part of their contract. Let's take a look at another example of a product that is available for those people who are uninsurable.

Marilee's Memo

If you are **uninsurable,** you are not able to purchase insurance due to health reasons. Someone who may be uninsurable for life insurance due to a heart problem may be easily insurable for long-term care insurance. Insurance companies look at different conditions to determine whether you are insurable for a particular type of insurance (see Chapter 13). Different companies have different guidelines. You may be considered insurable by one insurance company, and uninsurable to another.

Some insurers are offering deferred (asset) annuitied that add a long-term care benefit after a certain number of years. People who cannot buy long-term care insurance can buy this annuity, since there are no medical questions. The advantages and disadvantages of this type of long-term care coverage are relatively obvious. Let's start with the disadvantage: If the insureds need care before the long-term care benefit starts, they do not have coverage. On the flip side, though, if they need care after the policy's "waiting period" has passed, they have long-term care benefits that would not have been available to them otherwise, since they were uninsurable. A typical annuity with a deferred long-term care benefit would pay a percentage of the annuity amount (say a monthly LTC benefit of 1 percent of your initial investment) after 7 years. There is a cost to adding this benefit to your annuity. The terms of the rider varies between insurance companies. In my opinion, if someone is uninsurable for long-term care insurance and they were going to buy an annuity anyway, they should strongly consider this type of annuity, for its potential to help with future long-term care costs.

As you can imagine, these insurance products for uninsurables are not as strong as stand-alone long-term care insurance. There are a growing number of insurance policies for uninsurables. Because these are insurance products, they are subject to regulation by the state divisions of insurance, and their premium prices must be okayed before the policy can be sold.

Annuities and Long-Term Care Planning

Annuities can be important financial tools for sheltering assets in order to qualify for Medicaid, and these very specific types of annuities are discussed in Part 6. In this chapter, I'll discuss annuities for those who are looking to pay for their long-term care privately. Earlier in this chapter we discussed how some people use traditional immediate annuities to pay for their LTC insurance premiums or medically underwritten immediate annuities to pay for their long-term care.

What if you're healthy, and want to buy long-term care insurance? You may have heard of annuities that have a long-term care insurance rider attached to them. These annuities are designed for the insurable person who wants a product that will do "double duty," comparable to life insurance policies that have long-term care riders attached to them. (A *rider* is an addition to an insurance contract that adds benefits, normally at additional cost. For example, a waiver of premium rider is normally added to every individual life insurance policy. If the insured policyholder becomes disabled, this rider provides that no premium payments have to be made.) Even if the person never uses the long-term care insurance, he or she figures that either the life insurance or the annuity proceeds will be used.

The marriage of an annuity and long-term care insurance is, in my opinion, a match made in heaven. Why not combine your retirement savings with an insurance policy that kicks in if you need long-term care? Of course, compare the LTC benefits against a stand-alone policy to make sure you aren't trading off something important.

Combo Life Insurance/Long-Term Care Policies

Many people are happy to see a new type of policy is now becoming widely available. This policy combines a cash-value life insurance policy with a long-term care insurance policy. The combo policies are popular for a logical reason: The policyholder (or, more accurately, the policyholder or his or her beneficiary) benefits even if he or she never needs long-term care. That's because the policy will eventually pay: Although you may not need long-term care, you certainly will die.

Here's how these policies usually work. The policyholder buys a permanent, or cash-value, life insurance policy. He or she pays an additional premium for a long-term care insurance rider. This additional premium is usually less expensive than a stand-alone long-term care policy. The value of the rider's benefit is often limited by the amount of the *base* life insurance policy. For example, the LTC benefit may pay a maximum monthly amount of 2 percent of the life insurance's death benefit, for a maximum of 50 months. A $200,000 life insurance policy with that company would allow the purchaser to buy a $4,000 monthly long-term care benefit.

Marilee's Memo _____

A **base policy** consists of the primary benefit you purchased. For example, you may have a $150,000 life insurance policy designed to pay off the mortgage for your spouse if you died. You may add riders, or optional benefits, such as waiver of premium (waives the premium if you are disabled), or a long-term care insurance rider. Your base policy would be the $150,000 life insurance policy. The base is always the coverage to which riders are attached.

When the insured person dies, his or her beneficiary is paid the amount of the life insurance amountless any amount that the insured person collected on the long-term care rider. This kind of policy is not recommended when life insurance is needed to provide for survivors, because the life insurance amount can be compromised and even obliterated if the need for long-term care goes on long enough.

Combo life/long-term care policies are often designed so that the premium dollars paid in will be either paid out as a death benefit to the beneficiary or as a long-term care benefit for the policyholder. This can be an attractive option for people who want to make sure their premium dollars are not "wasted" if they don't need long-term care.

The taxation on these policies is straightforward. If the LTC benefit is tax-qualified, the benefit is tax-free, as long as the benefit received doesn't exceed your costs. Any life insurance proceeds at death are always income-tax free. The tax advantages of these products make them attractive when compared with some other ways of funding long-term care.

LTC Lowdown _____

With a combo life insurance/long-term care policy, often your long-term care benefit is a percentage of your life insurance death benefit. Because of this, your long-term care benefit may not keep pace with inflation. Make sure that you understand whether or not your whole long-term care benefit has inflation protection. Any shortfall would have to be funded out of other assets or income. This problem becomes more important for the young purchaser of a life/long-term care combination policy. Read Chapter 18 for more information on inflation.

Tailor-Made for Seniors

One of the shortfalls for younger people who plan to combine their long-term care insurance with life insurance is this: If the long-term care benefit is used, it reduces or even uses up the money that would have been paid to beneficiaries. For example, a 45-year-old buys life insurance with a long-term care rider, hoping to "kill two birds with one stone." He develops a debilitating problem, and needs years of long-term care before he dies at age 60. In that scenario, he might have used up all the life insurance benefit on long-term care, since the life insurance death benefit is reduced by the long-term care benefit. In that case, it would be as if he had no life insurance.

That's why I'm a fan of people using combination policies that don't necessarily need the death benefit. What do I mean? Imagine that you are 60 years old, with a $200,000 CD at the bank. It's your "rainy day money" that you plan on never touching, but want to leave to your kids or grandkids after you die.

You know that, if you need long-term care, the money is going to be used, and there'll be nothing left. So you purchase a whole-life policy with the $200,000. The initial death benefit is $372,201, so you've almost doubled the amount you'd leave to your kids or grandkids. But you've also taken out two long-term care riders on the policy. The first would pay up until the total death benefit (limited to 2 percent of the current death benefit per month, for 50 months) was used. If you needed care that exceeded that amount, your second rider would extend the benefit for another 50 months (a lifetime option is also available). The total LTC benefit on your policy is 100 months, or 8⅓ years of benefits.

Meantime, you've accomplished two goals:

- ◆ You've enhanced the amount to be left to your heirs, if you don't need care, or need a small amount of care.

- ◆ You've created a whole pile of money just for long-term care. This pile gives you more private-pay options than if you relied on your assets alone, and it protects your assets.

Only if you spent $372,000 on your long-term care would you heirs not realize a death benefit when you pass away. Let's say you needed $250,000 of long-term care over the next six years. If you had left the money in the CD and wanted to private pay, you likely would've spent the CD. Nothing would've been left. If you had purchased this type of policy, then needed long-term care, the rider would pay for the $250,000 of care, and your heirs would still receive the life insurance amount minus what was paid for care (approximately $372,000 – $250,000, or $122,000). By the way, the figures quoted reflect guaranteed values available the day the policy is purchased. As time passes, the death benefit may grow, so that, in 25 years (age 85), the amount left to your heirs if you don't need LTC is projected to be over $800,000. (Thanks to National Life Insurance Company, Montpelier, Vermont, for kindly providing figures for their LifeCare product for the example.)

For seniors who want to preserve assets to pass along, this strategy is worth looking at. It may or may not make sense for you, depending on your health and your whole financial situation.

Wisdom of the Aged

To buy a combination life/long-term care insurance policy, you must be healthy enough to qualify for both life insurance and long-term care insurance. Insurance companies look for different medical problems in evaluating an application for life insurance than for long-term care (LTC) insurance. Someone may be able to get LTC, but not qualify for life insurance, or vice versa. If your health is less than optimal, you may find that it is easier to get a stand-alone long-term care insurance policy. Read Chapter 13 for more information on the medical requirements for long-term care insurance.

Whether or not this is a good policy for someone depends on the answers to three questions:

- Is the long-term care insurance rider as high quality as what the person could get as a stand-alone policy?

- What are the other life insurance or investment options available, and how do they compare to the life insurance base of the policy?

- Does the idea of bringing these two products together make the person better able to sleep at night?

I have been a speaker for many years, and have spoken to thousands of people across the country about long-term care planning. One of the most common questions that I am asked about long-term care planning is, "What if I buy the insurance and I never need it? Is all the money I paid gone?" With traditional, stand-alone long-term care insurance, the answer is yes. Like auto insurance, homeowners insurance, or disability insurance, if you do not have a claim, the premium money is "gone."

Combining long-term care with life insurance policies or annuities makes the bitter pill of long-term care planning easier for many people to swallow.

If an adviser strongly puts down a product or strongly encourages you to acquire the product, ask why he or she feels that way. Ask him or her also to take the devil's advocate position and argue the opposite side. In the end, it's your decision. After all, it's your life and your money!

The Least You Need to Know

- Income annuities (immediate annuities) can provide a guaranteed income that you can't outlive.

- Some annuities have a type of LTC benefit that can be great for people who are otherwise uninsurable.

- Medically underwritten annuities are a new product that pay a higher income to those who aren't expected to live as long as others because their health is bad.

- Some people purchase income (immediate) annuities to pay their long-term care insurance premium, so that the premiums don't have to be paid from their regular budget.

- A life insurance policy with an accelerated death benefit *may be* a source of LTC funding. A LTC rider on life insurance is more likely to pay.

Chapter 7

"Thar's Gold in That Thar Life Insurance"

In This Chapter

- ◆ The living benefits of life insurance
- ◆ The ins and outs of surrendering your life insurance
- ◆ How to get a death benefit prior to death

Have you ever had a yard sale where you brought out all your forgotten treasures, and were amazed at the amount of money you had raised by the end of the day? From white elephants to green cash! How sweet it is when we are surprised that something is worth much more than we thought. There are many people who purchased life insurance to protect their children when their own kids were small, and now they are grandparents. Maybe they got a policy to buy out the business interest of a partner, if the partner were to pass away. Now that the business has been sold, the coverage is no longer needed. Those policies bought so many years ago can often be tapped today, providing money to pay for long-term care.

What is you don't have an old life insurance policy? These days, you can actually buy a life insurance policy with a long-term care benefit rider. If you don't need long-term care before you die, the policy will pay out eventually! That's the kind of insurance that you'd plan on keeping forever.

In the last 20 or so years, we've seen brand-new options in life insurance, including accelerated death benefits, viatical settlements, life settlements, and long-term care riders. These all accomplish the goal of getting cash before the person insured by the life insurance dies, but these options are not the same. These new advances, as well as the good old-fashioned cash that accumulates in many life insurance policies, can be used for your long-term care. That's right, you may be able to use life insurance to pay for long-term care or provide cash to buy long-term care insurance—possibly even on a tax-advantaged basis!

Life Insurance to the Rescue

If you are over age 40, you probably remember the early days of the late-night show *Saturday Night Live*. One classic skit was a parody of a commercial for an all-purpose cleaning product. Gilda Radner played a housewife who was cleaning the floor with a wax she squirted from an aerosol can. Her husband complained that they were out of dessert topping. While she squirted the product on his pudding, she happily explained to him that the product was not just a floor wax, it was also a dessert topping!

Life insurance can be the financial equivalent. We usually think of life insurance as paying an amount of money to a loved one when we die (the death benefit). However, there are many ways to use life insurance in your long-term care planning. It may sound odd, but life insurance is one of the most interesting and flexible financial vehicles ever invented. That has never been more true than today. Life insurance which was bought years ago to take care of the kids if something should happen may now be used to pay for your long-term care. Although cash-value, or permanent, life insurance offers the maximum number of planning options, some of the ideas in this chapter are also available with terminsurance policies.

Some seniors have hefty life insurance policies, but most don't. For this reason, many of these options will not be much help. According to the U.S. Census Bureau, the median cash value of life insurance policies for seniors is only $5,000. The ability to tap into $5,000 will not make a big difference in the overall scheme of financing long-term care.

The Types of Life Insurance

There are two basic categories types of life insurance: term insurance and permanent insurance.

◆ Term insurance is designed to provide life insurance for a specific number of years. It is pure protection only, and does not build up cash value. It's very inexpensive, unless you want to maintain it longer than it was designed for. You can buy term insurance that locks in the same flat premium for up to 20 or even 30 years. Most term insurance can be converted to a cash value policy with the same company with no medical questions.

♦ Permanent (or cash value) insurance is more expensive at first than term insurance. It is designed for a long-term need for life insurance (more than 20 years). The IRS encourages the purchase of life insurance by giving a number of tax breaks to the policies; for example, cash value inside life insurance grows tax-deferred. The most expensive form of permanent life insurance is called whole life, which also offers the strongest guarantee: Your premium will remain level, as long as you live. Other types of permanent policies are universal life and variable life.

If you are healthy, you may use your life insurance policy to generate money to pay for long-term care insurance, so that the premium doesn't come out of your regular budget. If you medically do not qualify for long-term care insurance, you may use the money in your life insurance to pay for your actual care. Perhaps you are planning on purchasing life insurance anyway, and are considering adding a long-term care insurance rider to the policy.

Marilee's Memo

An **accelerated death benefit** is an optional benefit on many life insurance policies. It lets the insured access some or all the policy's death benefit before he or she dies. In order to get this benefit, you must meet the terms of the contract. For example, the contract may require that you have less than six months to live, or that you are permanently confined to a nursing home.

Like any financing method, each option has pluses and minuses. Which one is right for you will depend on your health, your financial situation, the tax ramifications, and, most importantly, what you are looking to accomplish. As with any advice in this book, seek competent professional advice regarding your options. All the options listed in the following section have potential tax ramifications, which your financial and tax advisor can review with you.

How Life Insurance Can Be Used to Finance Long-Term Care

Life insurance can be used in various ways to finance your long-term care. The following options are available for both term and permanent insurance policies:

♦ Some life insurance policies have a rider (meaning an optional benefit) an *accelerated death benefit*. But beware—not all these riders are created equal. Since contract benefits vary, some policies require you be terminally ill to collect, so you may or may not qualify for payments under this benefit when you need long-term care. More attractive modern policies allow you to collect under this benefit if you need nursing home care, or better yet, if you need any type of long-term care.

♦ If you are terminally ill you could sell your life insurance policy using a viatical settlement (this option is discussed at length later in the chapter).

♦ If you are not terminally ill and you meet the criteria for a life settlement, you could sell your policy to a life settlement company (this option also is discussed later in the chapter).

♦ Some life insurance policies and annuities have a long-term care benefit attached to them. These rider benefits vary, so it's important to compare the benefits against a stand-alone long-term care policy to judge the quality of the contract. These policy riders were discussed in Chapter 6.

These options are only available with permanent life insurance:

♦ You could elect the "dividends paid out" option. If you own a traditional whole-life contract, it may pay an annual dividend. Instead of reinvesting the dividend in the policy, you may direct the insurance company to send you the check instead. This is similar to having your stock dividends sent to you each year, with one important exception: Insurance policy dividends are considered a return of premium paid, and are not taxable. The amount of money you would receive in dividends depends on the value and age of the policy. Some people use this "found" money to pay for their long-term care insurance premiums.

♦ You could cash in the policy to receive the surrender cash value (this may not be equal to the cash value of your policy, since there is sometimes a surrender charge). In this case, the policy is no longer in force.

♦ You could take a policy loan against the cash value in your life insurance. This can be a great option with a lot of flexibility, since you can choose to repay the loan at any time. There may be tax advantages associated with this strategy. Another advantage to a policy loan or policy withdrawal (see next item) is that you can get money very quickly—normally within a few days of your request. Remember that the amount of your death benefit is reduced by the outstanding policy loan. Also, although the loan does not have to be paid back, the performance of the policy will be hurt because of the loan.

♦ You could make a withdrawal from the cash value of the policy (with a whole-life policy, this would be called "surrendering adds"). The performance of the policy will be hurt because of the withdrawal.

Viatical and Life Settlements

When considering how to pay for long-term care, you may not think about the option of selling your life insurance. That's right, I said selling your life insurance, not surrendering the policy to get the cash value or taking a loan against the policy. Selling your life insurance policy, which can be done even if you are not seriously ill, is a relatively new type of financial transaction. Imagine having the option of selling a life insurance policy, for more than the cash value that you didn't want to keep anyway?

Life settlements and viatical settlements both result in you getting paid in exchange selling your life insurance policy. No future premiums payments are payable by the owner who sells his or her policy. Life settlements are usually available to people over age 65, in good or bad health, who have life expectancies of less than 12 years Viatical settlements are available to terminally ill people of any age who own life insurance.

Marilee's Memo

Surrendering a life insurance policy (or annuity contract) means to give up, or cancel, the policy. Any surrender value would then be sent to the policy owner. Once a policy is surrendered, it is no longer providing a benefit to anyone. It may, in fact, provide a big negative—a tax bill! Make sure that you consider the tax impact of any financial move, such as surrendering life insurance.

Here's how a viatical settlement works. The viatical company projects, based on the person's medical diagnosis, how long he or she is likely to live. The purchaser knows that once the person dies, the life insurance company will pay the amount of the life insurance (called the face amount, or death benefit) in a lump sum to the *beneficiary* of the policy. The purchaser of the policy will also be the beneficiary. The viatical company is willing to buy the policy for an amount less than the death benefit and continue making premium payments on the policy, knowing that when the person who sold the policy dies, they (the viatical company) will collect the death benefit.

Marilee's Memo

Terminally ill means that someone is expected to die within a specified time period, usually defined as less than two years in insurance company contracts. When someone is described as terminally ill, it usually means that the medical community has determined that there is no hope of recovery. Although many terminally ill people need long-term care services, the reverse is not true. Someone can need long-term care and not be terminally ill.

Here's an example. A 54-year-old woman is diagnosed with malignant cancer. Her life expectancy is 30 months. She has a cash-value life insurance policy with a death benefit of $250,000. Although the accumulated cash value is $12,000, the surrender cash value is only $5,000. Instead of keeping the policy in force and paying premiums, or surrendering it for $5,000, she chooses to sell the policy to a viatical company for $160,000. She uses the money to take her family on a dream trip to Hawaii, to modify here home to make it more comfortable for her illness, and to hire a live-in companion.

Don't Count on a Viatical for Long-Term Care

A relatively healthy person cannot count on a viatical settlement to pay future long-term care costs. Here's the reason: Viatical settlements are only available to the terminally ill individual, and many people who need long-term care are not terminally ill. For example, someone with severe osteoporosis or painful rheumatoid arthritis could need years of long-term care. But the same person's life expectancy is not impacted by the disease, and he or she is certainly not terminally ill.

Sometimes people us the proceeds of a viatical settlement to provide funds to pay for their medical treatment, possibly extending their life. Another option is to use the proceeds to make their quality of life better in the remaining time. Remember, though, if that policy is sold and the money used to pay for the person's long-term care, there is no death benefit paid to the beneficiary. The policy has been "used up."

To summarize, the usefulness of viaticals is limited to those people who are terminally ill, and who are willing to forgo the life insurance benefit for their beneficiaries.

Viaticals for the Rest of Us

If a company can figure out how much to pay for a life insurance policy on someone who is terminally ill, why can't they figure out what to pay for a policy on someone who is not terminally ill? Glad you asked! That new product is called a *life settlement*.

Here's how a life settlement works. The buying company projects, based on the standard life expectancy tables and medical information specific to the applicant, how long the person insured by the policy is likely to live. Some people own joint life insurance policies, which insure more than one person; these can also be used for a life settlement. Most life settlement companies will only purchase a policy from someone at least 65 years old, with a life expectancy of 12 years or less. In addition, the policy needs to have been in force for at least two years, which puts the policy out of its contestability and suicide-exclusion period.

Some settlement companies will not purchase *term insurance*, others will. Some companies will purchase term insurance only after it has been converted to a cash value policy. Consumer safeguards such as requiring that the life insurance policy's beneficiary sign his or her consent to the sale, and other disclosure requirements recommended by the National Association of Insurance Commissioners (NAIC), are utilized by some companies. Most companies have a minimum policy size, such as $100,000 or $250,000. Here's an example: A 75-year-old healthy man has a large

Marilee's Memo

A **life settlement** refers to the sale of a life insurance contract by someone who is not terminally ill. Often a senior drops life insurance because it is not needed or the premium is too expensive. Life settlements can be a great option in those circumstances.

life insurance policy that he bought years ago to cover some business loans. He doesn't need the $1,500,000 in insurance any more, and would prefer to have cash to use to supplement his retirement income or to pay for long-term care. The cash value of the life insurance policy is $132,314. If he were to surrender the policy (cash it in), he would receive a check for $131,689 (the cash value minus the surrender charge). He inquires about a cash settlement and learns that he can sell his policy for $294,000.

Wisdom of the Aged

Bet you didn't know that the owner of a life insurance policy, the person who is insured, and the beneficiary do not have to be the same person. In a viatical or life settlement, the policy owner signs an agreement to transfer all ownership rights to the viatical/life settlement company. Another agreement is also executed to make the viatical or life settlement company the beneficiary of the life insurance policy. Then, as the owner of the policy, the viatical company not only gets the premium due notices, but as the beneficiary the company also gets the death benefit paid when the insured person dies.

Earlier I mentioned that for a policy to be eligible for a life settlement, the insured person does not have to be terminally ill, but must have a life expectancy of 12 years or less. This is an important point as we consider whether to plan on the ability to sell our life insurance if we need long-term care.

A "healthy" 65-year-old woman who needs long-term care because of a crippling accident would not be able to sell her life insurance policy. She is not terminally ill, so cannot qualify for a viatical settlement. Her life expectancy is longer than 12 years; (in fact, it's 17 years according to a mortality tables used by some life insurance companies). Therefore, she wouldn't qualify for a life settlement. However, if the same person were 75 years old instead of 65, her life expectancy would be short enough (10 years) to qualify for a life settlement.

Although each case is evaluated on its own, in general, the older someone is (whether or not they have serious health conditions), and the older their life insurance policy is, the more they will get (higher percentage of death benefit) from a life settlement. As a rule of thumb, for those not suffering from a life-threatening condition, a woman may be eligible for a life settlement at age 75, a man at age 73. People between age 65 to 75 who have poor health or a life-threatening illness may also qualify for a life settlement.

LTC Lowdown

Why does it matter how old a life insurance policy is in determining the amount of a life settlement? The life settlement company has to figure out how much it will cost them to keep your policy in force. An older policy was bought when you were younger, so the premium is less, making it more attractive. Also, an older policy normally has higher accumulated cash values. These can be used by the life settlement company to reduce or eliminate their premium payments.

Regulation of Life Settlements

Although most states regulate viatical settlements, you can see in the following table there is far less regulation for life settlements. Life settlements are such a new product that it will take some time for both the regulatory community and the public to get their arms around this new option.

Regulation can be a double-edged sword. On the good side, regulation is critical so consumers can feel comfortable selling their life insurance for a life settlement. Good regulations help consumers know that they are being paid a fair price for their policy, and provide full disclosure of all aspects of the transaction. On the bad side, overregulation can create an unfavorable business climate for a particular product, which keeps businesses away and leaves consumers without choices. Note in the following table that just because a state regulates life settlements doesn't mean that life settlement companies have products available in that state.

States That Regulate	Viaticals	Life Settlements
Alabama	no	no
Alaska	yes	yes
Arizona	no	no
Arkansas	yes	no
California	yes	no
Colorado	no	no
Connecticut	yes	no
Delaware	yes	no
District of Columbia	no	no
Florida	yes	yes
Georgia	no	no
Hawaii	no	no
Idaho	no	no
Illinois	yes	no
Indiana	yes	no
Iowa	yes	yes
Kansas	yes	no
Kentucky	yes	yes
Louisiana	yes	no
Maine	yes	yes
Maryland	no	no
Massachusetts	yes	no
Michigan	yes	no
Minnesota	yes	no
Mississippi	yes	yes
Missouri	no	no
Montana	yes	yes*
Nebraska	yes	yes
Nevada	yes	yes
New Hampshire	no	no
New Jersey	yes	no
New Mexico	yes	no

continues

States That Regulate	Viaticals	Life Settlements
New York	yes	no
North Carolina	yes	yes
North Dakota	yes	yes
Ohio	yes	yes
Oklahoma	yes	yes
Oregon	yes	no
Pennsylvania	no	no
Rhode Island	no	no
South Carolina	no	no
South Dakota	no	no
Tennessee	yes	yes
Texas	yes	yes
Utah	yes	yes*
Vermont	yes	yes
Virginia	yes	no
Washington	yes	no
West Virginia	no	no
Wisconsin	yes	no
Wyoming	no	no

Montana and Utah regulate life settlements—but prohibit them. Maine law effectively makes life settlements impossible.

Source: Living Benefits Financial Services, LLC, Minnetonka, Minnesota

State regulation of insurance changes constantly, and by the time you look at these pages, the information here may no longer be accurate. For the latest information, please contact your state's insurance department (Appendix A) and the websites listed in the "Life Settlements and Viaticals" section (Appendix E).

As I've said before, it's important to consider the after-tax effect when you look at any way to pay for long-term care. When Congress passed the Health Insurance Portability and Accountability Act (HIPAA), which became effective January 1, 1997, it made viatical settlements not subject to income and capital gains taxes. Until Congress grants life settlements the same break as viaticals, tax advisors are debating the tax treatment of life settlements.

Wisdom of the Aged
Viatical companies have received bad press in the past. Here's one reason. The funds to pay those who are selling their life insurance policies have come from two sources: institutional investors and individual investors. Individuals who had no business investing in viaticals got burned when some people who sold their life insurance policies lived longer than expected (remember the miraculous new AIDS drugs that transformed terminally ill patients into long-term survivors? Imagine what that did to viatical investors who had planned on collecting death benefits over the short term.) Viatical settlements are not an appropriate investment for many individual investors. However, the viatical settlement of a life insurance policy can be a godsend for those who are terminally ill. As the viatical and life settlement industries mature, there is a growing trend towards funding which comes from institutional investors, not individual investors.

The life settlement industry explains the taxation in this way. It says there is no tax due on the amount received up to the amount of premiums you've paid. The amount of the settlement that exceeds this amount up to any cash surrender value (of the sold life insurance contract), if any, would be taxed as ordinary income. The settlement amount received that exceeds the policy's cash surrender value would be taxed as a long-term capital gain. Check with your tax advisor before making a decision.

The Un-Death Benefit

Some life insurance policies have a provision that allows the policy's death benefit to be received prior to death under certain conditions. If you have a life insurance policy with this benefit, it may be possible to use this cash to pay for your long-term care.

When you applied for your life insurance policy, there were likely optional benefits that were either applied for or not. For example, most life insurance policies have an optional benefit, or rider, called waiver of premium. If you buy this rider and become disabled while your life insurance policy is in force, this benefit suspends your premium payments as long as you are disabled.

Another common life insurance policy waiver is accidental death and dismemberment (AD&D). If you die as a result of an accident and your policy has the AD&D rider, your beneficiary will receive a much bigger payment than if your death was from natural causes.

The accelerated death benefit is another type of rider. Some insurance companies call them living benefits riders. This rider is not offered by all life insurance companies. It is a relatively new benefit, and has only been available for less than 20 years.

Truth & Consequences _____

An accelerated death benefit or living benefits rider is not the same as a long-term care rider. In general, a long-term care rider exists to pay for long-term care, while these other riders are geared toward paying the terminal ill policyholder, or the policy-holder who has a permanent confinement to a nursing home. There is no standard language among companies offering these riders. Read your policy closely to see what is, and isn't, covered.

The cost of the accelerated death benefit rider varies; some insurance companies offer the benefit at no additional cost. When looking at insurance policies, it is important to consider how the insured can collect on the policy. It's pretty straightforward with all life insurance policies: If you're dead, the insurance company pays! But how do you collect on an accelerated death benefit? The answer varies, depending on the policy you have.

For example, some insurance companies will pay an accelerated death benefit when you are terminally ill and a doctor believes that you have less than two years to live. In another policy, life expectancies must be as short as six months to qualify for an accelerated death benefit.

Like the problems associated with planning on a viatical settlement to pay for long-term care, this trigger is of no use to pay for someone not terminally ill. For example, let's consider the common example of someone who has suffered severe complications of diabetes and is wheelchair-bound and legally blind, or someone who suffered a stroke and will never regain the function of one side of the body. They are both disabled, but may have a projected lifespan of more than two years. If their life insurance had an accelerated death benefit, they would not yet qualify for it, and so couldn't use that money to pay for long-term care.

Other accelerated death benefit riders *will* pay their benefit if the insured person needs long-term care, even if he or she is not terminally ill (you remember that most people who need long-term care are not terminally ill). One contract may require that you be in a nursing home to collect under the long-term care provision of the rider; another insurance company may make payments to insureds who are receiving their care in their own home.

Since 1997, some accelerated death benefit payments are not subject to income and capital gains taxes, while others are tax-free up to certain limits, and still others may be taxable. You need to check on the specific policy features, and consult a tax advisor. Most insurance companies usually have someone who can explain the taxation of their benefit to you or your tax advisor.

The Least You Need to Know

- Your life insurance policy may have a variety of ways to provide easy cash to pay for long-term care insurance or long-term care.

- Before you stop paying premiums and discontinue any life insurance contract, consider whether the policy can instead be sold.

- Since many people who need long-term care are not terminally ill, do not count on products with that requirement to pay for long-term care (for example, viaticals and some accelerated death benefits).

- If you use up your life insurance for long-term care, remember the death benefit is no longer available for your beneficiaries.

- As with any long-term care funding option, check with your legal and financial advisors regarding the pluses, minuses, and suitability for your situation. Every option may have significant tax ramifications and Medicaid consequences.

Chapter 8

Do You Take Personal Checks?

In This Chapter

- ◆ Champagne toasts, caviar long-term care
- ◆ Cash is king
- ◆ The rich buy peace of mind
- ◆ It's deductible

To someone who is considering long-term care planning, it may appear that there are only two options available: Medicaid planning and long-term care insurance. Although these two options may dominate much of the discussion, there are other ways to pay for long-term care.

The General Accounting Office of the United States reports that 23 percent of long-term care is paid for by individuals who pay out of pocket—that means people who are writing personal checks against their income and savings. Should your plan be to pay for long-term care out of pocket?

Unfortunately, many people who are writing personal checks for long-term care cannot really afford to. They will eventually become what I call "long-term care bankrupt," and will then qualify for the Medicaid program for the poor. This chapter will help you determine if you afford to pay for long-term care out of your own resources. If you can, it will also help you decide whether or not to do any additional long-term care planning.

Can I Be My Own Insurance Company?

When I teach long-term care planning to certified public accountants (CPAs), there is one question that they always ask: "How much does someone have to be worth to not need long-term care insurance?"

The answer to this question is quite easy. But I want you to keep reading after you see my answer, because, I think that the question itself is the wrong one to ask!

All right, what's the magic number—how rich is too rich to need long-term care insurance? The answer is this: If you can write a check each month, indefinitely, for the kind of long-term care that you desire, and it doesn't bother you to write this check, then you don't need long-term care insurance. That's it.

Please make note of the fact that it is possible for more than one family member to need this type of care at the same time. Your spouse may need long-term care at the same time as a parent who is financially dependent on you.

Wisdom of the Aged
There's actually an alternate question to ask regarding whether or not you are rich enough to pay for your own long-term care. Here it is: "Do you care where you live when you need long-term care?" If you don't care, you may be able to reposition assets to qualify for the government's Medicaid program (see Part 6). Most people who are affluent enough to consider self-insuring long-term care do not want to rely on government benefits. They prefer to pay privately so that they have care options not available to Medicaid recipients.

In order for you to answer the self-insurance question for yourself, you will need to know your local costs of care. Remember that these costs will increase over time. (For more details on these costs, please refer to Chapter 2 and Appendix D.) Many people decide that, if they can pay for long-term care for themselves and their spouse out of income, without having to sell assets, they can self-insure. I agree. But wait: The next point is an important one.

Some accountants aren't happy with the answer above, and so they ask me again: What's the exact number? Exactly how much does someone have to be worth to not need long-term care insurance? Again, my answer is a question: How much does someone have to be worth to not need homeowners insurance ... or Medicare supplement insurance? The reason that I ask these questions is that we don't think of other types of insurance in terms of whether we have enough money to not need them. Think about it: There are many wealthy people who could afford to rebuild their home if it burned to the ground, and, in any event, the likelihood of that kind of total loss is minimal.

Wisdom of the Aged

Your property insurance agent will tell you that most house fires are small. They are confined to a limited area of the house, and the claim is settled for well under $60,000 (the national average cost of only one year in a nursing home, however, is over $60,000). Those of us with mortgages are required by the bank to carry homeowners insurance; however, once our mortgages are paid off, we continue paying for our homeowners protection. We don't even question the wisdom of continuing to pay our homeowners policy. If someone asked us why, we'd say, "I wouldn't want to have to pay to rebuild my house out of my own pocket."

Let's look at the idea of self-insuring long-term care another way. What would you say to someone who suggested that you cancel your Medicare supplement, your homeowners and auto insurance, and the extra insurance on your valuables such as jewelry, because you could afford to self-insure these risks?

What Insurance Can You Cancel?

You may want to take this opportunity to review all your insurance with a critical eye. There are often opportunities to save premiums or reposition your insurance premiums into policies that are better suited for the risks you face now.

For example, let's say that you have a valuable ring that a beloved relative gave you. You have it insured for its value, but, frankly, the sentimental value to you far exceeds the jeweler's appraised value of $7,500. What would you do if the ring were lost or stolen? It really couldn't be replaced. You may choose to save the annual premium of whatever it costs to insure the ring, because you wouldn't care to replace it anyway.

The concept of *risk management* is critical to your financial well-being. Risk management is simply deciding which risks you will insure on your own, and which you will transfer. Usually risks are transferred to an insurance company, when we pay premiums. I then urge the accountants that I train, and I'm urging you, to take a look at your whole insurance situation, and consider the following question: Do I need each one of the policies I own, or can I afford to go without insurance? This is called self-insuring, since you are keeping the risk of the loss or expense to yourself. This exercise is called a risk-review, should be done every few years by your insurance agent or financial advisor. It's the only way to know that you have the insurance that you need—and that you aren't paying for insurance that you don't need. Risk reviews should also be done whenever you have a major life event such as a move, a job change or loss, or a new dependent.

Marilee's Memo _____

Risk management is simply deciding which risks you will insure on your own (called self-insuring), and which you will transfer. Usually, risks are transferred to an insurance company, which we then pay premiums. When you buy homeowners insurance, you transfer the financial risk of your house burning down, or other types of covered losses, to the insurance company. If your house does indeed burn down, you have insured your income and life savings against the cost of having to pay for a new house.

You should have an insurance "checkup" with your insurance agent when you have a major change in your life (such as a new child or newly dependent family member, starting a new business or selling an old one, or when you buy or sell an insurable asset like a home or car). If nothing major has happened, you should still sit down in person with your agent every two to three years or so. If you are not sure that you should have a particular type of insurance anymore, ask your agent the following questions:

- If I don't have this insurance, what is the financial risk that I am running?

- Is there a way to reduce my premium, while still giving me the insurance that I need?

- Do you recommend that I make any changes in my insurance program?

If long-term care insurance is appropriate for you (as explained in Chapter 13), and yet you are thinking of *not* purchasing the coverage, take a look at all the other insurances that you carry, and critically answer this question: Do I need this insurance? Why would you pay for any insurance that you don't need? Let me play devil's advocate for a moment: Assuming that you believe in the value of insurance and own policies, why is long-term care insurance the one insurance that you won't buy?

It goes back to that bit of wisdom I referred to in Chapter 4: Financially successful people don't make the best decisions every time, but they also don't make big mistakes. Wealthy people don't like their money to be vulnerable. They believe in insurance to minimize risk.

Did you know that when Malcolm Forbes died, he had life insurance policies that he had bought less than 24 months before his death? Why would one of the richest people in the country buy life insurance at his age? Well, he never told me personally why he bought them, but I guess he wanted to increase the liquidity of his estate. For whatever reason, he obviously wanted more cash available when he passed away. And this financially brilliant man recognized that life insurance was the cheapest way to make the cash available. I wonder if he had long-term care insurance.

So I guess the question is this: At a minimum cost of some $50,000 per year, and rising, does it make sense for you to self-insure the risk of long-term care?

LTC Lowdown

If you are wealthy, your cost of care may be more expensive than that of your middle-class friends. Many wealthy people have extensive home health care through an agency. This can be more expensive than a nursing home, especially if around-the-clock care is needed. If you go to a facility, you will want a private room. Facilities that cater to the affluent have accommodations and prices to match. This kind of facility will cost much more than the averages that you see reported.

Can I Really Be My Own Risk Manager?

Okay, I know it doesn't sound like an exciting pastime, but proper insurance planning, or risk management, is the foundation of any solid financial plan. While most people would rather discuss the latest sexy stock offering, without solid risk management all your other best-laid financial plans can come tumbling down.

Imagine the 40-year-old husband and wife who are saving aggressively for retirement and their child's college education. If one of them passes away, the risk-management tool called life insurance can immediately fund both the surviving spouse's retirement and the child's education. I guess that you could call risk-management contingency planning—it protects you and your family against economic losses due to catastrophes like fire, hurricane, disability, or death.

Long-term care is not the only catastrophic cost you should consider self-insuring. Apply the same critical eye to all your insurance. Consider the potential financial loss, and determine if the loss is something that you could suffer and still be financially okay.

High-End Home Care

If you are wealthy, you are in great shape in terms of accessing care options at home. There is an army of services available to the wealthy senior for home care, from private-duty nurses through agencies that do not accept Medicare or Medicaid, to personal managers who will do everything from overseeing your plan of care to balancing your checkbook and bringing your dog to the vet.

Truth & Consequences _____

Before you cancel any insurance, consult with your insurance agent. Keep in mind that insurance coverage may protect you for losses that you are not aware of. For example, your homeowners or apartment dweller's policy will protect you against the theft of money in your wallet when you travel, and your auto insurance protects you against liability lawsuits that could arise if someone borrows your car and is in an accident. Ask your insurance agent for details.

As I mentioned in Chapter 2, the kind of care you deploy may cost much more than the most expensive nursing home. It is not unusual for people with around-the-clock care to pay more than $125,000 a year just in nurses' or health aides' salaries. Many people spend even more than that. I call this kind of care the "Katherine Hepburn plan." Miss Hepburn is still alive, living in her house on the Connecticut shore, with around-the-clock home care. Every year, on her birthday, the television news programs show her leaving the house for a rider, two nurses at her sides.

Wisdom of the Aged

Professor Smith, age 72 and a professor at an Ivy League school, met with an insurance agent to discuss long-term care insurance. He had substantial assets, and a six-figure income from teaching and consulting. The agent asked if he wanted to get the insurance for his wife. He replied, "That's why I'm meeting with you. My wife suffers from a neurological disorder and is not able to stay by herself in our apartment. I pay for a companion each day, but when I travel on consulting jobs I must pay for round-the-clock care by a nurse's aide. The care is costing me almost three-quarters of my income. As long as I'm working, we can afford it. But if I were to need care too, it would bankrupt us in a few years. I see the checks I write each month, and wish we had the insurance on my wife. I'm your easiest sale."

People who have the personal funds to pay for their own long-term care are in the catbird seat. The rest of us may be in the doghouse. They have all the choices in the world.

When Cash Trumps Long-Term Care Insurance

The wealthy even have some choices that most long-term care insurance policies will not pay for. That's true! Long-term care insurance policies are very specific in the kind of care that is covered. Most modern policies cover a broad number of care options, from care in your own home, to adult day care, to assisted living facilities, and, of course, nursing homes.

But the policies have limitations. In most policies, for example, home care is covered only if it is provided by a licensed home-care agency.

Other policies have a more liberal definition. They allow the insured to hire a home-health caregiver who is a freelancer (not connected with an agency), as long as he or she is licensed by the state. Home-health agencies have an extra level of oversight and care management than an individual can provide, and the costs for hiring someone through an agency are less expensive than hiring an individual directly.

Home-health agencies also take care of payroll-withholding taxes, workers' compensation, and provide bonding, which can reimburse patients who have items stolen from their homes. Agencies also have a greater likelihood of being able to send a replacement worker if the scheduled home-care worker is sick or doesn't show up for work. But if you want to hire someone who is not working through an agency, many policies will not reimburse you for their charges.

In some neighborhoods, it is commonplace to hire unlicensed home-care helpers. It is beyond the scope of this book to comment on the advisability of this practice. You can imagine that the potential for problems, including financial and physical abuse, may be more likely when you are hiring someone who has not been through an agency screening process, and whose work is not being monitored by an outsider.

 **LTC Lowdown** _____

Some people are on their way to being able to self-insure long-term care, but they aren't quite there yet. Until their financial situation is set, if they want private-pay options in the event they need care, they need to purchase long-term care insurance for the interim. Long-term care insurance is not a lifelong commitment, unless you want it to be. If your situation changes and you don't need or want the coverage any more, simply cancel the policy and stop paying. Just like you cancel auto insurance when you sell the car, you call the shots!

The advantage of hiring freelancers as opposed to someone through an agency is that they are usually less expensive. They may also be someone who you know, a neighbor or a friend. Even if they are not trained, the kind of care they give may be just fine for your situation. It's important to know that most long-term care insurance policies do not reimburse for pay you give to unlicensed home-care workers or to family members.

Your own personal funds, of course, do not have this restriction. You never have an argument over whether a care provider is covered when you go to your bank to withdraw money for your long-term care, or if you write a check to your caregiver. People who are paying for their care with personal funds have the ultimate in flexibility and choices.

A Long-Term Care Policy That Acts Like Cash

A true per diem long-term care policy will send you your policy's benefit amount as long as you satisfy the benefit triggers. This is just like cash—you can spend the money however you would like. For the ultimate in choice and flexibility, when purchasing long-term care insurance, per diem policies are valuable. The trade-off? You can count the number of true per diem contracts on less than one hand, and the policies are noticeably more expensive than traditional reimbursement contracts. Read more about per diem contracts in Chapter 19.

Cash Management as We Age

As we age, some of us have difficulty managing our finances, and some of us fall prey to people who do not have our best interests in mind. They want our money. Often these people are not who seniors are taught to be fearful of—they are not the telephone solicitor calling from a boiler room phone bank. Unfortunately, in many cases, they are our relatives and neighbors.

Setting up financial instruments such as trusts and naming an institution as trustee can limit our vulnerability to financial swindlers as we age. Professional money managers and trustees, such as banks and attorneys, have a legal obligation to always act in our best interests and follow the letter of the legal document that we draft, and can be a great safeguard as we age.

In addition to the federal income-tax deduction for long-term care, at the time this book was being written, Congress is considering legislation that will broaden the deduction for tax-qualified long-term care insurance, and will also provide a modest tax credit to caregivers.

 **LTC Lowdown** _____

Money spent on long-term care is tax deductible as a medical expense on your federal income taxes. In order to take any deduction, the amount of expense needs to exceed 7.5 percent of your adjusted gross income, and you must itemize. Other items that can also be used in this deduction are unreimbursed prescription-drug expense, Medicare supplement premiums, and the premium on tax-qualified long-term care insurance policies (see Chapter 12).

Consider Liquidity

Many affluent people have their money tied up in *illiquid assets*. This can be a problem if they plan on using the proceeds to pay for long-term care, since the money may not be immediately available. A business may be worth a lot, and it could be sold. But even in a good economy, this transaction can take time.

Some assets have a value which is highly dependent on timing. Although an illiquid asset may be worth a lot on paper, if it needs to be sold quickly, it may only sell for a fraction of its paper value. Someone may not want to sell an asset if the timing is not right. For example, a vacation house in a recession will not fetch the highest sale price.

Marilee's Memo

Illiquid assets are assets that are difficult and costly to sell. Two examples are homes and fine jewelry. The most liquid asset is cash, which can be used immediately. Another liquid asset would be a savings account at the bank; it's easy to get the money out. Illiquid assets' values may also fluctuate more than other assets.

Are Your Assets High Enough to Self-Insure?

What if you know that you can't self-insure from your income, but you think that maybe your assets are high enough to pay your long-term care bill? How do you know if you can go that route to self-insure?

The first step is to look at your income, and decide how much of it (if any) you are willing to use on long-term care. Compare this amount to the cost of the kind of care you'd want. If you're not sure what this is, you may want to take a look at the private-room rates at the nicest nursing home in town, or call a home health-care agency and ask what around-the-clock care by a nurse or nurse's aide costs.

Subtract the income you are willing to use from the cost of care. The shortfall is what you'd make up by selling assets, or converting them to usable income. List your assets, in the order you would be willing to sell. Be sure to take a look at the liquidation value, which would decrease the value of the asset to pay for taxes and expenses such as early withdrawal penalties. Here's a partial list of the assets to consider:

- Home (a sale or a reverse mortgage)
- Vacation home
- Money in bank—savings and checking
- Certificates of deposit

- Mutual funds/stocks/bonds

- Qualified plans—IRAs, 401(k)s, etc.

- Deferred annuities

- Life insurance policies (to sell or use cash value)

- Other assets that you own and are willing to part with

Your financial advisor can run an analysis showing the cost of long-term care over time, and also the increase in the value of your assets. But the most important work has to come from you: Look at the income and assets that you have, and decide what, if any, you are willing to use to pay for long-term care. Compare the resources that you are willing to spend to the cost of care. See how many years of care you can pay for privately. Then, decide if you'd rather transfer some or all this risk to an insurance company by purchasing long-term care insurance.

To read additional information on long-term care insurance, please refer to Parts 4 and 5.

In summary, taking a critical look at your financial situation and deciding how you would pay for long-term care is an important exercise if you believe that you have enough money to pay for long-term care. Comparing the risk and cost of LTC to other risks you choose to insure will help you decide whether you should buy long-term care insurance.

The Least You Need to Know

- Before you decide that you can self-insure your long-term care, compare the potential expense of extended care to other risks that you buy insurance for; is long-term care a risk you want to keep?

- If you are married or are financially responsible for other family members (such as parents), consider their long-term care needs when doing your planning.

- If you have decided to self-insure with personal assets, keep in mind that their value may fluctuate, and make sure that you are looking at their after-tax liquidation value.

- Long-term care expenses paid out of pocket for you and any dependents are deductible under the federal income-tax health-expense deduction.

Part  3

Government Programs

During our working years, we pay into a variety of government programs. Medicare and Social Security are our retirement safety nets. They provide health insurance when we're age 65, and a retirement income benefit. If we become totally disabled before age 65, these programs are there to help. Veterans enjoy the promise of health care for life.

But these programs fall far short of providing long-term care when we need it. Coverage is limited under Medicare. Veterans benefits are evolving to include community-based long-term care, but availability is a problem.

Many states and the federal government have incentives, such as tax credits and tax deductions, to encourage us to buy long-term care insurance. In this part, I take a look at government and incentives to buy long-term care insurance. Understanding what is available through the government should make it easier for you to do your planning.

Chapter 9

Veterans' Benefits

In This Chapter

◆ The Department of Veterans' Affairs in brief

◆ Who is eligible for the veterans' benefits

◆ The TRICARE for Life program

◆ Facility and community-based LTC for veterans

If you are a veteran, you have heard a lot about the promise of "health care for life." You may think that the Department of Veterans' Affairs (VA) will provide long-term care for you. The truth is, some veterans will have the VA to count on when they need long-term care, and others will not.

This chapter is here to encourage any veteran who is counting on the VA system to provide long-term care to examine the programs that are available. Only by understanding what is available to you can you do smart long-term care planning.

In some areas of the country, there are more resources for veterans than in other areas. Look into the availability of resources in your area before you plan on the VA for long-term care. This task is made difficult because not only can benefits change at any time, but there are currently initiatives in place that will decrease resources in some states and increase them in others. Before making a decision based on the information in this book, verify all information through official sources.

The Veterans' Affairs History

With more than 250,000 employees and a budget in the millions of dollars, the VA is there to help veterans and their dependents. Approximately one third of the country's population is eligible for benefits and services from the VA, because of dependent and survivor benefits.

In 1812, the Philadelphia Naval Home was founded to provide medical care for disabled veterans. Two soldiers' homes followed in the 1850s. Soldiers' homes, or state veterans' homes, as they are often called, exist in most states today. Although the VA pays a portion of the daily cost of care in state veteran's homes, the states establish both eligibility and admission criteria.

The VA was created by Congress in 1930. The agency had among its many responsibilities providing medical services for veterans, and disability compensation, life insurance, and retirement payments for veterans and their eligible civilian family members.

The VA and Long-Term Care

In 1975, the VA started responding to the increasing number of older veteran patients by opening up the first geriatric Research, Education and Clinical Center (GRECC). In 1980 there were eight in operation.

The veteran population is currently about 24 million. Although it is expected to decline to 20 million by 2010, the elderly veteran population has been growing. More than 9 million veterans are age 65+. According to a 1999 statement by John R. Vitikacs, VA assistant director, the VA is meeting the LTC needs of only 21.4 percent of disabled and poor veterans. In congressional testimony, Vitikacs reported that "several VA nursing homes have recently closed and many other long-term care beds have been reduced. Many veterans are having their VA nursing home contracts reduced to 60 days or less, prior to placement in a community-based facility." It was also noted that "despite high quality and continued need, long-term care is perceived to be an adjunct entity, unevenly funded and undervalued."

Marilee's Memo

The Former Prisoner of War Benefits Act of 1981 entitles former POWs to hospital and nursing home care without regard to their ability to pay. These veterans are also eligible for VA outpatient treatment for any medical condition, with a priority basis second only to that of a service-connected veteran.

Can a veteran count on VA long-term care benefits? The VA has a long history of striving to serve a large population within the funding appropriated by Congress. Priority in the VA system is given to those veterans whose need for care is service-related. The issue of priority is complex. When veterans enroll in VA, they are enrolling in a bene-fits package—a defined set of services for which all enrolled veterans are equally eligi-ble and for which they have equal priority once enrolled. Not all long-term care services are included in the benefits package, although many are available on a discre-tionary basis.

After service-related needs for care, the next level of priority is given to those veter-ans whose do not have the income and ability to pay for care. In the last few years, many more veterans have been relying on the VA for their health care. This has put a further strain on the system.

As we have seen in nonveteran government benefits, there is a strong desire to tie any future benefits to low income, as a way to limit participation and cost. Another way that programs limit the cost of funding is to charge a copayment. There has been pressure to increase the amount of VA copayments.

However, the VA is sensitive to the needs of aging veterans. I think we will see more programs to serve the LTC needs of veterans, but these programs may not be avail-able for middle-class to well-off veterans who do not have service-connected disabili-ties.

Recent Legislation

In October 1996, Congress passed Public Law 104-262, the Veterans' Health-Care Eligibility Reform Act of 1996. This legislation established seven priority groups that are eligible for the VA medical benefits package. When you apply for enrollment, you will be assigned as a member of one of these priority groups once it is determined that you are eligible for benefits:

♦ **Priority Group 1:** Veterans with service-connected disabilities rated 50 percent or more.

♦ **Priority Group 2:** Veterans with service-connected disabilities rated 30 percent or 40 percent.

♦ **Priority Group 3:** Veterans who are former POWs; veterans with service-connected disabilities rated 10 percent or 20 percent; veterans discharged from active duty for a disability incurred or aggravated in the line of duty; veterans who received the Purple Heart; and veterans awarded special eligibility classifi-cation under 48 U.S.C., Section 1151, "benefits for individuals disabled by treat-ment or vocational rehabilitation."

◆ **Priority Group 4:** Veterans who are receiving aid and attendance or house-bound benefits; veterans who have been determined by the VA to be catastrophically disabled. (The VA defines catastrophically disabled as "individuals who have a severely disabling injury, disorder, or disease which permanently compromises their ability to carry out the activities of daily living to such a degree that they require personal or mechanical assistance to leave home or bed, or require constant supervision to avoid physical harm to self or others.)

◆ **Priority Group 5:** Nonservice-connected veterans and noncompensable service-connected veterans rated 0 percent disabled, whose annual income and net worth are below the established dollar thresholds. (Nonservice-connected means "an eligible veteran who has been discharged from active military duty and does not have an illness or injury that has determined to have been incurred in or aggravated during military service.")

◆ **Priority Group 6:** All other eligible veterans who are not required to make copayments for their care, including:

LTC Lowdown _____

The Veterans Millennium Health-Care and Benefits Act, which was passed by Congress in late 1999, expanded health programs in the VA to enrolled veterans. The highest priority is given to veterans whose disability is service-connected, and it mandates nursing home care for certain veterans. The services expire December 31, 2003, and so Senator Jay Rockefeller (D-WV) has introduced a bill to extend benefits until 2008.

◆ World War I and Mexican Border War veterans.

◆ Veterans seeking care solely for disorders associated with exposure to herbicides while serving in Vietnam; or exposure to ionizing radiation during atmospheric testing or during the occupation of Hiroshima and Nagasaki; or for disorders associated with service in the Gulf War; or for any illness associated with service in combat in a war after the Gulf War or during a period of hostility after November 11, 1998.

◆ Compensable (meaning, a veteran who has been rated by VA as being service-connected and who receives monetary benefit) 0 percent service-connected veterans.

◆ **Priority Group 7:** Nonservice-connected veterans and noncompensable 0 percent service-connected veterans with income and net worth above the established dollar thresholds and who agree to pay specified copayments (meaning, a specific dollar amount of a covered health service expense for which a veteran is responsible to pay).

The TRICARE for Life Benefit

The TRICARE for Life benefit, which was implemented in October 2001, is a great health insurance benefit for retired military personnel and their eligible beneficiaries who are on Medicare. TRICARE for Life is a permanent entitlement program, and as such does not require annual authorization or funding by Congress. This benefit is here to stay.

The National Defense Authorization Act for Fiscal Year 2001 extended TRICARE (the military health-care plan) to 1.4 million Medicare-eligible military beneficiaries. The new program is a free benefit for Medicare-eligible retirees of the uniformed services, their family members (does *not* include dependent parents and parents-in-law), and survivors. Retired guard and reservists are covered by the new benefit, as are widows and widowers. There is no disability requirement or low-income requirement for someone to qualify for TRICARE for Life.

More information on the TRICARE for Life program is available by calling 1-888-DOD-LIFE (that's 1-888-363-5433), or online at www.tricare.osd.mil.

Wisdom of the Aged

Many people are eligible for TRICARE for Life but may not know about the program. Some former spouses will receive the benefit if they were eligible for the traditional TRICARE program before they turned age 65. There are many older widows who may not realize that they qualify for this great program. Please note that widows/widowers lose their eligibility when they remarry—unless, of course, their new spouse is a military retiree.

To find out if you are eligible for TRICARE for Life, call the Defense Manpower Data Center Support Office Beneficiary line at 1-800-538-9552.

There is a requirement that the beneficiary be enrolled in both Medicare Part A and Part B in order to receive TRICARE for Life.

In the past, although military retirees lost their health coverage when they turned 65, they had the right to free medical care through the VA, subject to the limitations described earlier in this chapter. Most older veterans instead relied on Medicare and supplemental policies or plans such as Medicare HMOs. But these options were often costly, as was the option of self-insuring.

TRICARE and Medicare

For eligible beneficiaries, Medicare is their primary payer, with TRICARE for Life being secondary. TRICARE for Life will normally pay Medicare deductibles and coinsurance for services that both plans cover. Many Medicare-eligible military beneficiaries are canceling their Medicare supplement or Medicare + Choice plans, which are being replaced by the free benefit of TRICARE for Life. Those beneficiaries who keep other health insurance will find TRICARE becomes their third payer, behind Medicare and their other health plan.

The TRICARE pharmacy benefit started in April 2001, and does not require all Medicare beneficiaries to enroll in Medicare Part B to be eligible for the prescription-drug benefit. This benefit will give many seniors a welcome break from the high cost of prescription drugs. Not only does the plan cover prescription drugs at military treatment facilities, but also at retail pharmacies and through a national mail-service program. There are very reasonable out-of-pocket expenses—less for mail-service and network pharmacies, more for non-network pharmacies.

Truth & Consequences

Many seniors are replacing their costly Medicare supplements and Medicare plus choice plans with TRICARE for Life. Before you cancel any existing coverage, make sure that you first look into what, if any, benefits you may give up.

The Defense Enrollment Eligibility Reporting System (DEERS) record file reflects a code that shows your eligibility for TRICARE for Life. Your DEERS address must be kept current so that you can be notified of changes in benefits. For questions regarding your DEERS record, call the telephone center at 1-800-538-9552 (0600 to 1530 PST, Monday through Friday—that's 6 A.M. to 3:30 P.M. for you civilians out there).

TRICARE for Life and LTC

Like Medicare, there is no coverage for custodial long-term care under TRICARE for Life. Although TRICARE for Life does cover some things that Medicare doesn't (such as care outside the United States), it is a health insurance, not a long-term care program.

The VA currently funds LTC services to about 68,000 veterans a day (in 2001). In some cases, the VA system provides the services itself; in other cases, the VA pays for care by non-VA providers. the federal advisory committee on the future of VA long-term care reported that the VA meet only about 20 percent of the need for long-term care nationally among veterans with service-connected conditions and those with low incomes. Most veterans use other systems for LTC services.

LTC Lowdown

To learn more about what's happening on Capitol Hill in the veteran's world, visit the U.S. House of Representative's Committee of Veterans' Affairs at www.house.gov/va and the U.S. Senate Committee on Veterans' Affairs at www.senate.gov/~veterans.

The VA and Facility-Based Long-Term Care

VA nursing homes are usually located on the grounds of VA medical centers. In some cases, such as when a community nursing home provides services that a VA nursing home does not, the VA has a history of placing veterans in community nursing homes (non-VA facilities). In these cases the VA subsidizes the care of veterans. Even though there may be an out-of-pocket cost, these alternatives to VA nursing homes can be a great thing if a veteran does not live near a VA nursing home, or if the VA facility is full. As VA centers close, and the elderly veteran population booms, the VA may increase their reliance on outside care providers.

VA employees may help veterans who are enrolled in the VA system and their families find privately run long-term care facilities. This benefit is often available even if the veteran is ineligible for VA funding of his or her care. Take advantage of this benefit, and ask for help!

Traditionally, if you qualified for inpatient VA medical care, you qualified for the VA nursing homes. But it used to be that VA nursing homes, more than VA hospitals, had to make decisions based on the availability of space. No one was guaranteed admission to a nursing home, as they may be guaranteed mandatory inpatient care if they were in the right categories.

The Veterans Millennium Health-Care and Benefits Act requires the VA to provide long-term nursing care to veterans rated 70 percent disabled or greater, and to veterans who need the care for service-connected disabilities. For other veterans, if the VA chooses to offer care, the Act requires the VA to collect a copayment.

Under the State Extended-Care Facilities Grant Program, the VA provides construction funding to encourage the building of more nursing home rooms to meet increasing veteran demand. For example, in California, the VA estimates the number of beds needed to be 5,754; there are currently only 2,007 beds. The California shortfall is more than 3,000 beds.

The VA and Community-Based LTC

The Veterans Millennium Health Care and Benefits Act requires VA to provide greater access to community-based LTC programs.

These programs include geriatric evaluation, adult day health care, respite care, and other noninstitutional alternatives for nursing home care.

The Least You Need to Know

- ◆ TRICARE for Life is a no-premium health insurance policy for retired military personnel on Medicare and some dependents; it does not offer a long-term care benefit.

- ◆ Overall, the VA system prioritizes those who may be eligible for benefits. Middle-class veterans who need long-term care for conditions that are not service-related may find it difficult to access VA benefits for long-term care.

- ◆ All veterans, especially low-income veterans or veterans with a service-related disability, should investigate whether the VA will provide them long-term care.

- ◆ Former prisoners of war and veterans whose need for long-term care is service-related are likely to receive VA benefits for long-term care.

Chapter 10

Medicare and Medicare Supplements

In This Chapter

- ◆ Medicare: The health insurance for the elderly
- ◆ Medicare and the 100-day clock
- ◆ What Medicare covers and doesn't cover
- ◆ How Medicare covers Alzheimer's disease

Medicare is the health insurance plan that covers 95 percent of America's aged population. Medicare is like the health insurance most of us have during our working years. It is designed to pay for treatment of illness and injury, and some preventative care. In keeping with the focus of this book, I'm going to talk about when Medicare will pay for home health care and limited nursing home care, not how Medicare covers doctors, hospitals, surgery, and other medical expenses.

Many people mistakenly think that Medicare will cover their long-term care. Medicare does not pay for most long-term care. Another government program, Medicaid, is the nation's largest payer of long-term care costs. Though the names are similar, Medicare and Medicaid are very different programs. (For more details on Medicaid, please refer to Chapter 21.)

Others know that Medicare can't be counted on to cover long-term care, but they mistakenly think that their Medicare supplement or Medicare + Choice plan (such as an HMO) will cover long-term care expenses. However, in this chapter you'll discover that Medicare covers very little long-term care. If you are planning on Medicare to pay for your long-term care, wake up and smell the coffee. It's not going to happen.

Medicare's History and Future

Medicare was created in 1965 under Title XVIII of the Social Security Act. Medicare is administered by the Centers for Medicare and Medicaid Services (CMS), an agency of the U.S. Department of Health and Human Services. In addition to providing health insurance for those age 65 and older, Medicare also covers some younger people: the eligible disabled, and people suffering from end-stage renal (kidney) disease, and Lou Gehrig's disease (ALS). Prior to Medicare, retirees typically had no health insurance. When they suffered health problems, they were often quickly impoverished by the expense. The Medicare program is a critical component in ensuring financial security for seniors in this country.

Medicare benefits to retirees are funded by payroll taxes paid by current workers and their employers. Increasing life spans and increasingly expensive medical technology have combined to place intense financial pressure on the Medicare program. Retired workers are collecting the "free" Medicare Part A benefit for more years. This problem will become much worse as the baby boomer generation turns age 65, since there are fewer workers younger than them to support their Medicare benefits. Workers are paying into the system at rates not able to support increasing life spans and rising medical expenses.

In 1999, the National Bipartisan Commission on the Future of Medicare observed that, without reform, the Medicare trust fund will be bankrupt in 2008. Their suggested reforms have not been implemented. No one can observe this situation and honestly think that Medicare will add coverage for long-term care in the foreseeable future.

Back in the 1980s, seeking to control the growth in Medicare spending, Congress enacted a change in the way that Medicare paid hospitals for care. Medicare adopted what is called the Diagnostic Related Group (DRG) system for reimbursing hospitals. At the risk of oversimplifying, here's how the payment system works: When a Medicare beneficiary enters a hospital, a diagnostic code is assigned. Medicare reimburses the hospital a flat amount based on that code, regardless of the amount of services that one beneficiary receives. Whether the person stays 1 night or 10 nights, Medicare pays the hospital the same amount.

Prior to this system, Medicare paid hospitals based on the actual services provided. What this change to the DRG system did is shift the risk of financial loss to the hospital and away from the taxpayer-funded Medicare program. It is argued that, over the large Medicare beneficiary popu-

LTC Lowdown

Home health-care coverage under Medicare has no deductibles or copayments.

lation, payments to hospitals are fair. Some Medicare patients are moneymakers for the hospital, while other Medicare patients cost the hospital money. Clearly, the change gives hospitals an incentive to push Medicare beneficiaries out as soon as possible.

Medicare did the same thing with home health-care providers on October 1, 2000. Instead of paying home health-care providers for the actual amount of time spent with each Medicare beneficiary, Medicare went to a capitation program. Again, at the risk of oversimplifying, here's how Medicare now reimburses for home health care: Under the new program, a home health-care agency is paid per person served, regardless of the amount of time spent with that person.

Patients with complicated health-care needs, who require a lot of care, were favored under the old payment system: The more care the agency provided, the more revenue it collected. That has now changed. The way that home health-care agencies increase revenue is by increasing the number of Medicare beneficiaries served. This change gives home health-care agencies an incentive not to take on complicated cases.

Medicare-approved home-care agencies have the right not to take on a case so long as they do not discriminate. In other words, they cannot take my case and refuse yours, if you have the same health-care situation that I do. Have you noticed that in the late 1990s many home health-care agencies closed? Or that they moved into hospitals or other businesses to save on rent and other overhead? That happened because they were preparing for the change in Medicare home health-care payments.

Another result of this change in Medicare reimbursements is the explosion of private-pay home health-care agencies. These agencies do not accept Medicare (or Medicaid). They provide those with the ability to pay privately with the care they desire. In many areas, these agencies have hired some of the best nurses in their region. They pay the nurses and other professional medical staff more for a work schedule that is less harried and stressful. Instead of running in and out of the car trying to squeeze in as many patients as possible, these medical workers have a less frantic work life—paid for by their well-to-do patients. As our population ages and medical science comes up with new treatments, it will clearly be harder for Medicare to and pay for adequate care without raising taxes or out-of-pocket payments.

When Medicare was started, prescription drugs were not an important part of treatment. Today, prescriptions are as important as doctor's visits and hospital stays. Some members of Congress are trying to add a prescription-drug benefit to Medicare, but to date they have run into opposition over the cost involved.

Truth & Consequences

Medicare only covers nursing home stays, home health-care services, and medical equipment and supplies provided by Medicare-approved vendors. Most nursing homes are Medicare approved, but not all are. To avoid billing problems and surprises, make sure the services that you use are Medicare-approved. If you are in a Medicare managed-care plan, or a Medicare + Choice plan that limits coverage to certain providers, you must make sure that the providers that you use are on the plan's list.

Medicare's Home Health-Care Coverage

Medicare pays for home health care for the treatment of an illness or injury, for beneficiaries who meet all of these four conditions:

◆ Your doctor decides that you need medical care in your home and makes a plan for that care.

◆ You need at least one of the following: intermittent skilled nursing care, physical therapy, speech language pathology services, or occupational therapy.

◆ You are homebound, which means normally unable to leave home. When you leave, it must be infrequent and for a short time, such as a doctor's visit (adult day care is an exception here).

◆ The home health-care agency must be Medicare-approved.

Truth & Consequences

Medicare pays for some home health care and nursing home care, but it doesn't cover any assisted living facility costs.

Please note that, unlike Medicare's nursing home benefit, you do not need to be admitted to a hospital first in order to be eligible for Medicare home health care.

Most people who need long-term care need custodial care only. Custodial care is not covered by Medicare. But, here's where it can become confusing for people: If you qualify for Medicare's skilled home-care benefit, there can be a benefit for home-health aides, who provide custodial care. This benefit is covered only if you are also getting skilled care. The home-health aide services must be a part of the home-care treatment for your illness or injury. The aides provide services that support the skilled services that the nurse or therapist provides. These services can include custodial care, such as help with bathing and using the toilet.

Marilee's Memo

Medicare beneficiary is someone covered by Medicare. If someone were covered by private health insurance, he is usually called an "insured." Medicare uses the word beneficiary. Medicare beneficiaries are always over age 65, unless they qualify for coverage at younger ages because of a disability.

There are two parts to the original Medicare: Part A and Part B. Part A has no cost to people (or their spouses) who have 40 or more quarters of Medicare-covered employment, and are age 65 or older. Part B costs $54 per month (as of 2002). Medicare used to cover home health care under Part A (hospital insurance) exclusively. On January 1, 1998, Medicare moved some home health care under Part B (doctor's visits and outpatient, optional coverage). Home health care now covered under Part B is that care which is not associated with a hospital or nursing home stay. Most, though not all, Medicare beneficiaries purchase Part B coverage, which is optional. Everyone on Medicare has Part A coverage.

Low-income Medicare beneficiaries may be eligible for free Part B coverage and free coverage for expenses not covered by Medicare. There are a number of benefits under the states' Medicaid programs. Qualified Medicare Beneficiary (QMB) programs and Specified Low-Income Medicare Beneficiaries (SLMBs) are the most popular programs. (For more information, contact the offices listed in Appendixes B and C.)

Changes in the funding of Medicare home health care discussed earlier in this chapter have meant that workers providing Medicare home health care are juggling tremendous workloads. They are under pressure to see as many Medicare beneficiaries as possible. This is because Medicare, which used to reimburse for the amount of time they spent with a beneficiary, now pays the home health-care service by the number of people served. The result has been that Medicare home health-care agencies have had to become more efficient providers, which means that they have less time for each patient.

If you have experience with a friend or relative who received Medicare home health care in the past, you may think that there is a substantial benefit for home care under Medicare. In general, if you qualify for Medicare home health care, you will receive much shorter visits than were common even in the early 1990s.

Truth & Consequences

Medicare covers personal care by home-health aides only if you also need skilled care. Medicare never pays for homemaker services such as shopping, housecleaning, and laundry. Smart long-term care planners know that they may qualify for Medicare home health care and still need to pay for additional custodial care in order to live comfortably and safely in their homes.

Medicare home health care does not provide 24-hour care; in most cases it does not cover an eight-hour full shift of home care. The nurse or other health-care professional comes to your home, provides the treatment needed, and then leaves. How long does a visit last? Medicare allows up to 28 hours of home care a week, with a daily limit of less than eight hours. However, I'm told by home health-care workers that a typical visit lasts anywhere from 20 minutes to two hours, with most lasting closer to 20 minutes.

In most cases, Medicare limits its home health-care benefit to 21 days. The Medicare home-care program is designed to serve beneficiaries who need intermittent care. Intermittent care is part-time care, for a relatively short period of time. Intermittent care is usually not given on a daily basis. Beneficiaries who need daily skilled care can receive this benefit from Medicare in a Medicare-approved nursing home.

Once you are receiving Medicare home health care, your plan of care will be reviewed at least every 60 days. If your health changes and skilled care is no longer required, the home-health agency will notify your doctor, who will alert Medicare. At that point, your home care will no longer be covered by Medicare.

When this happens, in many cases, the individual and their family are shocked. The person may still need a lot of help every day. He may be unable to go from a bed to a chair unassisted. He may be unable to bath or get dressed by himself. But, once his health has stabilized and he is not responsive to medical treatment, his care is no longer called skilled. That's when Medicare stops paying. That's also when any Medicare home-health-aide services stop, even though the custodial care provided may still be needed.

If you think that care was stopped in error, check with your doctor first to see why service was discontinued. Talk with the home health-care agency, too.

Beneficiaries in original Medicare have the right to appeal discontinuation of services by Medicare. See the back of the Explanation of Medicare Benefits or Medicare Summary Notice for your appeal rights.

If you are in a Medicare Plus Choice, such as a Medicare HMO, the plan is required to cover home health care. If you have questions about coverage, call your managed-care plan, not Medicare.

Medicare's Nursing Home Coverage

The AARP reports that 55 percent of people recently surveyed thought Medicare paid for nursing home care. As AARP clarified to its members, "Medicare does not cover long-term care in a nursing home, which is defined as more than three months of regular care for a chronic condition." Medicare will pay for up to 100 days of care in a Medicare-approved skilled-nursing facility (SNF, pronounced "snif" by medical people and Medicare personnel), if all of the following conditions are met:

- The move to the SNF must be within 30 days of a hospital stay.

- The hospital stay must have been for at least three days (I like to say four days, since Medicare doesn't count the day of discharge).

- Care must be medically necessary (skilled-nursing or skilled-rehabilitation care).

- The patient must need skilled care for a medical condition that was treated in the hospital or started in the hospital.

Medicare was not designed to cover long-term care. In some cases, Medicare will cover up to 100 days of skilled nursing care in a nursing home. However, most people who need nursing home care do not need skilled care and so do not qualify for Medicare coverage. Remember, skilled-nursing care is medically necessary, and it either improves your condition or maintains your condition and prevents it from getting worse. Of those who need skilled care, most find that their need for skilled care ends within the first 20 days, and Medicare stops paying the bill at that point.

In addition to the skilled care requirement, there are other criteria a Medicare beneficiary must meet to have Medicare pay for his or her long-term care in a nursing home. For example, the beneficiary must have first spent three days in the hospital (not counting the day of discharge). Do not count on Medicare to pay when doing long-term care planning.

LTC Lowdown

Medicare's benefit for skilled-nursing facilities (nursing homes) is a maximum of 100 days per benefit period, not per year or per lifetime. A benefit period begins when the beneficiary enters a hospital and ends when there has been a break of at least 60 consecutive days since inpatient hospital or skilled nursing care was provided.

Medicare pays 100 percent of your first 20 days of the nursing home bill for eligible stays. For days 21 through 100, Medicare covers all but $101.50 per day. This

$101.50 per day is your copayment, which would be covered by a Medicare supplement policy, if you owned one. After 100 days, there is no coverage by Medicare or Medicare supplements.

It is possible for Medicare beneficiaries to collect under this benefit several times over their lifetimes. Keep in mind, though, that most people do not require 100 days of skilled care in a nursing home. Usually, after a couple weeks of skilled care, they have stabilized, and their care is now custodial, not skilled. In most cases, Medicare pays for less than three weeks, not for 100 days.

Medicare Supplements

Although Medicare does not cover long-term custodial care, some people think that this care is covered by their Medicare supplement (sometimes called Medigap) policy. These policies in most states (though not all), are identified by the letters A–J. They are designed to cover the deductibles and copayments in Medicare. They do not cover long-term care.

Plans H, I, and J also have a prescription-drug benefit. Visit the Medicare website or call 1-800-MEDICARE to find out what supplemental plans are available in your state. Your state's division of insurance (see Appendix A) can advise you on insurance company policies to cover gaps in Medicare. Every state has a SHIP (Senior Health Insurance Program) program whose counselors advise you—for free—on questions ranging from help choosing a Medigap insurance company policy or Medicare Part C plan, to long-term care insurance. To find your local SHIP counselors, call the Medicare program (see Appendix E) or your state's Executive Office of Aging (see Appendix C). *Medicare beneficiaries* who are retirees of the uniformed services, survivors, or eligible family members can get no-premium Medicare supplemental coverage called TRICARE for Life. Read Chapter 9 for more information. Like all Medicare supplements and Medicare managed-health plans, TRICARE for Life does not cover long-term care costs.

> **Wisdom of the Aged**
>
> What if you take your social security retirement income benefit early—before age 65—can you get Medicare then? No. You must be age 65 to enroll in Medicare, unless you meet the criteria to be eligible because of disability, Lou Gehrig's disease, or end stage renal (kidney) disease.

With the limited exception of prescription drugs on some plans, Medicare supplement policies do not pay a benefit for charges that Medicare has not approved. So, for example, once you have been in Medicare-approved nursing home for 100 days, your Medicare skilled-nursing facility coverage has run out for that benefit period. Therefore, your Medicare supplement would not pay a benefit.

However, during the 100 days that Medicare would provide a benefit (as long as you required skilled care), your Medicare supplement would pay then, too. So from days 21 through 100, Medicare will pay for skilled care, but there is a copayment of $101.50 (2002 figure). This is the charge that your Medicare supplement covers. So instead of having to write a personal check for the approximately $100 per day that Medicare doesn't pay, your Medicare supplement pays that portion of the bill.

Medicare + Choice

Medicare + Choice (sometimes called Part C) gives Medicare beneficiaries options not available under original Medicare (Part A and Part B). The Medicare + Choice plans are as follows, and may or may not be available in your location:

- Coordinated care plans—includes health maintenance organizations (HMOs), provider-sponsored organizations (PSOs), and preferred provider organizations (PPOs)

- Fee-for-service programs

- Religious fraternal benefit plans

- Medical savings account (MSA) plans—which provide benefits after a single high deductible is met

All Medicare + Choice plans (except MSA plans) are required to provide the benefits under the current original Medicare benefit package, excluding hospice services. Many plans offer additional services not covered by original Medicare. For more information on Medicare + Choice plans, see our resources section (Appendix E).

Like Original Medicare, Medicare + Choice plans do not cover long-term care.

Medicare and Alzheimer's Disease

In late March 2002, the Centers for Medicare and Medicaid Services (formerly the Health-Care Financing Administration, or HCFA) announced that Medicare would cover Alzheimer's disease. There was immediate confusion in the long-term care planning world, as consumers and their advisors tried to understand the implications of the new policy.

Did this mean that the *custodial care* in homes, assisted living facilities, or nursing homes would now be covered by Medicare for Alzheimer's patients? No. The ongoing, often 24-hours-a-day supervision and/or assistance that Alzheimer's patients often need is still not covered by Medicare.

Truth & Consequences _____

Do not make the mistake of thinking that Medicare covers long-term care for Alzheimer's patients. There has been a lot of confusing information reported about this topic. People with Alzheimer's usually require nonskilled custodial care for long periods of time, sometimes years. This type of care is not covered under Medicare. Medicare covers reasonable and necessary medical treatment, or skilled care, but it does not cover the long-term care needs of Medicare beneficiaries, even those with Alzheimer's.

This new policy changed nothing in regards to long-term care planning. Here's what the change did do: In the past, many companies that paid Medicare claims for the government automatically rejected claims submitted on behalf of a Medicare *beneficiary* with Alzheimer's disease. So for example, a speech-therapy or physical-therapy claim would automatically be denied, under the premise that treatment would not benefit an Alzheimer's patient.

If patients appealed the denial, often the claim was paid after a fight. Advocacy groups had lobbied for this change. It's reassuring to know that now Medicare claims for Alzheimer's patients will not be automatically denied; however, there is still no coverage for long-term care under Medicare for Alzheimer's patients.

The Least You Need to Know

- Medicare covers 95 percent of the aged population in America for care by doctors, hospitals, and other medically necessary health care.

- Like other health insurance plans, Medicare does not cover long-term, chronic, custodial care.

- Although 55 percent of people recently surveyed thought Medicare paid for nursing home care, Medicare does *not* cover long-term care in a nursing home.

- Reforms in the way that Medicare reimburses home health-care agencies have led to shorter home care visits.

- As our population ages and medical science develop new treatments, there is a clear conflict between providing the care and paying for the care without raising taxes or out-of-pocket payments. A plan for Medicare to cover long-term care is not even being discussed. Instead, some politicians are discussing raising the Medicare eligibility age to save money.

Chapter 11

Social Security and Medicaid

In This Chapter

- ◆ A word about the Social Security retirement program
- ◆ Social Security's two disability programs
- ◆ What you must know about disability insurance
- ◆ Tomorrow's Social Security

For many years, we have heard about the "three-legged stool" of proper financial planning for retirement. The third leg is our own personal savings. The second leg is the retirement pension that we may receive from a former employer. That brings us to the first leg—Social Security.

The Social Security Administration (SSA) is a federal agency that administers the program that provides both retirement benefits to workers and their survivors, and benefits for disability to covered workers. There is no long-term care benefit through Social Security. However, a basic working knowledge of the program can help you in your long-term care planning, especially if you are lower-income or disabled and not sure what income benefits may be available to you. Financially vulnerable individuals should contact their state's Medicaid office (see Appendix B) to see if they qualify for free health insurance and/or for free Medicaid coverage of their long-term care. (For more information, see Chapter 21.)

Did you notice that the standard retirement planning stool is missing two very important legs? The first leg that is missing is the Medicare health insurance program, which is crucial to almost everyone's financial security in retirement (see Chapter 10). The last missing leg is a plan to pay for long-term care.

If you don't have a financial leg to stand on, the federal government's means-tested programs can give you a leg up: Social Security's Supplemental Security Income (SSI), which is described in this chapter, and the Medicaid program as administered by your state (please read Chapter 21 for the details).

Social Security Retirement Income

Most people are aware of Social Security's retirement income program. We have payroll taxes during our working years from our paychecks that go to the Social Security program. Workers born before 1938 can receive Social Security retirement benefits as early as age 62. By waiting until age 65, their full retirement age, they will receive a bigger benefit. Workers who collect benefits before age 65 are penalized by getting a smaller benefit—they will receive between 20 to 30 percent less than if they had waited until full retirement age, depending on the year that they turn 62.

Alternately, workers who wait beyond their full retirement age may delay collecting Social Security retirement benefits. They are rewarded for the wait, with a permanently increased benefit. Depending on their year of birth, their eventual benefit will be increased between 4.5 percent to 8 percent for every year they delay benefits between their full retirement age and age 70.

The full retirement age has increased for workers born in 1938 or later. For example, someone born after 1959 has a full retirement age of 67, not 65.

If you decide to collect your Social Security retirement benefit before full retirement age, your benefit amount may be reduced if you have earnings above a government-stated limit. Contact the Social Security Administration or ask your financial advisor or tax preparer for more information.

> **Wisdom of the Aged**
>
> Curious what your social security retirement check will be each month? You should receive in the mail each year a Social Security Statement that estimates this number. To request a copy, either call or write the Social Security Administration (see Appendix E), or request the statement online at www.ssa.gov. There is usually a two- to four-week wait to get your statement.

Social Security Disability Programs

When you work and pay into the Social Security program, you are probably thinking of Social Security as providing a monthly check in retirement. However, if you are disabled before age 65, Social Security has a benefit for you.

How does Social Security's disability benefit differ from the disability insurance that you may get for free at work, or from the disability insurance that you bought on your own? Most people don't even think about their disability benefits until it's too late—they are disabled when they crack open their coverage, and read about it's limitations. If your need for long-term care occurs before age 65, it is likely to impact your ability to earn a paycheck. If you are sick or hurt and unable to work, your disability benefits can be transformed—from a coverage you never took the time to look into, to the one thing that will provide the cash to pay your mortgage and your bills. Look into your disability coverage now, to make sure that you're well protected.

Social Security Disability Insurance Program

Some working-age adults who need long-term care will qualify for Social Security's disability insurance program. Do not confuse this benefit with long-term care insurance. Social Security sends a monthly check to you to help with living expenses. It certainly doesn't pay enough for you to cover long-term care—and, for many people, Social Security's disability benefit won't even cover their mortgage payment. The maximum monthly benefit in 2002 for Social Security disability is $780 per month for the nonblind, and $1,300 per month for the blind.

Truth & Consequences

According to Social Security, it usually takes two to three months to find out if your submitted claim has been approved or not. Then, if approved, Social Security pays disability benefits in the month after they are earned. So you would receive your February benefit in March. If you are relying on Social Security for your disability protection, you had better have a cash cushion to live on for the first few months!

To qualify for Social Security disability, your disability needs to be long-term and total. This means that you are unable to work at any job for at least a year, or that the disability is expected to result in death. Benefits will be paid until you are able to work again, or until you turn age 65.

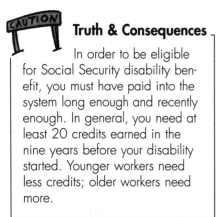

Truth & Consequences

In order to be eligible for Social Security disability benefit, you must have paid into the system long enough and recently enough. In general, you need at least 20 credits earned in the nine years before your disability started. Younger workers need less credits; older workers need more.

It is much more difficult to qualify for Social Security's disability benefit than for other disability benefits that you may be familiar with. For example, no benefit is payable until the first full month after you have been disabled for six months. Social Security never pays a disability benefit for partial disabilities. Disability insurance that you have bought on your own or through an employer often covers partial disabilities and usually starts well before six months of disability. Workers who are hurt on the job may qualify for worker's compensation benefits, in addition to any disability insurance benefits.

If you turn age 65 while collecting Social Security disability benefits, your disability benefits automatically become retirement benefits, and the amount you collect remains the same.

You can earn a maximum of four work credits per year, with every $870 of your income earning one credit (2002 number). Your spouse and child or children may be eligible for disability benefits even if they have not paid into the system and are not disabled.

If you are receiving Social Security disability, and your income and assets meet the requirements, you may also qualify for SSI (Supplemental Security Income). SSI is available to those people with disabilities who are financially vulnerable. It is even available to children. The next section describes SSI.

The federal government reports that a 20-year-old worker has a 3 in 10 chance of becoming disabled before retirement age. Smart long-term care planning during your working years includes a high-quality disability policy. Disability insurance replaces your earned income that is lost because you are sick or hurt. Long-term care insurance covers the additional cost of any long-term care that you need. When shopping for disability insurance, seek out a policy that includes the following:

◆ Benefit to age 65 (lifetime, if available).

◆ Partial disabilities covered (without a requirement of total disability first).

◆ Portable if you change employers.

◆ Benefit increases once your are on claim to keep pace with inflation.

◆ Future purchase options to allow your benefit to increase with your earnings.

◆ Strong definition of disability (pays a benefit if you are unable to perform your own job—not any job).

◆ Noncancellable (the policy cannot be changed and the premium cannot be increased, as long as you pay your premiums).

Depending on your occupation and the insurance company whose disability policy you are considering, all the above features may or may not be available. Working age adults who are unable to buy disability insurance, or unable to get a high enough disability benefit, may want to consider purchasing a true per diem or indemnity long-term care insurance policy.

Why would someone be unable to get disability insurance? There are a lot of reasons. Disability insurance is among the toughest type of insurance for which to qualify. In addition to proving your medical health, you must also prove your earnings. People in high risk occupations, or who engage in high risk , (such as piloting private planes or S.C.U.B.A. diving), sometimes have trouble purchasing high quality disability insurance. Someone who has just started his or her own business and cannot demonstrate earnings probably can't get disability insurance until stable earnings can be shown. Sometimes, a medical condition will make disability insurance hard to get, while LTC insurance may be attainable.

CAUTION Truth & Consequences

Long-term care insurance is not a substitute for disability insurance. There are claims that would be paid under a disability policy that would not be covered by long-term care insurance. But, if someone can't get disability insurance, per diem/indemnity LTC insurance can be a practical purchase. Hopefully, the situation is temporary, and disability insurance can be secured. Meanwhile, at least the person has a policy that will send cash to their mailbox under certain circumstances.

Here's why a per diem/indemnity LTC contract can be helpful in these situations. With a true per diem policy, once you have triggered benefits, the insurance company sends you a check to use as you'd like, even if you are receiving informal LTC from unpaid caregivers. This is like disability insurance, which sends you a check (as replacement for your earned income) to use as you'd like. As you'll read in Chapter 19, true per diem policies are much more expensive than traditional LTC insurance. Some people are calling per diem LTC "cash benefit" LTC. If you can't get disability insurance, consider buying a much large benefit on your per diem/indemnity LTC policy than your would purchase for traditional LTC purposes.

Supplemental Security Income (SSI) Program

The Supplemental Security Income (SSI) Program is a different program than the Social Disability Program. Payments under the SSI program are not based on employment; they are based on financial need. The program is run by Social Security, but funding does not come from Social Security taxes. SSI payments are paid by the federal government using general tax revenues.

To qualify for SSI's monthly payment, you must have low income, have few assets, and be blind or disabled. You must also be a U.S. citizen, certain lawful permanent resident, or eligible noncitizen (contact Social Security or visit the web site for details).

The maximum monthly federal SSI payment in 2002 is $545 per individual, and $817 per couple. Some states supplement this federal amount with their own payment.

Truth & Consequences

Seniors who qualify for SSI will likely qualify for Medicare's important programs for financially vulnerable seniors, such as Qualified Medicare Beneficiary (QMB) programs and Specified Low-Income Medicare Beneficiaries (SLMBs).

Most people who qualify for SSI also qualify for Medicaid programs and food stamps. Contact your state's Medicaid office (see Appendix B) and ask about both health insurance and long-term care benefits.

Qualified Medicare Beneficiary programs provide subsidized or free Part B coverage and free coverage for expenses not covered by Medicare. For more information on low income and asset programs, contact the offices listed in Appendixes B, C, and D.

The Future of Social Security

The future of Social Security is not on as solid footing as most of us would hope. Similar to Medicare and Medicaid, the program is facing the problem of inadequate funding given the booming population of retirees and their increasing life spans. This problem has been on the horizon for many years, yet there seems to be little political will to either cut benefits or increase payroll or other federal taxes. Payroll taxes were raised in 1950 and 1977 to avoid a shortfall in revenue. In 1983 a number of reforms to Social Security were made, including the increase of the retirement age for those born in 1938 and later.

Back in January 1997, AARP's magazine *Modern Maturity* ran a cover story titled "Can We Save Social Security?" The debate is still raging. In December 2001, a bipartisan Social Security commission chartered by the President delivered a series of options to save Social Security. Their timing couldn't have been worse; they spoke to a federal government preoccupied with a recession and the new war on terrorism. It seems that the time is never right to take a hard look at the problems with the Social Security program—and take the tough steps necessary to put it on secure footing.

My crystal ball tells me that Social Security retirement ages may have to be raised again, and that benefits may even have to become means-tested. If either one of these things happen, it's another blow to the middle class and upper-middle class.

I suspect that the readers of this book who are not rich or poor will find less and less government benefits in the future, despite the fact that they are basing their current retirement and long-term care planning on the promise of these programs. The younger that you are now, the more this potential problem is likely to affect you. Congress is unlikely to make abrupt cuts in programs for those already collecting or on the threshold of collecting.

The Least You Need to Know

- Current Social Security retirement program funding is inadequate to meet future obligations, as the baby boomers retire and life spans increase.

- The Social Security retirement age is currently 65 for people born before 1938, and older for those born later.

- Seniors with few finances may qualify for the Supplemental Security Income Program (SSI). Some states supplement this federal payment.

- The maximum monthly benefit in 2002 for Social Security disability is $780 per month for the nonblind, and $1,300 per month for the blind—not enough to pay for LTC.

- You do not have to be retirement age to collect disability benefits from Social Security.

Chapter 12

Government Incentives to Buy LTC Insurance

In This Chapter

- ◆ TQ or not TQ—that is the question
- ◆ Tax incentives for individuals and businesses
- ◆ State incentives and partnership programs

For many years, some states have offered incentives for their citizens to purchase long-term care insurance. The reason is straightforward—if someone has LTC insurance, he or she is less likely to be on Medicaid. Medicaid is a government program to pay the health and LTC costs of the poor (as discussed in Chapters 21–24); about half of the Medicaid payments come from state taxes.

Starting in the 1997 tax year, the federal government offered a tax break to many people with LTC insurance. A bigger tax deduction is pending in Congress as I am writing this book. As Congress debates the increased deduction, more and more states are giving their citizens an incentive to purchase LTC insurance. The federal government is not just handing out tax breaks—in 2002 it rolled out a payroll-deduction LTC insurance program to an estimated 20 million employees and members of the federal family (for more details, see Chapter 15).

No one should make the decision whether or not to buy LTC insurance based solely on governmental incentives. But it's not every day that you are rewarded with a tax deduction or other benefit for purchasing insurance for yourself or a family member. Let's take a look at what's available.

Federal Incentives

The *Health Insurance Portability and Accountability Act* (HIPAA) was signed into law August 21, 1996. It included broad new protections for people covered by employer-sponsored health insurance, tried to eliminate Medicaid planning, and had many items pertaining to long-term care insurance. Effective January 1, 1997, the law mandated criteria for a new class of long-term care insurance: tax-qualified policies. It also included the first tax deduction for long-term care insurance.

A tax-qualified policy (TQ) is one that meets the standard outlines in HIPPA. Examples of some of the standards for TQ policies are:

Marilee's Memo

A **benefit trigger** is a specified event or circumstance that allows someone to access benefits under an insurance policy. In a life insurance policy, the benefit trigger is the death of the insured. In a TQ LTC insurance policy, benefit triggers are the loss of two activities of daily living (from a standard list of five or six), or a cognitive impairment (such as Alzheimer's disease).

- Mandates activities of daily living (ADLS), including bathing, continence, dressing, eating, toileting, and transferring.

- Mandates the loss of two activities of daily living (from a list of five or six) and cognitive impairment as the only ways that policyholders qualify for benefits (called benefit triggers).

- Disallows cash value long-term care insurance policies.

- Mandates a 30-day free look period (after policy delivery, the policyholder can return the policy within 30 days for a full refund).

- Disallows claims payments for claims expecting to last fewer than 90 days.

TQ and NTQ LTC Insurance

By creating tax-qualified (TQ) policies, Congress gave an incentive for insurers and consumers to embrace long-term care insurance.

Many insurance companies only offer TQ contracts. Some people argue that consumers are better off buying policies that are not restricted by the TQ guidelines in

HIPAA. These policies are called nontax-qualified (non-TQ, or NTQ) policies. On the positive side, NTQ policies can offer benefits that TQ policies are not allowed to; on the negative side, there is no federal tax deductibility for NTQ policies, and the taxation of benefits is uncertain.

For example, HIPAA defines a chronically ill individual as someone certified by a licensed health-care practitioner as being *unable to perform at least two activities of daily living (ADLs) for at least 90 days*, or a person with a similar level of disability. Non-TQ policies typically do not have the 90-day precertification requirement, so claims under those policies would be eligible for payment, even if they're expected to last less than 90 days.

As you just read, TQ policies require the loss of at least two ADLs to trigger benefits. Non-TQ policies are not bound by the HIPAA language, and so may, for example, have in their policy that only the loss of one ADL is required to trigger policy benefits. Here's how that might work. Your mother has severe arthritis in her hands, and so she is unable to dress herself without assistance. She can still handle all the other ADLs on her own, but buttons, snaps, and zippers are too small for her arthritic hands to work with. With a TQ policy, she needs the loss of another ADL in order to trigger policy benefits. If she had a non-TQ policy that had one ADL benefit trigger, since she needs assistance dressing, she would be eligible for benefits.

Not all non-TQ policies have only one ADL loss as a benefit trigger, but some do. Some offer it as an optional benefit for an additional premium. The previous example is given for you to see how a non-TQ policy is not bound by the TQ standard contract; benefits may be easier to access in non-TQ policies.

Truth & Consequences

HIPAA provides a list of six standard ADLs: bathing, dressing, eating, continence, transferring, and toileting. Tax-qualified policies must list at least five ADLs from this standard list of six. It is commonly accepted that the first ADL that most people need assistance with is bathing. If a policy lists only five ADLs, look to see if bathing is included. Policies that list the bathing ADL are likely to trigger benefits sooner than those that don't.

HIPAA provides a second trigger besides ADL impairment. A person may be considered chronically ill in a TQ policy if he requires substantial supervision to protect himself from threats to his health and safety due to a severe cognitive impairment (such as a dementia like Alzheimer's). Proponents of NTQ policies point out that such coverage often can have a third trigger which is not allowed on TQ policies:

"medical necessity." The medical-necessity trigger allows your doctor to say that care is needed to begin policy benefits. This third trigger may be included on a NTQ policy as a basic part of the policy, or as an optional benefit when you apply, for additional premium.

The Precertification Period

For any claim to be paid by a TQ LTC policy, there is a precertification requirement. To satisfy the requirement, a licensed health-care practitioner must first certify that the person looking to collect benefits is expected to need at least 90 days of care. This requirement is separate and distinct from the *elimination period*, or waiting period. If you have a TQ LTC policy and do not meet the standard for precertification, no benefit will be paid, even if you have satisfied the elimination period.

Marilee's Memo

The **elimination period** (EP), sometimes called waiting period (WP), is like a deductible. It is the number of days that must be waited before a policy's benefit starts. Typical elimination periods are 30, 60, or 90 days. Since most policies require that the EP be satisfied with days of paid professional care, if you have a policy with a 60-day elimination period, you must be able to pay for the first 60 days of care out of your own pocket.

Even if your policy has a short elimination period, say 30 days, and you suffer a fall and need 60 days of care, a TQ policy can't pay benefits. This is because you will not meet the 90-day precertification requirement. If you owned a NTQ policy with a 30-day elimination period, with or without a medical-necessity trigger, it is likely that claim would be paid.

LTC Lowdown

How do you know if an LTC insurance policy is tax qualified? The policy will state so, probably on page one. If you are unsure, call or write your agent or the insurance company and ask if your policy qualified as a tax-qualified contract under HIPAA. If your policy issue date is after December 31, 1996, make sure that your policy clearly states whether it is tax qualified or nontax qualified.

Which Is Best for Me: TQ or NTQ?

Which policy is best for you: TQ or NTQ? It's quite a debate. A consumer considering a non-TQ LTC insurance policy needs to weigh the potential for easier access to LTC benefits against no federal tax deductibility, and the potential for benefits to be taxable. Let's look at some additional considerations:

♦ Short-term (fewer than 90 days) claims can never be paid under TQ. But this isn't a consideration if you have a 90-day deductible.

♦ The tax deduction is great for business owners, but many individuals can't take advantage of the current federal tax deduction. This is because the current federal tax deduction for long-term care insurance is part of the medical expense deduction, which can only be taken by people who itemize and whose unreimbursed medical expenses exceed 7.5 percent of their adjusted gross income.

♦ I previously discussed easier benefit triggers, such as the loss of one ADL. Some people argue that if you have the loss of one ADL, it will shortly be followed by the loss of a second, so the TQ trigger is not a burden. However, there could be claims where one ADL versus two makes a big difference to a policyholder.

♦ Some states offer a tax credit or deduction only for TQ policies. Other states allow a deduction for both TQ and NTQ policies.

♦ Concern about rate increases in NTQ policies.

Here's a last consideration in the TQ vs. NTQ debate. One of the reasons that HIPAA imposed such strict limits on TQ policies was in hopes of encouraging rate stability of LTC policies. Though many consumers find this hard to believe, there are people who were (and are) nervous that insurance companies made it too easy to collect on LTC policies relative to the premiums being charged. By adding the 90-day precertification requirement to TQ policies, Congress eliminated a huge number of potential short-term claims. This philosophy is in line with the idea that LTC insurance is for long-term care needs (more than 90 days). TQ policies with short elimination periods (such as 20 days) can pay claims before 90 days of care are received, so long as the need for care is expected to last at least 90 days.

Then, how can NTQ policies be priced similar to TQ policies, while at the same time, their benefits are easier to access? Are consumers who purchase NTQ policies setting themselves up for future premium increases? The debate is intense in the insurance industry, and I don't have any easy answers for you here. I wish that I did. Why should a consumer worry that an insurance company priced its product too low? The truth is that consumers do have to be worried about low rates when buying long-term care insurance, because future rate increases are a real possibility.

Marilee's Memo

Guaranteed renewable means that, as long as you pay your premium, your policy is in force. But, while you can't be singled out because of a change in health or because you have submitted a claim, the premiums are not guaranteed to remain flat. Only a noncancelable policy means that premiums are guaranteed never to change.

This is because the vast majority of long-term care insurance policies are what is called *guaranteed renewable*. This means that, while you can't be denied renewal because of a change in health or a claim, the premiums are not guaranteed to remain flat. The insurance companies cannot single you out for a rate change; if a premium rate increase happens, it must apply to your fellow policyholders, too.

Most insurance companies do not offer non-TQ policies, so many people are not even aware that there is a decision to be made. If the deduction for TQ policies is expanded, as most observers expect to happen, or the benefit of non-TQ policies is deemed taxable, which may or may not happen, I expect that non-TQ policies will become even less available. Meanwhile, your insurance agent and/or financial advisor are the best people to help you make a good decision on this matter.

Federal Tax Incentives for Individuals

The federal tax deduction for LTC insurance applies to TQ policies, or policies that were grandfathered (issued prior to January 1, 1997).

Pending legislation, the Long-Term Care and Retirement Security Act of 2001 (HR 831, S 627) would provide for an above-the-line tax deduction on TQ LTC policies. It would also, for the first time, allow LTC insurance to be included in employer-sponsored cafeteria plans, sometimes called flexible benefit plans, which let employees use pre-tax money to purchase certain benefits. The pending legislation would also provide a modest tax credit for eligible caregivers. These bills, as of spring 2002, have not yet passed.

Current tax code allows TQ LTC insurance premiums, subject to limitations, to be included as an unreimbursed medical expense. Unreimbursed medical expenses, such as prescription drugs, are combined with items such as Medicare supplement premiums, and now TQ LTC premiums, and are added up by the taxpayer. If this total amount exceeds 7.5 percent of adjusted gross income (AGI), the taxpayer *who itemizes* can take a deduction for the amount that exceeds 7.5 percent.

The amount of premium which can be applied as an unreimbursed medical expense for federal income-tax purposes is limited, and depends on the insured's age at the end of the tax year. The limits increase each year; the 2002 limits are shown in the following table.

Attained Age Before the Close of Tax Year	Tax Limitation of Premiums Calendar Year 2002
40 or younger	$240
41–50	$450
51–60	$900
61–70	$2,390
71 and older	$2,990

Let's look an example. Mrs. Smith, age 70, has a TQ long-term care policy that costs $1,900 a year. Her adjusted gross income in 2002 is $40,000, and she itemizes deductions on her federal income tax return. Her unreimbursed medical expenses are $2,300 for the year, which include the premium on her Medicare supplement policy. When it's time for her to file her 2002 taxes, she sees that, based on her age, she can deduct up to $2,390 of TQ LTC insurance—so her whole premium of $1,900 can be included as an unreimbursed medical expense. Adding the $2,300 to the LTC premium ($1,900), we have total unreimbursed medical expenses of $4,200. The amount that exceeds 7.5 percent of her AGI ($40,000 × 7.5% = $3,000) can be deducted. This means that Mrs. Smith has a deduction of $1,200 ($4,200 − $3,000).

Federal Tax Deductibility for Businesses

Since HIPAA classified LTC insurance as accident and health insurance, 100 percent of the premium for TQ policies paid for employees, their spouses and dependents, and retirees and their spouses is deductible to a C-corporation as a business expense. The employer's premium payment is not included as taxable income to the individual. The deduction is not limited by the age-related numbers previously shown.

Employees of a not-for-profit company are treated like the employees of a C-corporation (100 percent deductible). Please note that there are no discrimination rules for employer-provided LTC coverage. LTC coverage can be an effective tool in employee recruitment and retention, as discussed in Chapter 14.

For self-employed individuals (such as sole proprietors, partners, and shareholders with more than 2 percent shares of subchapter S-corporations), the premium expense for TQ policies is deductible, just like health insurance to a self-employed individual. The eligible deduction in 2002 is 70 percent of the age-based limit noted in the preceding chart for individual taxpayers; from tax year 2003 on, the deduction is 100 percent of the age-based limit. In addition to the business deduction, self-employed individuals may include the remaining percentage of eligible premiums as medical expenses on their personal federal income-tax return. Premiums paid for spouses and dependents are treated in the same way.

State Incentives

Twenty-four states have either tax deductions or tax credits for LTC insurance. In some states, the deduction or credit is limited to policies that meet the federal definition of TQ. In other states, the tax break is extended to non-TQ policies. Some states do not offer a tax deduction, but they offer other incentives to purchase LTC insurance. For example, in Massachusetts, there is a special exclusion from Medicaid recovery of your home if, before you enter the nursing home, you have a LTC insurance policy (TQ or NTQ) that meets the state's requirements. Even if you eventually end up on Medicaid, to reward you for having the LTC policy, the state will not place a Medicaid lien on your primary residence.

You may wonder, why would I end up on Medicaid if I had LTC insurance? Let's say that you had a policy with a five-year benefit, yet you needed eight years of care. First, your policy would pay for five years. Then, you would likely use personal assets or have already protected those assets through Medicaid planning (see Chapter 22). At that point you would qualify for Medicaid. Was it worth having the LTC insurance?

Well, the insurance gave you five years of private-pay choices before you had to invade your life savings—five years of time to form a plan to protect your assets. And, of course, five years of controlling your destiny, just as if you had a big bank account to cover five years of care. Then the state of Massachusetts lets you keep your house in your name, and leave it to whoever you'd like, to reward you for having the insurance.

The following figure shows which states have a tax credit or deduction for long-term care insurance policies. Check to see if the LTC policy that you are considering purchasing (or already own) is eligible for a tax credit or deduction in your state. Each state has its own requirements for policies that qualify. This map is current as of March 2002; things may have changed since then.

Check with your insurance agent, company, or your state's division of insurance for details on other government incentives to purchase LTC insurance that may be available in your state (see Appendix A for your state insurance department contact information).

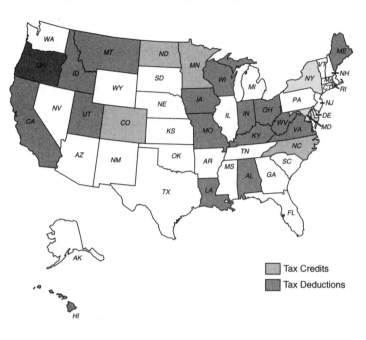

State Tax Incentives for Purchase of LTCI

Tax Credits
Tax Deductions

Long-term care insurance: state tax credits and tax deductions.

(Source: Health Insurance Association of America (HIAA), March 2002)

Partnership Programs

In addition the long-term care policy benefits, five states offer special long-term care policies available through what are called partnership programs. By purchasing a partnership policy, people in these states can protect assets that otherwise would need to be spent before they would qualify for Medicaid.

These states are California, Connecticut, Illinois, Indiana, and New York. The Robert Wood Johnson Foundation was instrumental in making this program possible, to encourage the development of private-funding sources for long-term care. The partnership programs each specify a minimum policy design, such as a minimum daily benefit and required built-in inflation protection, in order for a LTC policy to be bought under the program.

If you owned a partnership policy, your state would allow you to keep some assets that would normally have to be spent down—liquidated and spent—to qualify for Medicaid (see Chapter 21). In California, Connecticut, and Illinois, the protection is dollar for dollar. For every dollar of benefits your long-term care partnership policy provides, you can keep one dollar of assets that otherwise would have to be spent down. Let's say that you are single, and your state's Medicaid office says that single people must have no more than $2,000 in countable assets (your primary residence and some other assets are not included here) to qualify for Medicaid. Your partnership policy provides $200,000 in benefits. Your state's Medicaid office would allow you to qualify for Medicaid long-term care benefits, even though you had $202,000 in countable assets.

In New York, the benefit of a partnership policy is even more profound. Once you have used up your long-term care partnership policy benefits, you automatically are eligible for Medicaid from an asset point of view, without having to spend down any assets. The protection is not tied into the policy benefit at all—an unlimited amount of assets can be protected.

Indiana residents who own a partnership LTC insurance policy may have either dollar-for-dollar asset protection, or unlimited asset protection (like New York). It depends on when the policy was purchased, and the design they chose for the policy.

Why are we combining the topics of LTC insurance and Medicaid? Aren't they mutually exclusive? Isn't the reason that people buy LTC insurance to make sure that they never have to go on the government's Medicaid program? Yes and no. If you buy a LTC insurance policy with any benefit less than lifetime, you run the risk that your need for care lasts longer than your policy benefits. Using our same example from the previous section, let's say that you own a policy with a five-year benefit, but you need eight years of care. The policy pays the first five years, then you would look to your income and life savings. Eventually, you could end up on Medicaid.

Check with your state's insurance department (Appendix A) for more information on partnership policies if you live in California, Connecticut, Illinois, Indiana, or New York. You can also find information at the following websites:

- California: www.dhs.cahwnet.gov/cpltc

- Connecticut: www.CTpartnership.org

- Illinois: www.state.il.us/INS/Ship/seniorHealth.htm

   (Download the booklet "Long Term Care Partnership Policies Shopper's Guide" from www.state.il.us/Aging/pub-2.htm.)

- Indiana: www.in.gov/fssa/iltcp

- New York: www.nyspltc.org

Truth & Consequences _____

By the way, the special protections offered by partnership policies only work if you end up receiving your LTC in the state where you bought your policy, or in another partnership state with a reciprocal arrangement (Connecticut & Indiana have such as agreement). Although a partnership LTC policy will pay benefits in any state, the protection from Medicaid spend-down is usually limited to the state where you bought the policy. For example, if you live in New York (a partnership state), but plan on retiring in Arizona, a New York partnership policy gives you no special benefits if you are not in New York when you receive long-term care.

Taxation of Benefits

The federal tax deduction is limited to premiums for tax-qualified policies. Some states offer a state tax deduction for TQ policies only; others allow a deduction for NTQ policies that meet state guidelines. But how is the benefit paid by a LTC policy taxed?

Benefits from a life insurance policy are received free from income tax. But HIPAA clarified that LTC insurance is a type of health insurance. Are LTC benefits taxable? We know for sure that benefits paid by a TQ LTC insurance policy are tax-free, with certain limitations. TQ benefits are tax-free as long as they do not exceed the actual cost of care, or are less than $210 per day (2002 number). In other words, if a TQ policy pays more than $210 per day, the amount of benefit paid which exceeds the actual cost of care would be taxable.

HIPAA is silent on the tax treatment of benefits from an NTQ LTC insurance policy. Until Congress or the IRS clarifies how these benefits will be treated, conservative planners will plan on the worst: that benefits paid under a NTQ LTC policy will be taxable.

How will the IRS know that benefits have been paid to you by a LTC insurance company? Beginning in January 1997, when any insurance company pays a benefit under any long-term care contract, that company is required to report to the IRS using form 1099-LTC. This requirement applies to all contracts, whether TQ or NTQ. If an accelerated death benefit was sold, marketed, or issued as long-term care insurance, benefits under that life insurance rider must also be reported.

The Least You Need to Know

 - ◆ Whether to buy a tax-qualified or a nontax-qualified LTC policy is a hotly debated issue.

 - ◆ The federal tax deduction for LTC insurance applies only to tax-qualified policies (if your policy is dated before January 1, 1997, it is grandfathered).

 - ◆ Partnership policies, which are available in five states, allow people to qualify for Medicaid while preserving assets that otherwise would have to be spent down.

 - ◆ Many states have tax credits or deductions—check into what policies qualify if you are buying insurance.

 - ◆ The federal tax deduction for TQ LTC insurance is only available to taxpayers who itemize.

 - ◆ Businesses have substantial tax-planning benefits from purchasing TQ LTC insurance.

Part 4

The Truth About LTC Insurance

Okay, you're thinking that long-term care insurance is the best way for you to plan for long-term care. Can you even get it—from a health point of view? Is the purchase appropriate, given your financial situation? Assuming that you're healthy enough, and can afford it, now you have a lot of choices. This part of the book will help you decide where to purchase long-term care insurance. In the spirit of the devil's advocate, in Chapter 17 I highlight for you what I think are the five biggest problems with this type of insurance.

Should you buy the program offered by your employer or an association that you belong to? You may qualify to purchase coverage from the biggest group program in the country—the federal government's program. Is that where you should look, or should you meet with an insurance agent? What should you look for in an agent? Read Part 4 and understand.

Chapter 13

LTC Insurance—Is It Right for You?

In This Chapter

- ◆ The health that fits the bill
- ◆ LTC insurance and the elderly
- ◆ What you should know about modified offers
- ◆ The truth about underwriting and combo policies
- ◆ What is financially appropriate—and what is not

The first step in determining the optimal way for you to finance long-term care is an assessment of your options. To know whether long-term care insurance is an option in your planning, you first need to know if you can even qualify to buy the product. There are a lot of people who wish they could get long-term care insurance, but they have a health problem and can't get approved.

There are other people who are healthy enough to be approved for the Insurance. They can't afford the premium. You see, there are two different ways to determine if long-term care insurance makes sense for you.

The first is medical in nature. If you want long-term care insurance, will your health allow you to buy it? The second consideration is financial. Financially, is this an appropriate purchase? Can you afford it?

How is it that saying goes … we can't always get what we want? The reality is that long-term care insurance is not a product for everyone. Knowing the information in this chapter before you even speak with an insurance agent could save you both a lot of heartache and hassle. Let's start with whether you can even get long-term care insurance, then take a look at whether you can afford to buy it.

Are You Healthy Enough?

There's a saying in the insurance industry: Money pays for long-term care insurance, but your health buys it. This means that, even if you have the money to pay the insurance premium, you may not be able to buy a policy because of health problems.

Just as the banks love to lend money to people who really don't need it, the insurance companies love to sell policies to people who don't think they will ever collect. It has to be that way, or insurance wouldn't work. If we all waited until we knew we had a health problem before we bought long-term care insurance, the insurance company could not possibly charge us enough for the insurance. Insurance is based on the reality that not everyone will have a claim.

For example, the life insurance company knows that a certain percentage of people who are age 25 and healthy today (and think they will never collect) will die before the normal life expectancy. Their families will collect on their life insurance. But most 25-year-olds who medically qualify for life insurance today won't die for many, many years. That's why a healthy young person can buy life insurance, for less than the price of a daily cup of coffee, that will pay his family a million dollars if he dies.

That's what insurance does. It takes a risk that would be catastrophic for an individual (such as a house burning down or needing years of long-term care), and shifts the risk off the shoulders of the individual to the insurance company. The individual shifts the risk by paying a premium in exchange for a contract, or promise to pay, from the insurance company. The insurance company collects premiums from a large number of people with the same concern, earns profits by managing the risk well, or loses money if claims are higher than expected. Some of the people in the insured group will collect on their policies in any given year; most will not.

Are You the Right Kind of Healthy?

The life insurance company knows that everyone will eventually die. When they look at an application they try to figure out if the person has a higher chance of dying sooner than the average person. If so, they must charge a higher premium to cover the higher risk—the higher likelihood that they will have to pay out a claim sooner because of your health problem.

When you apply for long-term care insurance, the insurance company tries to evaluate your risk of needing long-term care.

The process of looking at someone's health and making a decision about issuing insurance is called *underwriting*. Although underwriting technically refers to evaluating other aspects of an insurance application, such as financial suitability, when most people talk about underwriting, they are referring to medical underwriting.

Wisdom of the Aged

An insurer sets premium rates based on an average person, with average health. Some people will die without ever needing long-term care. Others will pay their premiums for many years, and only collect for a short while. Still others will cancel their policies before care is needed. Money collected on all these policies is used to pay for claims. The most expensive claims are those that are long in duration, and that start before the insured has paid in for many years.

For example, a 45-year-old woman buys a long-term care insurance policy and soon after is hit by a car on her daily jog. She suffered massive injuries, is wheelchair-bound, and cannot take care of herself. This woman, who didn't plan on collecting long-term care benefits for 30 or so years, will collect an incredibly large amount of money compared to the small amount of premiums she paid.

Most people are familiar with the underwriting for life insurance policies, but few know how long-term care underwriting works. Many people are surprised to find out that even though they may be able to purchase life insurance, they do not qualify for long-term care insurance. The opposite is also true. Someone who is turned down for life insurance can often purchase long-term care insurance.

Put bluntly, when you apply for long-term care insurance, the insurance company does not care how long you will live (mortality risk), it only cares about your odds of needing extended long-term care (morbidity risk). Someone with severe rheumatoid arthritis, whose hands are crippled and frozen, may need years of long-term care. However, the illness will not affect how long he lives. His neighbor, however, had triple-bypass heart surgery a year ago. For the rest of her life, she may not be able to qualify medically for standard life insurance at prices she can afford. However, her application for long-term care insurance may be approved, with no more premium than someone with no heart problems.

Marilee's Memo

Mortality risk is the phrase that insurers use to describe our chances of dying. **Morbidity risk** is the chance that we will be disabled. A long-term care insurance company is concerned with morbidity, while a life insurance company is concerned with mortality. The underwriting health criteria for long-term care insurance is totally different than that for life insurance.

Red Flags in an LTC Application

If you were diagnosed with terminal cancer yesterday, you know that you couldn't buy a new life insurance policy today. What are the conditions that prohibit someone from purchasing long-term care insurance?

Declinable conditions for LTC insurance include the following:

- Parkinson's disease

- Alzheimer's or other dementia

- Multiple sclerosis

- Osteoporosis, if it has resulted in fractures

- Muscular dystrophy

- Diabetes, with complications such as eye problems or amputation

- ALS (Lou Gehrig's disease)

- Anyone already in need of help with everyday activities such as dressing, bathing, and walking

Yellow Flags in an LTC Application

Many other conditions may be acceptable … or not. It depends on the company that you are applying to, as well as the details of your particular situation. One person with high blood pressure may be able to get long-term care insurance, while another person may not be able to, since his doctor's records indicate that his condition is not well controlled. Peg had breast cancer and was able to get LTC insurance; Deb, who had the same kind of cancer, could not, since less time has passed since her last cancer treatment ended.

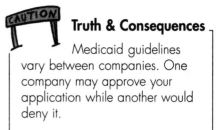

Truth & Consequences

Medicaid guidelines vary between companies. One company may approve your application while another would deny it.

Do you have more than one yellow flag? Then your situation is likely much more complicated. Underwriters refer to multiple yellow flags as comorbidities. Simply put, if you have two yellow flags, your risk of needing long-term care may not be doubled, it may instead be tripled or quadrupled. One yellow flag by itself may be unimportant, but add two others and your application may be declined.

Examples of *yellow flags* which may or may not be problems when applying for long-term care insurance include the following:

◆ High blood pressure (level of control is important)

◆ Smoking (by itself, not considered a problem)

◆ Obesity (or, as I prefer to say, you are too short for your weight)

◆ Your doctor has recommended tests or surgery (the decision by the insurer would be delayed until the test or surgery is done)

◆ Cancer history (prostate cancer and benign skin cancers are generally not a worry)

◆ Diabetes (how well controlled is important, as are medication levels)

◆ Emphysema

◆ History of falls

◆ Episode of memory loss, TIA (transient ischemic attack—mini-stroke), or stroke

◆ Currently taking many prescribed medications

◆ Has given up driving/leaves house rarely

The company's underwriting guide is the first place your agent will look to see if a condition may be a problem in getting long-term care insurance. Your agent may also speak with someone in underwriting at the insurer's home office. If one company denies your application, get a written explanation why, and look for other coverage.

LTC Lowdown _____

Do not try to figure out if you qualify for long-term care insurance on your own. If you have any health problems, ask how the company or companies you are considering will look at the condition. An insurance agent will not be able to guarantee you that your application will be approved, but he or she should be able to explain how this company has treated other applications like yours.

According to AUL LTC Solutions in Avon, Connecticut, leading causes of declinations among LTC-policy applicants include the following:

♦ Cognitive impairments

♦ Stroke with residuals or multiple TIAs

♦ Cancer

♦ Diabetes, either uncontrolled or with complications

♦ Severe or debilitating musculoskeletal disorders

♦ Comorbidities

Older Applicants

There is a direct correlation between the age when you apply for long-term care insurance and the likelihood of the application being approved. Most of us do not get healthier with age. On average, when people between the ages of 50 to 60 apply, only 5 to 10 percent are declined. But at age 70 to 80, the declination rate jumps to between 18 and 30 percent. Does this mean that you shouldn't apply if you're older? No. However, younger readers should keep in mind these facts when they decide whether to apply now or wait awhile.

Most companies require what is called a "face-to-face assessment" for any applicant over age 70. The insurance company will send an examiner, who is usually a nurse, at its expense to your house to ask you some questions. Sometimes the exam can be done over the phone. The examiner is simply trying to make sure that you do not suffer from Alzheimer's or another cognitive impairment.

This screening is very important to the insurance industry, since claims arising from cognitive impairment can be very long, and can strike at relatively young ages. As part of the face-to-face assessment, the examiner will ask you questions, and ask you to repeat a list of words. Don't worry, you don't need to remember every word to pass the exam! Ask your insurance agent ahead of time if you have any questions about this exam.

A Weighty Matter

I've already talked about how underwriting guidelines vary from company to company. One company may approve your application while another one would decline it. What's too much weight on an individual for one company may be acceptable to another.

Some companies offer special, lower premiums for very healthy people. These rates are usually called preferred. Your height and weight must fit the company's underwriting guidelines for your application to be approved. And remember, it's not just your bathroom scale's number; think back to what your doctor's records will say!

Please note that the weight guidelines do not just list a maximum—they list a minimum, too. Some people may not qualify for long-term care insurance because they are too light.

Let's take a look at the weight guidelines for two different companies for a variety of applicants. If you are overweight, if it's at all possible, make sure that your statistics fit into the published guidelines of the company. Most companies will decline an applicant whose weight exceeds the guidelines. Note that Company #2 has unisex height and weight standards, while Company #1 has one table for men and one for women. As the following table shows, a man six feet tall who weighs 230 pounds would qualify for preferred rates with Company #1, but only standard rates with Company #2.

	Company #1 Weight Range	Company #2 Weight Range
Female Applicant Height	Preferred/Standard	Preferred/Standard
5'0"	102–178/179–208	88–164/165–205
5'4"	112–196/197–229	100–180/181–227
5'8"	125–215/216–251	113–199/200–253
6'0"	139–244/245–282	127–219/220–282
Male Applicant Height	Preferred/Standard	Preferred/Standard
5'0"	111–180/181–213	88–164/165–205
5'4"	123–198/199–232	100–180/181–227
5'8"	136–220/221–257	113–199/200–253
6'0"	152–244/245–285	127–219/220–282

Modified Offers and Rated Policies

Most long-term care insurance companies will either approve or reject your application. But what if your application isn't black or white from a medical point of view? Perhaps you are a smoker who is very overweight. We know this puts you at a higher risk for stroke than the average person. Many companies would decline this application. However, some companies take different approaches.

Wisdom of the Aged

Do insurance companies have any sources of information on applicants beyond what you put on your application? Absolutely. Whenever you sign an insurance application, you give the insurance company permission to get copies of your doctor's records. You also authorize the release of information to the Medical Information Bureau, or MIB. The MIB is a database that records information "flags" submitted by member insurance companies, such as health conditions and other underwriting considerations. If an application is denied because of a MIB report, you can get a free copy of your report to take a look. Otherwise, it costs $8.50 to get your report. For more information or to order a report, visit www.mib.com or call 617-426-3660.

The Mod Squad

When a company makes you a modified offer, it is offering you a policy with a different design than you applied for. However, you will not pay more for the policy; you will pay standard rates. So, for example, someone who has a history of osteoporosis may be offered a policy with a longer elimination period (deductible) than she had wanted. A six-month elimination period would mean that shorter claims would not be paid. Or the insurance company might offer someone who applied for a lifetime benefit period a policy that only pays a maximum of three years. This limits the insurance company's risk.

What should you do if you get a modified offer? The natural human response is to say, "Forget it!" In many cases, the insurance company is hoping that you'll do just that. If you pass on the coverage, you are still uninsured for the cost of long-term care, only now you know that your risk for needing the care is higher than for the average person. See the following "Why Should I Take a Modified Offer or a Rated Policy?" section for suggestions on how to proceed.

My Life Is Rated PG-13, My LTC Insurance Is XXX

What is a rated policy? If a company offers you a rated policy, this means that you will pay a higher premium rate than someone with better health. Like movie ratings, some ratings carry more weight than others. A typical rating would be 25 percent or 40 percent. If you were offered a 25 percent rating, that would mean that your premium would cost 25 percent more than an standard applicant whose health was standard. If your original policy premium was quoted at $1,600 per year, with a 25 percent rating, the actual premium would be $2,000. The insurance company charges this additional premium to compensate for the additional risk that it believes your medical condition brings.

If you have a complicated medical situation, your best bet to get LTC insurance may be with one of the few companies that offers the ability to rate their long-term care policies. Although the ability to offer rated life insurance policies is universal among insurers, most insurance companies do not offer rated LTC policies. They have a yes/no policy for dealing with applications, so if your health doesn't fit into their general guidelines, they'll decline your application.

Marilee's Memo

An insurance company that offers rated (higher premium) policies may approve a policy that another insurance company would decline. If your health situation is worse than the average person's, but not as bad as an application that would automatically be declined, a company that offers rated policies may be your best bet to get long-term care insurance.

Why Should I Take a Modified Offer or a Rated Policy?

When we are told by an insurance company that we can't get what we applied for, or that we can but it will be more expensive, our natural response is to say "Forget it. No deal."

I recommend a different response. Take the insurance company up on its offer—temporarily. By doing so, you have transferred a big risk to it for pennies on the dollar. Do not pay a full annual premium, because you may not be keeping this policy for a year. Instead, pay monthly (most insurance companies will require this be done directly through your bank account), quarterly (although most insurers don't offer a quarterly payment choice), or semiannually. This buys you time to research your options and perhaps apply to another company. You would generally ask that the new policy start the day before the premium is paid up to on your current policy. Never stop paying on an existing insurance policy until you know the new policy you are replacing it with is in force.

If your health situation changes for the better and you own a rated policy, you can ask to have the rating removed. When you accept policy, ask when the insurance company would be willing to reconsider the rating, and under what condition(s) it might be removed. The answer may be something like, "Once you have lost 30 pounds and have kept the weight off for six months, we will reconsider."

Truth & Consequences

When you apply for long-term care insurance, you will be given the option to make a premium payment with your application. You should do this. Here's why: If you put down a deposit, once the application is complete you have what's called conditional coverage. This means that you have frozen your health. If your health declines before you receive your policy, the policy must still be issued, back to the day the application was completed, or as explained in the conditional receipt.

Freeze Today's Health with Conditional Coverage

Some people are reluctant to pay premiums before they know that they are approved. As explained in the Truth and Consequences box above, it's to your advantage to do so, since it gives you conditional coverage and freezes your health.

Few of us get healthier as we age. If you are healthy enough to consider long-term care insurance, any health news flash that you are likely to get will not be good news.

As mentioned earlier, the application must be completed before conditional coverage is in effect. Most companies require applicants over a certain age (typically around ages 70 to 74) to have a face-to-face interview as part of the application process. If the company requires this, your application is not complete (and your health is not frozen) until you have met all the conditions required to complete an application. So once you've decided to apply for insurance, don't dawdle!

Truth & Consequences

Do not let anyone convince you to lie about a medical condition or on any other question that the insurance application asks; a false statement could mean your policy could be canceled retroactively back to when it was issued.

What if your application for insurance is declined after you have made out a check to the insurance company? You will receive a complete refund for the exact amount of your deposit check. Just in case you are wondering, you do not receive interest on this money.

By the way, when you make out a check to submit along with an insurance application, always make the check payable directly to the insurance company, not to the person you're meeting with or their company.

What if you paid a premium with your application, the policy was issued, and then you change your mind? The vast majority of long-term care insurance policies have a 30-day free-look clause. Tax-qualified long-term care policies *must* have this provision. Here's how it works: If, for any reason, you change your mind within 30 days after receiving your policy, you can return the policy to the insurance company or its authorized agent to receive a full refund of any money that you paid. Of course, at that point, the insurance is no longer in force.

So you see, there is virtually no downside to making a check out when you apply for long-term care insurance. In fact, it is in your best interest to do so.

> **LTC Lowdown** _____
>
> How long does it take for me to know if my application is approved? Once your application has been sent to the insurance company, in most cases the underwriter orders copies of your doctor's records. Once the underwriter has the doctor's records, a decision is usually made within a week. Depending on whether your doctor responds quickly or slowly, the whole process can take anywhere from three to eight weeks and more! By the way, the insurance company pays the doctor for the copies of your medical records.

If you are returning a policy under the free-look provision, consider sending it via certified mail or some other trackable way.

Underwriting and Workplace Policies

Some employers offer long-term care insurance policies. In most cases, coverage is paid through payroll deduction. Some plans offer relaxed underwriting or even guaranteed issue. This means that employees, who otherwise would not qualify medically for a policy if they applied on their own, may be able to obtain a policy through their workplace. Read more about workplace policies in Chapter 14.

Combo Policies and Underwriting

You know that insurance companies are worried about a different list of medical conditions for life insurance versus long-term care insurance. This means that, if you are applying for a policy that combines both coverages, you need to qualify from both a mortality and morbidity point of view. Do you have to be Superman (or Superwoman) to buy a combo policy? No, but if you have health problems that make it tough to get life insurance, a savvy insurance agent will steer you clear of a life/LTC combo policy.

Financial Underwriting

Your body may qualify for long-term care insurance, but does your *balance sheet*? Many different organizations have different guidelines to help people decide if long-term care insurance is financially appropriate. Some organizations talk about minimum levels of assets (not counting your house) of $20,000, $50,000, or $100,000, as a threshold that should be met to consider long-term care insurance. Others talk about spending only a percentage of income, say to a maximum of 5 or 10 percent.

I take a very practical approach. I would say that those who can afford the premium for long-term care insurance, without having to change their lifestyle, are financially qualified. If someone wants long-term care insurance and she feels that she can afford it, she probably can. Can you afford a new car, or a kitchen renovation? Most people know exactly what they can—and can't—afford.

Marilee's Memo

A **balance sheet** is a statement of financial worth. It shows your assets (what you own), and it shows your liabilities (what you owe). This information, coupled with your income and budget or spending information, gives a good picture of what you can and cannot afford.

Should people consider dipping into their savings principal to buy the coverage? Probably not. However, if they have low income but savings in excess of $50,000, the earnings on their life savings could supplement their income to pay for the premium.

People whose income is not high enough to buy long-term care insurance comfortably may want to consider other sources of money for the premium, such as reverse mortgage, life settlements, and annuities. (For more details, refer to Part 2.)

LTC Lowdown

Is the policy that you are considering properly designed with a high enough daily benefit and proper inflation protection? Make sure that you are not sacrificing proper design in order to make the policy affordable. Another possibility is that you are considering too big a long-term care policy, and that the premium is higher than need be. Read Chapter 20 to sanity check the design of any policy that you are considering.

Make sure that you can comfortably afford the premium on any policy that you are considering. Remember, most long-term policies are "full pay." This means that you will pay the premium as long as you have the policy. Because the premium can increase, *it's important that you are not biting off more than you can chew.* Imagine that your premium went up every 10 years by 5 to 10 percent. Would it still be affordable? This scenario is highly unlikely, but I think it's a great way to make sure you are purchasing an appropriate policy.

If, after considering all the ways to free up money to pay for long-term care insurance, you cannot afford it, you may want to consider asking your children to chip in. Many children worry about the eventual long-term care needs of their parents, but are uncomfortable bringing up the subject. They may welcome the chance to help you get a policy that gives you the same options that someone with more money enjoys.

The Least You Need to Know

- You should not buy long-term care insurance if you need to change your lifestyle to afford the policy.

- Keep in mind your long-term care premium could increase.

- Find ways to pay for long-term care insurance besides your regular budget: Review your whole insurance program to see if you can find savings; consider a reverse mortgage; use or sell life insurance policies; use earnings off your "rainy day" money pay for the insurance.

- Medical underwriting guidelines can vary dramatically among different insurance companies.

Workplace and Association LTC Insurance

In This Chapter

- ◆ Why you should look into LTC insurance
- ◆ Who can purchase workplace LTC insurance
- ◆ The benefit of relaxed underwriting
- ◆ A case of self-funded insurance plans

More and more workplaces are offering long-term care insurance. Should you buy coverage through your workplace? Maybe. If you think that you're a good candidate for long-term care insurance, read through this chapter to help you decide whether to grab your employer's offer or an association offer, or whether to pursue coverage on your own.

Most employees are working because they need the money. They could not afford to pay for long-term care if they were sick or injured and needed that type of care. Neither could they afford to jeopardize their financial well-being by taking the time needed to be a parents (or spouse's) primary caregiver. For employees (and their parents who aren't wealthy) long-term care insurance can be an important part of their financial plan.

Employees and their families can now often purchase long-term care insurance at their workplace, or through an association that they belong to.

Why Businesses Like LTC Insurance

Nearly two thirds of family caregivers work. Employee absenteeism among family caregivers can't be ignored. Employee caregivers are preoccupied and exhausted. Employers are waking up and realizing that it's not only families that will benefit from long-term care insurance: Their business benefits from higher productivity. Everyone benefits when employee's parents have done long-term care planning and have long-term care insurance. When these elders need long-term care, their daughters and sons will have a big part of the burden of caregiving lifted off their shoulders. Their parents will have the money to pay for care.

They will have the *care-coordination services* that are such a lifesaver for time-pressed adult children, who may not live near Mom or Dad. Care-coordination services are a standard benefit on many long-term care insurance policies. The Federal Long-Term Care Insurance Program (kicked off in 2002) includes a care-coordination benefit. This benefit extends even beyond the insured member of the federal family who needs care. The person with the insurance can ask the care coordinator questions about an uninsured family member, for example.

Marilee's Memo

Care-coordination service representatives/care coordinators are people who I describe as wedding planners for long-term care. If you've ever planned a wedding, you know there's a steep learning curve. You don't know who to call for flowers, a band, invitations, etc. The same is true when a loved one needs long-term care. Especially when children don't live nearby, a care coordinator, in addition to accessing the situation and recommending prescreened services, can be the kids' local eyes and ears.

A report published by the MetLife Mature Market Institute reported that "holding other factors constant, those caring for disabled elders with long-term care insurance are nearly two times as likely to stay in the workforce than are those caring for noninsured disabled individuals."

What I find particularly interesting is this: The study found that working caregivers of elders with long-term care insurance spent about the same amount of time with their disabled elders as working caregivers of uninsured elders. But, the caregivers of those with insurance devote more quality time with the elder. They spend more time in companionship and less time assisting the elder with activities of daily living. I think that's what we would all hope for when we need long-term care—that we could have our loved ones around us, but hire someone to do the "heavy lifting" of our care. What a gift it must be to be able to shift the most physically exhausting and least emotionally satisfying parts of caregiving to trained caregivers.

When they talk about long-term care planning, I often hear people say, "I'll never put my kids through what I went through." Well, avoiding "what you went through" either involves a lot of planning, a lot of luck, or, most realistically, a lot of planning and a little luck. By doing long-term care planning, you give your children a tremendous gift—to be able to care for you and visit you without the relentless burden of caregiving.

Nearly half of all large companies (companies with 1,000 employees or more) offer some kind of elder-care assistance. Information and referral services are most the most likely assistance, not long-term care insurance. The referral services are often as part of an Employee Assistance Program (EAP).

Who Can Buy Workplace LTC Insurance?

Many employers open up their programs to family members (such as parents) and retirees. In most cases, if someone is not an employee, they will go through stricter underwriting than an employee would. This is to protect the insurance company against what is called *adverse selection*.

Marilee's Memo _____

Adverse selection describes the fact that people who are at the highest risk for an event are the ones who try to buy insurance protection. So, for example, if you have 100 retirees from a workplace and 20 have existing health problems, those 20 are much more likely to apply for long-term care insurance than the 80 healthy retirees. To compensate for this fact, insurance companies are likely to ask more questions of all eligible nonemployees applying for workplace insurance.

How Young Is Too Young?

If someone is working full-time, at what age should he or she consider long-term care insurance? That's a tough question, since most people do not have adequate disability and life insurance. But I can make a compelling argument no disability insurance program is complete without long-term care insurance. Most employees recognize the value of disability insurance (DI). DI is designed to replace pay or salary that is lost when you're sick or hurt and can't work. But if you have the "wrong kind of disability" and also need long-term care, you're in trouble. Your health insurance won't pay for custodial care. There's no insurance besides long-term care insurance that's designed to pay for the long-term custodial care that you might need. At the same time, a younger worker has to balance the need for retirement accumulation (saving money for retirement) with the need to manage the risk of long-term care.

Regardless of age, if a person fits all three of the following descriptions, that person should look into long-term care insurance:

♦ Someone who already has health insurance and adequate disability insurance

♦ Someone who has enough life insurance (if there are financially dependent family members or other people who you'd want to leave insurance proceed to)

♦ If still working, someone who is starting to save for retirement; if retired , someone who has adequate income and/or assets to afford the insurance

LTC Lowdown _____

Some people are finding that, with limited insurance budgets, combo policies are just the ticket. For a younger person, life insurance with a long-term care benefit may feel right. Compare any combo long-term care benefit with a stand-alone policy. And be aware of this: Any long-term care benefit paid is subtracted from the policy's death benefit. This could be a big problem for the family of the younger person who needs long-term care and then dies.

"I'm Worth More Dead Than Alive!"

Here's my thinking. If someone suffers a debilitating accident or illness before he or she has had a chance to save enough for retirement, the long-term care insurance is the safety net. It will provide for him or her to receive care in a desirable setting, if there is a qualifying claim. Imagine the 40-year-old executive with a wife, two kids, and early-onset Parkinson's disease. He may have enough life insurance to take care of his family if he were to pass away; but the way that many people have structured their insurance, their family is very vulnerable to a disability and need for long-term care.

Have you ever heard people say about their insurance program (or maybe you've said it yourself), "I'm worth more dead than alive"? Our families should not be financially worse off if we need long-term care, but don't die! Most people don't do proper disability and long-term care planning because these insurances are very expensive. Can you guess why? Because the odds of collecting on disability or long-term care are higher than the odds of dying before age 65.

The Priceless Benefit

There are some people whose health does not allow them to purchase insurance individually. For these people, the offer of a workplace or association long-term care insurance policy can be a lifesaver. You see, workplace or association programs often have relaxed underwriting.

In addition, if you start a job with a new employer who has long-term care insurance, you also usually have a specific time period (such as 30 days or 60 days) from your start date to apply for guaranteed-issue long-term care insurance.

If you think that long-term care insurance is appropriate for you, I urge you to apply for coverage during any opportunities for relaxed underwriting. Once you have the coverage, you can always continue to research other long-term care insurance, and make a switch if you can pass the underwriting for the new policy. Of course, never cancel an existing insurance policy until the new policy has been confirmed in force.

LTC Lowdown _____

If you are not sure whether you will be keeping a long-term care insurance policy and are planning to continue researching your options, do not buy a policy with accelerated payments. These policies have you pay a higher premium today in exchange for an eventual paid-up policy that requires no additional premium payments (for example, a 10-pay, where you pay premiums for 10 years, a 20-pay, or pay to age 65). If you feel you may cancel the policy, pay as little as possible.

Here are the common types of relaxed medical underwriting:

- **Guaranteed issue.** This means that you will get exactly the policy that you applied for, regardless of your health.

- **Guaranteed-to-issue.** This means that you will be offered something. Depending on your health situation, you may get the policy you apply for, or, for example, someone with health problems may be offered a policy with a smaller daily benefit and/or a smaller benefit period than he or she wanted.

- **Simplified issue.** In this case, the insurance company does not ask as many questions as a regular, fully underwritten policy. However, your application may be rejected.

Is It Group Insurance?

Most benefits offered at a workplace, whether health insurance or payroll-deduction disability insurance, are group policies. Not so with long-term care insurance.

Many long-term care insurance policies being sold in workplaces or through associations are individual policies. Sometimes you will hear the words "endorsed group discount," or "association discount." That means that, because of the size of the group, the insurance company is giving an across-the board discount to any member of the group (maybe a workplace or an association) that buys an individual long-term care policy.

This can be very confusing to employees or association members. From their perspective, they know that the group health insurance that they have through work is of better quality than what they could buy on their own. They assume this is true with long-term care insurance—that the group plan at work is better than what they could get on their own. That's often not true. Individual long-term care policies are often better quality policies than group long-term care policies.

If you are being offered a discounted individual policy at a workplace or an association, you should ask the following two questions:

1. If I leave this employer (or if I am no longer a member of the association), do I keep my discount, or does the premium go up?

2. How does this coverage compare to what I could buy on my own?

Truth & Consequences

If you have important questions about your long-term care insurance, get your answers in writing, hopefully as a part of your policy. When push comes to shove, if it's not a contractual part of your policy, you can't count on it. If someone says, "Don't worry about it, they never enforce that," or similar words, beware. Twenty or thirty years down the road, when claims experiences may be bad, any insurance company will look at its contracts to see where it can cut claims expenses.

If the policy is a group policy (technically, you do not get a policy, as a group member you have an individual certificate of a group policy), ask these questions:

◆ Is the policy portable if I leave this employer, or if I am no longer a member of the association? If yes, is it portable with the exact same benefits and premiums?

- What are the scheduled premiums for this policy? Is the premium designed to increase over time, or is it designed to remain flat? If there are planned premium increases, ask to see a page showing all the planned increases (keep in mind that your premium can be increased beyond these increases, if the division of insurance in the state that holds the master policy grants a rate increase).

- How exactly does the inflation protection work on this policy? Is it comprehensive, built-in protection, or does it have limitations, such as a cap?

- How does this coverage compare to what I could buy on my own?

Is Group Insurance Always Better and Cheaper?

True group insurance is often less expensive, in theory, than individual insurance. This is because of cost savings for a variety of reasons. Insurance companies do not put applicants through rigorous, expensive underwriting, since they figure that, overall, working younger people are healthier than the older people who apply for individual coverage. Agents are paid a lower commission rate, since they do not incur the high costs of advertising to the public at large; generally it is easy for them to reach the workplace or association group. Group plans do not normally offer as many design options as individual policies, so that agents don't have the long one-on-one meetings that are normally associated with individual sales.

In reality, the potential savings to the consumer through true group insurance may or may not be realized. Younger, healthier people are often able to "do better" pursuing individual long-term care insurance outside of the group. This is true for two reasons. The relaxed underwriting (that is a typical part of true group long-term care) means that some people whose health doesn't qualify them for individual policies can get group long-term care insurance. Premiums must be raised for all group members to account for those with higher expected claims.

Secondly, the premiums for long-term care insurance are highly competitive. It is not usual for premiums to vary by 20 percent or more even among insurers offering similar policies and similar financial strength. The healthy consumer who has his or her pick of companies can often snag a more competitive price.

LTC Lowdown

Nearly all employers who offer worksite long-term care insurance use one insurer. Most have no more than three options and four benefit amounts. Almost all plans offer some kind of inflation protection, and almost all are employee-pay. Long-term care insurance cannot be included in a workplace cafeteria-benefit plan.

Consumers who buy individual long-term care policies at a workplace or through an association can benefit from the best of both worlds: individual coverage at discounts not otherwise available. However, keep in mind that a 10 to 15 percent association discount may not be a bargain if a comparable insurance company's premiums are 20 percent less to begin with.

Insurance with No Insurance Company

A small number of very large private employers and municipalities are providing long-term care coverage without an insurance company. You see, if a group is large enough, it can do what is called "self-insure." When a company self-insures, it takes on the responsibility for paying claims itself. Large employers have been doing this for health insurance for many years.

Some self-funding employers hire professional administrators. They handle the applications, premium billing, and claims paying. Often, especially in the early years of a program, the employer purchases insurance with a very large deductible, to limit the company's payments in the event of a bad-claims year, or years.

These self-funded plans are usually offered through payroll deduction, just like other workplace long-term care programs. Since there is no agent compensation paid and no insurance company profit built into prices, fans of self-insurance report that they can offer richer benefits at competitive prices. Remember, plans that offer benefit triggers that are more liberal than federal guidelines must be non-tax-qualified (for the pluses and minuses of this, refer to Chapter 12).

The Least You Need to Know

- ◆ Long-term care insurance completes a worker's health and disability insurance plan, so that all the financial costs of an illness or injury will be taken care of.

- ◆ Many policies being sold in workplaces to employees are individual, not group, policies.

- ◆ Self-funded, employer-sponsored long-term care plans are an interesting option for large employers.

- ◆ If bad health does not allow you to purchase insurance individually, relaxed underwriting workplace/association policies can be a lifesaver.

- ◆ Many employers who offer long-term care insurance open up their programs to family members (such as parents) and retirees.

15

The Federal Government's LTC Insurance Plan

In This Chapter

- ◆ The government view of long-term care
- ◆ The cost of the Federal LTC Insurance Program
- ◆ What's special about the Federal Program
- ◆ Should you buy a federal program policy

If you are a federal-government employee or a member of the uniformed services, you have no doubt heard about a benefit that became available in the spring of 2002: payroll-deduction long-term care insurance. U.S. citizens and employers may have heard about this program and wondered what it might mean for the benefits offered at their workplace.

If you or a relative works for the federal government, you may be wondering if you should buy this coverage. Should your eligible family members get coverage through the federal plan? What if you already have a policy—is the federal program better? This chapter will help you answer these questions.

The fact that the federal government is now offering long-term insurance systemwide to its employee base is important. As the largest group long-term care policy offering in the country, the federal government's long-term care program is a sort of "bully pulpit" for employers. When the federal government offers a benefit, other employers stand up and take notice. The federal decision to promote long-term care insurance is being reported as the "coming of age" of long-term care insurance. No longer a new, odd product misunderstood by many, long-term care insurance is now a mainstream benefit, recommended for people even under age 65.

A Little History

One of the major reasons that many consumers decide *not* to buy long-term care insurance is this: They are waiting for a new federal program that would make this coverage unnecessary.

When President Clinton proposed massive health insurance reform in 1993, many people thought the plan would cover long-term care. There were provisions for long-term care in the proposed program, but the long-term care benefits were based on financial need, and were therefore not available to many Americans. As you know, the proposed health-care reform didn't pass. Proposed legislation since then has revolved around modest tax credits for family caregivers and incentives to purchase private long-term care insurance.

However, there persists even to this day a perception among many Americans that the limited long-term care coverage available through Medicare and Medicaid will someday be enhanced through a new government plan. "Take a look at the statistics," they argue. "Americans are getting older, they need long-term care. They want to receive care in their own home, not in Medicaid nursing home beds. Hard-working Americans shouldn't have to bankrupt themselves paying for long-term care. The current system doesn't make sense, and the federal government will have to respond with new programs." All these statements make sense, but, in my opinion and the opinion of many others, it's not going to happen.

LTC Lowdown

There are two places to get the latest information on the federal LTC insurance program:

- Long-Term Care Partners, LLC, the administrator of the federal program (the insurance is offered by John Hancock Life Insurance Co. and Metropolitan Life Insurance Co.) website: www.ltcfeds.com, or by toll-free telephone at 1-800-LTC-FEDS (that's 1-800-582-3337)
- The U.S. Office of Personnel Management website: www.opm.gov

Congress Mandates Long-Term Care Offering

The Federal Long-term Care Insurance Program is a clear message from Washington that a new government program to pay for long-term care is highly unlikely. Congress passed the Long-Term Care Security Act unanimously, and it was signed into law on September 19, 2000. This law instructed the U.S. Office of Personnel Management (OPM) to make long-term care insurance available to the federal employees, and to what is referred to as the "federal family." OPM started rolling out this program for early enrollment on March 25, 2002. The federal long-term care insurance benefit is not free to employees; 100 percent of the policy cost is paid by the purchasing employee.

Marilee's Memo _____

Members of the federal family refers to federal employees, members of the uniformed services, certain retirees, and family members. As the program evolves, other groups may become eligible. Check the program web sites to get up-to-date information on which members of the federal family are eligible.

This new program encourages the federal family to take personal responsibility in planning for their own long-term care. By encouraging the millions of federal employees eligible for this plan to buy long-term care insurance, the message to all Americans is clear: There will be no new federal long-term care program to pay for your care. The federal government is encouraging us to buy private insurance now.

Who Qualifies for the Federal Program

An estimated 20 million members of the "federal family" are eligible for this program, including federal and postal employees and annuitants, members and retired members of the uniformed services, and qualified family members.

As defined in the Long-Term Care Security Act, the federal family includes ...

- ◆ Federal employees and members of the uniformed services, including employees of the U.S. Postal Service and Tennessee Valley Authority.

- ◆ Part-time employees and members of Congress.

- ◆ Federal annuitants, or surviving spouses receiving a federal survivor annuity.

- ◆ Individuals receiving compensation from the DOL who are separated from the federal service.

- ◆ Members or former members of the uniformed services entitled to retired or retainer pay.

- ◆ Gray reservists (retired military reservists at the time they qualify for an annuity).

- ◆ Current spouses of employees and annuitants, and some surviving spouses.

- ◆ Adult children of living employees and annuitants.

- ◆ Parents, parents-in-law, and stepparents of living employees (but not annuitants).

Not included are employees of the District of Columbia government. If you have any question about whether you are eligible to apply for the Federal Long-Term Care Insurance Program, contact the OPM or the program.

Medical Eligibility

Everyone who wants long-term care insurance under the federal program must apply for coverage. Not everyone who applies will be approved. An application will be approved or declined based on the applicant's medical situation.

LTC Lowdown _____

Abbreviated (or relaxed) underwriting describes an easier process than is normally required to get insurance. Underwriting is the process the insurance company uses to decide whether or not to approve an application for insurance. With abbreviated/relaxed underwriting, the number of medical questions asked is much shorter than in full underwriting, and medical records are usually not obtained. Since the insurer does not have access to as much information, some applicants will be approved who would otherwise be declined.

Like many employers, the Federal Program offers abbreviated (sometimes called relaxed) underwriting. This is a wonderful benefit that's not available if you are looking for a policy on your own. In the federal program, only eligible employees and their spouses are eligible for abbreviated underwriting, and only during certain times (such as Open Season—7/1/02–12/31/02, or when a new employee is first hired); check to make sure you understand your deadlines.

The federal program abbreviated underwriting application is a much shorter application; it asks only seven medical questions for employees and nine for spouses. These extra two questions focus on whether the applicant is already receiving care, uses medical devices, or suffers from what I call red-flag diseases (such as M.S. and Alzheimer's). Most people who apply using the abbreviated underwriting application will be approved. Some of the people approved on the relaxed underwriting application would not be eligible for coverage if they were subject to full underwriting. This means that they could get coverage through the federal program that they couldn't get on their own.

Eligible for abbreviated underwriting are …

- ◆ Federal employees and their spouses.

- ◆ U.S. Postal Service employees and their spouses.

- ◆ Members of the uniformed services and their spouses.

Eligible, but with full underwriting are …

- ◆ Federal or postal annuitants and their spouses.

- ◆ A surviving spouse receiving a survivor annuity from the uniformed services (includes Dependency Indemnity Compensation).

- ◆ Retired members of the uniformed services and their spouses.

- ◆ The adult child (age 18 and older, includes adoptees and stepchildren) of living federal or postal employees or annuitants, or living or retired members of the uniformed services.

- ◆ The parent, parent-in-law, or stepparent of a living federal or postal employee, or living member of the uniformed services.

Is the Federal Program a Bargain?

Due to the large group size and the negotiating power of the federal government, the federal LTC insurance program is being described as a bargain. Is it? It is clearly a bargain for people who otherwise could not purchase long-term care insurance on their own. Many perfectly healthy people will decide that the Federal Program is a good buy, too.

Many people who have conditions that would make it difficult or impossible to get long-term care insurance through other programs can qualify for the fed program during open season. Examples of some medical conditions that are not a problem under abbreviated underwriting include obesity, uncontrolled high blood pressure, and/or recent cancer history.

But what if you are in perfect health? Then is the Federal Program a bargain? Bear with me, but I have to give you an answer that you're probably not going to like. Here it is: The Program is probably a bargain, though you may be able to get a lower price buying your own policy somewhere else.

Why can't I make it simpler? Because this program includes a few spectacular benefits not available in most policies (read about these in the next section). So, if you were to "shop it out" and run prices with other companies based on similar coverage designs, you would not be comparing apples with apples. Read on to understand what you should consider.

For example, the vast majority of policies do not cover care outside the United States; the federal policy does. The vast majority of policies do not pay a cash benefit if family members take care of you; the federal policy does (subject to limitations).

For a single 60-year-old, with no children or close relatives, the family caregiving benefit is not of much value. For the person who plans on living in the United States, the foreign coverage isn't important. But in many other cases, these tough-to-get benefits are very valuable. Read the following section, "What Makes the Federal Program Different?" to help you in your comparisons. You may also want to read Chapter 18, which explains how to compare different policies.

On the flip side, the federal program does not have a spousal discount available. For married couples who each want a policy, this discount can be substantial, taking 5 to 20 percent—and sometimes even more—off the cost of each policy. The lack of spousal discount could make the federal program more expensive for some couples.

Also, insurance premiums vary dramatically between insurance companies. It's not unusual to see prices for the same person with the same policy design vary as much as 30 percent with different insurance policies. So the healthy person who is a bargain hunter may be able to get less expensive coverage on his or her own. But remember, this coverage would likely be different than the federal program.

Finally, let's take a look at some sample premiums. Remember, since the federal program offers almost one-of-a-kind benefits, it's tough to compare any other policy with this one.

The following table provides a comparison of a typical policy with a three-year benefit. The coverage is up to $150 a day, with a 90-day waiting period and automatic compound inflation protection.

	Federal Program	**Typical Private Insurance**
Premium age 40	$516	$514–$610
Premium age 50	$744	$648–$817
Premium age 60	$1,116	$897–$1,344

Truth & Consequences _____

   Pursuing the rock-bottom, lowest-cost long-term care insurance may be penny-wise and pound-foolish. Almost all LTC insurance contracts reserve the right for the premium to be increased, if the company loses money on the policies and state regulators allow an increase. Look for insurance companies that have a history of rate stability in their long-term care insurance products, and have priced their product fairly (for more information, please refer to Chapter 19).

What Makes the Federal Program Different?

There are a few benefits on the federal program which are highly unusual. For example, most long-term care insurance does not cover care given by any unlicensed person or by any family member, even if he or she is licensed. The federal program instead provides a benefit for certain family members or informal caregivers.

Informal Caregivers

The federal program is unusual in that it covers approved home care given by nonlicensed caregivers who don't normally live in your home. So, for example, if you have a neighbor or friend who provides your care, this care can be covered. Care by nonlicensed caregivers is called informal care. It is estimated that 80 percent of the long-term care provided to patients is informal caregiving given by family and friends. Often this care is provided at great financial sacrifice, as people cut back on hours worked or even quit their jobs to be caregivers.

When informal care is provided by family members, the federal program limits coverage for this care to 365 days. Approval for informal caregiving must be coordinated and approved by the federal program long-term care coordinators. These care coordinators are available for all federal enrollees. Using the care coordinators is optional; the only time that their use is mandated is under the informal caregiver benefit.

Inflation Options

The inflation protection benefits under the federal program are much like many other policies, at first glance. The automatic compound inflation option increases your daily benefit amount (and, therefore, the total value of your policy) by 5 percent every year without increasing your premiums (before and after claim). The future-purchase option allows you to buy more coverage in the future, at additional premium.

There are two nice features of the future-purchase option. Most insurers limit their option amount to the increase in the Consumer Price Index (CPI). Some years, the overall CPI can be very low, while long-term care costs increase at a higher rate.

The federal policy says it will initially offer increases based on the medical Consumer Price Index, which is based on the increase in medical costs. This index is usually much higher than the overall CPI, so it should be easier to make sure that your policy maintains its ability to pay for your future care. The contract may not always offer increases based on the medical CPI; it may use another index agreed to by the Office of Personnel Management.

Similar to other future-purchase options, the federal program's option does not continue once you are on claim, so your benefit is frozen at claim time. Also, if you turn down the future-purchase option three times, you will not be offered additional options without new underwriting. The federal program's future-purchase option is like one of those book or music mail-order clubs: The program presumes that you always want to take the higher benefit—it's thrown on automatically every two years and added to your bill unless you reject it in writing ahead of time.

The federal program also has another unusually attractive feature built into the future-purchase option. Whenever you are offered the ability to use this option, you can switch to the automatic compound inflation option (with no medical questions), as long as you are not on claim. If you made the switch, your benefit would therefore increase 5 percent a year on a compound basis, even when you are on claim. Your premium would be increased to cover this additional benefit, but it would not increase each year.

No Upper Age Limit

Many insurance companies limit new policies to those under a certain age, such as 75, or 85. The new federal program has no maximum age limit. A healthy 86-year-old who is receiving a survivor pension from the federal government could apply for and be approved for this policy (if her health was good enough). The minimum issue age is 18.

Right to Appeal

One of the most common questions asked about long-term care insurance has to do with claims paying. People want to know if their claims will be paid as promised in the glossy brochures, or if there will be a hassle (or heartbreak) at claim time. Under the federal plan, if the insured disagrees with the insurance company's decision at claim time, the insured has an unique contractual benefit. The insured can ask for an independent, third-party review of the company's claim decision. This offers the best of both worlds: The decision is binding on the insurer, but a claimant still has the right to sue in court if not satisfied.

Home Health Care

One limitation of the federal program is that home health-care and adult day-care costs are reimbursed in full but only up to 75 percent of the daily benefit amount. Many other plans offer 80 percent or 100 percent of your daily benefit to cover these charges. Since adult day-care costs are usually much less expensive than nursing home costs, the 75 percent limitation on adult day-care costs should not be a problem.

But, if you are planning on receiving your long-term care at home, limiting the benefit to 75 percent of your daily benefit could be a problem. That's because home health can cost just as much as a nursing home. If you hire a home health care aide for more than one eight-hour shift, it's not unusual for that care to cost as much, or more than a nursing home. In that case, you would wish you had your full daily benefit available for a home-care claim.

Catastrophic Coverage Limitation

An unusual limitation in the federal plan reads like this: "If there were a Catastrophic Event, the length of time during which you could receive benefits could be shortened, in consultation with OPM. A Catastrophic Event is an event or series of events affecting such a significant number of enrollees that it threatens to undermine the financial stability of the Program." In light of the number of active federal employees, postal workers, and servicemen expected to be covered by this program, I can understand why this kind of limitation would need to be included in the policy. However, contracts offered outside of the federal program do not have this limitation.

LTC Lowdown _____

If you are a member of the federal family who is considering long-term care insurance, check to make sure that you are aware of any application deadlines. Federal employees and their spouses are eligible for abbreviated underwriting *at certain times only*. As this book is being written, details of the federal program in 2003 have not yet been finalized. Check the websites listed at the beginning of this chapter for current information.

Foreign Coverage

The vast majority of long-term care insurance contracts do not cover care outside the United States. Some limit foreign coverage to Canada, or to the Americas. The federal program covers care received internationally. This care benefit is limited to 80 percent of the maximum amount that would otherwise be available. The remaining 20 percent would be available if you came back to the United States, its territories, and possessions.

A Good Game Plan

If you are a member of the federal family who feels that long-term care insurance is appropriate for you, take a look at the federal program and compare it with the coverage that you can get on your own. Chapter 13 will help you determine if you are a good candidate for long-term care insurance. Keep in mind that some benefits under the federal program are not available in most other policies.

If you are eligible for abbreviated underwriting, it is smart to apply and lock in the federal program. If you have any health problems or your health changes, getting coverage under the abbreviated underwriting program may be your only chance to get private long-term care insurance. Once you have the federal-program coverage, you may want to look into other policies. Based on your research, you will either confirm your decision to purchase the federal program, or you can switch to a policy that is better for you. Be sure that you do not cancel any existing coverage until you know that the new one is in force.

The Least You Need to Know

- The federal long-term care insurance program signals to all Americans that long-term care insurance is an important part of their financial and insurance planning.
- Members of the federal family may find that the Federal Long Term Care Program offers good coverage at a competitive price.
- The program allows *some* federal government employees (and their spouses), whose health otherwise wouldn't allow them to buy other long-term care insurance, the ability to buy LTC coverage.
- The federal program offers benefits not available in many other long-term care insurance policies, such as worldwide coverage and the ability to pay family members and other unlicensed caregivers.
- Many family members of federal employees and retirees are eligible for the federal program.

Chapter **16**

Choosing an Insurance Agent

In This Chapter

- ◆ How to tell a good agent from a bad one
- ◆ How to find an agent who's right for you
- ◆ What agents cost
- ◆ How to read insurance designations

Do you have an insurance agent who you like and trust? Someone who has proven himself or herself to be professional, and acts in your best interest? Then you can probably skip this chapter, which is about choosing an insurance agent. Those of you who are lucky enough to have good insurance agents will call them for help concerning long-term care insurance (or even other financial means to pay for long-term care). If your agent doesn't sell long-term care insurance, he or she can likely recommend someone who does.

The insurance company that you choose will probably be greatly influenced by the agent that you work with. A professional insurance agent who keeps up with long-term care is likely to know more than you ever will in terms of choosing an insurance company. That's good. Just like the internal medicine doctor who recommends a surgeon or the computer consultant who recommends a software program, these professionals, if they have made long-term care a serious part of their business, have access to information and experiences than any member of the public does.

Find a good insurance agent. Work with him or her. You'll both benefit.

When and Why to Use an Agent

I know people who will put off buying a new car, simply to avoid the process of stepping into a car dealer showroom and being "sold." GM has turned the perceived negative of a dealership into a positive with its "no haggle" Saturn line of dealerships, with no-pressure salespeople and a family-like corporate atmosphere.

I'm sure that the same is true with long-term care insurance. To avoid having to find an agent, many people either put off the whole process indefinitely, or try to go it alone. Do-it-yourselfers may arm themselves with websites and consumer reports, but buying long-term care insurance isn't like choosing a shampoo brand or even a car; it's much more complicated. And you can be stuck with a lemon long-term care policy longer than a "lemon" car, if your health declines.

The pace of innovation—which for LTC insurance means new policies introduced—is dizzying. Add to this company consolidation (some major insurance companies have sold their LTC blocks of policies, or are looking to sell them), different health requirements, and state- and federal-pending legislation, and the consumer is at a distinct disadvantage trying to go it alone.

Read on for some tips on how to find an insurance agent who can help you in your search for the right LTC insurance policy.

Just like any other occupation, there are good and bad insurance agents. A good insurance agent can be worth his or her weight in gold in helping you manage the financial risks that you personally face. A good agent combines the following traits:

- Honesty and integrity
- Competence
- Desire to serve your best interest
- In the occupation over the long run

 **LTC Lowdown**

Some insurance agents hold educational seminars to attract new clients. These can be excellent, low-pressure ways to check out a potential agent. They typically speak for about an hour, giving you plenty of time to size up if they sound knowledgeable, and also giving you some insight into their personality. Ask questions at the seminar that are not specific to your situation only, and see how they do.

Long-term care insurance is, without a doubt, the most confusing type of insurance that a person will ever purchase. There is no question that the more you know about long-term care insurance, the more likely you are to appreciate the help that an agent can bring to the table.

If you don't already have an agent, ask your friends and relatives who they have used to purchase insurance, and why. If you are fortunate enough to have a good working relationship with any of the following professionals, they may be able to recommend an insurance agent:

- Your property and casualty insurance agent

- Your lawyer

- Your tax preparer, banker, or stockbroker

Any of these professionals may also be licensed life, accident, and health insurance agents and sell long-term care insurance.

How an Insurance Agent Makes Money

Most insurance agents are paid by commission only. This means that they are paid a percentage of your premium when you decide to apply for insurance through them, your application is approved, and you pay your premium. Some insurance agents are fee-based; they charge a fee for working with you, and then receive a commission if you buy coverage through them.

A small number of insurance agents are fee only. This means that you pay them a fee for their work, and when you buy insurance, the commission would go to another person. They are usually described as fee-only financial planners or registered investment advisors. Sometimes fee-only financial planners will charge a fee for advice, then introduce you to an agent they recommend to help you with purchasing long-term care. The agent, not the fee-only planner, will receive the commission.

Truth & Consequences

Which is better, fee or commissions? Each method of compensation has potential problems. Commission-only planners are motivated to sell product; fee-only planners are motivated to sell reports or consultation time. In the end, given the same level of competence and honesty, the client ends up with similar recommendations. My advice? Interview thoroughly and follow your gut. I haven't seen evidence that agents who are paid partially or totally by fees are more competent, or more caring, than those paid by commissions.

If you are choosing an insurance agent based on an advertisement, such as the Yellow Pages, or a seminar, you may want to check his or her reputation with others, such as the professional people listed above. You may also ask for a biography listing the professional accomplishments of the person, and/or a list of clients who have agreed to be referral sources.

Request an appointment to decide if you want to work with this insurance agent. If you have more than one agent on your potential agent list, you will want to meet with each one. Ask if there is a charge for the initial meeting, if the meeting lasts less than 20 minutes. Usually there will not be a charge. If there is, you will have to decide whether to pay or to look for another agent.

Here are some suggestions for questions that might help you decide who to work with. You may decide to ask these questions over the phone, or in person:

♦ **What is the profile of a typical client served by your firm?**

The closer that your situation matches the answer to this question, the better.

♦ **How do you charge for your services?**

Make sure that you absolutely understand the answer. Don't be shy about asking this question. If you have any reservations about the method the agent is paid, ask him or her to explain further.

♦ **How many long-term care insurance policies do you write on a monthly basis?**

I think that, in order to have a basic competence level, the agent should be writing at least one to two applications per month. If an agent does nothing else but long-term care insurance, I would expect the response to be a much higher number. Just as a CPA can't keep up with the tax-law changes for every kind of client (individual, business, nonprofit, and so on), insurance agents focus their ongoing education in the areas which they frequently do business. An agent who is regularly selling long-term care insurance will keep up with new products, developments, and is likely to know how the insurance companies treat their policyholders.

♦ **Why do people pick you instead of other insurance agents?**

Here you will learn his or her perceived strengths, and also it's a great question to test your basic compatibility and ability to work together well. Two alternate questions would be: How long have you been an insurance agent? How did you decide to get into this business?

♦ **Will you tell me exactly why you are recommending a certain policy design, or a certain company?**

If the answer is no, run!

Does it matter if you choose a lawyer from a referral or from a list on a website? Not necessarily. As I say in Chapter 21 about choosing an elder law attorney, "Just like a single person looking for a spouse, some couples meet at concerts and others are fixed up by friends." Overall, you should feel good about your insurance agent. If you feel unnecessarily rushed or intimidated, keep looking.

Just like any other occupation, there are some bad eggs out there. Report any improper or insulting behavior formally to the state's insurance department (see Appendix A for contact information); it's the only way to protect others from the same situation!

LTC Lowdown

An insurance agent can only be your best ally in purchasing appropriate LTC insurance if he or she has good, honest information from you.

If you hide information about your health, for example, or your ability to purchase LTC insurance through an employer, you put the agent in a situation where his or her advice may not be right for you. You wouldn't lie to a doctor about symptoms, or you might get the wrong prescription. The potential for a bad insurance "prescription" exists, too.

The Cost of Using an Agent

Many people think that by not using an insurance agent, they will pay a lower premium. In theory, this would make sense, but, in real life, it's not true! Here's the scoop: If you are buying an individual LTC insurance policy (most policies sold are individual policies; some, usually sold at workplaces and through associations, are not), you will pay the same price whether you purchase the policy through an agent or directly with the insurance company. The prices on individual policies are approved by your state's division of insurance, for a particular insurance company for a particular design.

> **Truth & Consequences**
>
> Websites, far from being objective information sources, are often sponsored by particular insurance companies, or by marketing organizations that are looking to sell a specific policy or policies. At this point, and this may all change tomorrow, it is virtually impossible to get the information needed to do a meaningful comparison of insurance contracts for free on the web.

So, for example, let's say that I've been quoted a policy from ABC insurance company with a $150 daily benefit, 90-day waiting period, five-year benefit, and built-in compound inflation protection, for a premium of $1,094 per year. It makes no difference in my premium price if I apply through an insurance agent for the coverage, or if I call the insurance company directly. Assuming the policy design is the same, and assuming that we are talking about the same product, ABC insurance company charges the same premium, as required by my state's insurance department. If I apply to the company directly, the insurance company keeps the commission, instead of paying it to an agent. So I've paid the same premium, without benefiting from the free advice given by an insurance agent.

If an advisor strongly puts down a product, or strongly encourages you to acquire the product, ask why he or she feels that way. They may have had a bad experience with one company with another client, while another company has outstanding customer service. In the end, it's your decision. After all, it's your life and your money!

Designations, and What They Mean

You may have noticed that many financial advisors have initials after their names. Most of these initials signify that they have received advanced degrees or designations. Let's take a look at some of these designations.

For many, many years, there were two designations that were used to prove the competence of insurance agents:

♦ Chartered Life Underwriter (CLU)

♦ Chartered Financial Consultant (ChFC)

In terms of the weight that they carried, they were sometimes compared to a CPA. To pass either exam, there was a requirement that the designee take a series of 10 exams, each requiring approximately 40 hours of study. Completion of either designation usually takes two to three years. These designations are issued by the American

College, in Bryn Mawr, Pennsylvania, through correspondence classes and national exams. I am a CLU, and proud of it!

Approximately 30 years ago a new designation was "born." This designation came into being just when the occupation and practice of financial planning was embraced by the American public. A Certified Financial Planner (CFP) is someone who has taken five courses and passed a grueling, national exam, held over two days. The designation is bestowed by the Certified Financial Planner Board of Standards in Denver.

> **Wisdom of the Aged**
>
> If an insurance agent does not have a designation, does that mean he or she is incompetent in the area of advising on long-term care insurance? Not necessarily. Some agents have had years of selling long-term care insurance before the new long-term care designations even existed.

In the last five years, there have been newer designations that have cropped up.

- ◆ The Certified Senior Advisor (CSA) has taken a three-day class which takes a broad view of helping seniors plan for the future. Topics including aging, Alzheimer's, housing, funeral planning, Medicare, and senior spirituality are all covered. Students are taught by a team of several faculty members, typically including a medical doctor, geriatrician, financial planner, and someone from the Social Security Administration. I am proud to say that I teach three modules for this designation: Medicaid, Medicare, and Long-Term Care Planning. The day after attending the CSA classes, designation candidates take the exam.

- ◆ The Certified in Long-Term Care designation (CLTC) is also a three-day class with an exam at the end. Owned and run by an elder law attorney, this course is specific to long-term care.

- ◆ The Health Insurance Association of America and the American Association of Long-Term Care Insurance, both nonprofit organizations, have announced that they are kicking off the Long-Term Care Professional (LTCP) designation, scheduled to start in fall 2002.

Any formal education from a respected organization is always good. Classes taken, advanced degrees, conferences attended, and designations all indicate that agents believe in education and are serious about staying "on top of their game." But keep in mind that the real-life experience of an agent who has advised clients over a number of years can be more valuable to a consumer than a particular designation.

The Least You Need to Know

- The most important things to look for when choosing an insurance agent are technical competence and a desire to serve clients.

- You have a right to know how any financial advisor is paid; I have found no correlation between method of pay and integrity.

- If you are considering workplace or group long-term care, ask the agent to compare his or her programs against the other offerings.

- Never apply with an agent because you feel intimidated or afraid; report such behavior to your state's department of insurance.

- A good insurance agent will help you find coverage with strong companies that have stable rates and good customer service.

Chapter **17**

The Top Five Problems with LTC Insurance

In This Chapter

- ◆ The level premium that isn't
- ◆ Short claims need not apply
- ◆ Long-term care that isn't long-term
- ◆ Not another insurance bill
- ◆ It depends on what you mean by bathing

Many middle-class and upper-middle-class people who want choice and control when they need LTC decide to purchase LTC insurance. They exchange their premium dollars today for the promise of an insurance company to pay for care.

But LTC insurance is not a perfect solution to the problem of how to pay for LTC. There are some distinct risks to the policyholder in deciding to use insurance to plan for long-term care.

I believe that most people who think about the pluses and minuses of LTC insurance, Medicaid, and paying out of their own pocket will want LTC insurance to pay for their care. However, I think it's important that the decision is made from the standpoint of full disclosure. When you understand some of the potential problems with LTC insurance and Medicaid planning, you can make an informed decision.

#1: The Premium Is Expensive and May Increase

Long-term care insurance is not cheap. Buying long-term care insurance requires a noticeable allocation of funds that could otherwise be invested or spent.

No One Likes Paying Premiums!

As baby boomers delay having children, dollars to spend on long-term care insurance must compete with other financial goals such as retirement funding and college funding. Many people do not have enough life insurance or disability insurance to take care of their families if they died prematurely or couldn't work. Companies no longer routinely provide pensions and retiree health insurance, so workers feel more pressure to save for retirement. All these financial priorities compete for the same dollars. Some consumers are unwilling to spend money on basic insurance that they know they need. Even more consumers are unwilling to buy a coverage that they may not need for 20 or 30 years.

Of course, one of the reasons that LTC insurance is so expensive is because long-term care is so expensive. A man who buys a $100 daily benefit policy at age 45, with a three-year benefit and built-in inflation protection, would pay an annual premium of $510 with one insurer. If he has a claim at age 80, he would have paid in a total of $17,348 over 34 years. The daily benefit would have grown from $100 to $525, to keep up with inflation. His policy maximum benefit is $567,362—that's right—with $17,348 in premium he's bought a pile of money to use for long-term care worth $578,362!

Investing the Premium Instead

We know that cash offers the ultimate flexibility; you can pay for any type of care you desire. Since long-term care insurance is so expensive, some of you may be thinking, "I'll invest the money I would've spent on premium and build up my own special long-term care fund." It's a great idea—but it doesn't make sense. Here's why.

Continuing the example from above, if the same man had decided to save the $510 (premium amount) each year to try to pay for his own long-term care, the balance after 34 years (assuming a 7 percent after-tax return) would be approximately

$67,000. The LTC insurance benefit is over eight times bigger than his investment-plan balance would've been. And, if he had a claim anytime earlier, the difference would be even more dramatic. Someone with insurance who has a claim, say, a month or a year after buying his or her policy, will point out the obvious: You may not have the ability to pay in long enough to self-insure. Looking at the numbers, even if you could, it doesn't make sense.

CAUTION **Truth & Consequences** _____

If you want to be your own insurance company, look into the numbers first. Even if you invest well for years, you will not have accumulated nearly as much to pay for long-term care as a policy would provide. And what happens to your plan if you need care at an younger age than you thought you would? If you're lucky, you'll have built up enough money to pay for a month or two of care!

Premiums May Increase

What confidence does a long-term care policyholder have that his or her premium will remain flat? Contractually, very little. Financially conservative people may want to build in a 5 to 10 percent premium rate increase every 10 years. That thought can be scary to many people—myself included! But you can take heart that, even with a 10 percent premium rate increase every 10 years, the insurance is still a bargain if you end up needing long-term care!

There are many high-quality insurance companies that have been selling long-term care insurance for many years, that have had no rate increases. Others have had only modest rate increases. On the other hand, some people have been burned by huge rate increases—30 percent and more! I see two reasons for potential rate increases. One you can protect yourself against. The other you can't.

Some insurance companies, based on the premium rate increases they have requested, have obviously mis-priced their long-term care insurance policies. This means that the premium that they filed with the states' insurance divisions (for individual policies, premiums and policies must be approved for sale state-by-state) was not high enough to cover their expenses and claims. Their long-term care insurance may be priced like other companies, but their underwriting was easier—so they approved policies on a group of people that was less healthy. Then the claims hit, and money got tight. Or maybe their underwriting and policies were similar to other insurers, but their pricing was lower. In any case, it results in a policy that was "too good to be true"—the premium wasn't high enough to support the promises being made.

By the way, the National Association of Insurance Commissioners (NAIC) is very concerned about the long-term rate stability of long-term care insurance, and is actively working on regulations that would make it tougher for long-term care insurers to raise rates. There's more information on choosing an insurance company in Chapter 16. Meanwhile, here are some tips to help you pick a policy that's priced right:

- Ask to see a 10-year rate increase history for all the insurer's long-term care policies. Keep in mind that sometimes insurance companies have had reasonable rate increases because they were adding benefits to policies that had been outdated (for example, they did not cover home health care, or assisted living facilities). Also, some insurers who have taken over policies from other companies (in a sale, or as the result of insolvency), have raised premiums because the original company did not price the product correctly.

- Check out the financial ratings of the company (see the resources listing in Appendix E for information on how to find ratings). If the company that you are considering is not in the top tier of the rating services, ask why. Small- to mid-sized companies are somewhat handicapped with the rating services. The ratings services worry about smaller companies ability to weather bad claim times. Some companies are selling another company's product—in their company's wrapper. If they are taking advantage of the underwriting expertise and policy design experience of a strong, stable company with a good long-term care insurance track record, this should inspire confidence. Some insurance companies have an agreement with another company to back up their claims payment in the event that claims are higher than they expect. That's called reinsurance, and can be reassuring!

Some policies promise not to raise premiums for a set amount of time—perhaps three years, or ten years. Some limited pay policies (you pay a higher premium for a certain number of years only) and some life insurance/ltc combo policies offer premium rate guarantees not available in traditional, full-pay, long-term care policies.

In the end, an insurance policy is a contract between you and the issuing company. You should check them out as much as they check you out!

#2: The Insurance Is Confusing to Buy

Many people decide not to buy long-term care insurance because it's such a complicated product relative to other insurance products a consumer buys. This criticism is understandable, but to a great extent unfounded. If you were to see all the coverage options on your auto insurance policy, you would be similarly overwhelmed. A good insurance agent will help you hone in on what's important and what's not. In Chapter 20, I try to do the same thing.

There are 130 insurance companies that sell long-term care insurance. If you decide to purchase this insurance, rely on the expertise of an agent who is familiar with the product.

LTC Lowdown

According to Health Insurance Association of America (HIAA), 46 percent of people who looked into LTC insurance mentioned one important reason they didn't buy: confusion in figuring out which policy was right for them.

It is very difficult to figure out your best long-term policy if you are working with more than one agent at the same time. This can make the process seem more confusing. One agent will not have visibility to what the other one has said, and you will be left trying to figure out your options from a pile of illustrations and brochures. Most people will come to their best decision by first choosing an agent that they are comfortable working with (see Chapter 16), and then looking into coverage.

#3: You Must Be Healthy to Buy LTC Insurance

OK, you're smart enough to know that you can't buy auto insurance to cover the accident that just happened, or life insurance once your doctor tells you that you have six months to live. It's the same with long-term care insurance. Unfortunately, many people wait too long before they decide to buy long-term care insurance. In Chapter 13 I review the medical underwriting requirements and how they work.

Don't assume that you can't qualify for LTC insurance because you've been turned down for life insurance. The medical requirements are very different for these two types of policies. Read Chapter 13 to find out more.

Wisdom of the Aged

Don't forget that saying in the life, accident, and health insurance industry: Money pays for the insurance, but health buys it. While you may have the health to buy insurance today, that could change tomorrow.

#4: Your Care Choices May Be Limited

I like to describe long-term care insurance as "a pile of money for long-term care." But, unlike the pile of money you're envisioning, this pile has a chain link fence around it, with a door. The only way that you are allowed in to use the pile of money is if you meet the definitions in your policy and if you are receiving care that is covered by the policy.

Care outside the United States is excluded by most LTC policies. Some companies will cover care in Canada and/or Mexico, also. Very few policies will cover care abroad. The federal long-term care program is an exception. For members of the federal family with this coverage, their care is covered worldwide, but the benefit is limited to 80 percent of what otherwise would be available (see Chapter 15 for more information).

Care provided by a family member is usually excluded from most long-term care policies as well. Some policies make exceptions if your family caregiver is a licensed medical professional, or if he or she is hired through a licensed home health-care agency. However, such policies are rare. There are two notable exceptions.

The first exception is the federal long-term care program. It does cover care by family members, but the benefit is limited (again, see Chapter 15 for more information).

The second exception is a *true* indemnity or per diem contract. Out of 120 insurance companies that sell long-term care insurance, you can count the number of insurance companies that offer this type of policy on one hand. A true indemnity or per diem contract is one which, once you qualify for long-term care benefits (through the loss of ADLs or because of cognitive impairment), the insurance company sends you a check each month. It does *not* ask for proof that you are receiving long-term care. It's very much like disability insurance. You can do with the check what you'd like. What's the catch? These policies are more expensive (an extra 25 to 100 percent!) than traditional policies. Also, be aware that if the benefit that you receive exceeds the amount that you pay for your care, it may be taxable (see Chapter 19 for more details on per diem contracts, and Chapter 12 for more details on their taxation).

Wisdom of the Aged

The typical family caregiver is a spouse, or a daughter in her late 40s. The daughter works, and has had to make financial sacrifices to be the caregiver. From unpaid time off, to passing up promotions, to leaving full-time for part-time work, the financial sacrifices working caregivers (both sons and daughters!) make are substantial. Their family life is likely to suffer, as time with a spouse and children is squeezed. The emotional price of long-term caregiving is largely paid by the spouse and children of caregivers, and a financial price is paid by the sacrifice of the caregiver's financial security.

In many families, there are people who would love to be able to take care of the person needing care, but they can't for economic reasons. They can't afford to quit their job to take up caregiving, and the insurance policy will not pay them.

#5: It May Not Pay for Care You Need

As I wrote in Chapter 8, cash is king. When you are paying with cash, no one can tell you that the care you desire or the caregiver you select doesn't qualify for payments. That said, most of us do not have the ability to pay out of our own pocket for the kind of long-term care we are likely to need. Long-term care insurance will pay for our care, subject to the limitations in the contract. Let's take a look at some claims where LTC insurance typically doesn't pay.

Short Claims

For any benefit to be paid under a tax-qualified policy, a licensed health-care practitioner must first certify that you are expected to need at least 90 days of care. This requirement is separate and distinct from your *elimination period*, or waiting period. If you have a tax-qualified (TQ) policy (see Chapter 12) and do not meet the standard for precertification, no benefit will be paid, even if you have satisfied the elimination period.

The representative of one insurance company reported to me that 70 percent of its home health-care claims have a duration of less than 60 days. This company has a lot of zero-day deductible plans that were purchased before the HIPAA TQ precertification requirement. Anyone with a TQ policy must be aware that his or her LTC insurance is not designed for short-term, acute claims. This can be very difficult for single people (or widows and widowers) who live alone and may need temporary care after a hospital stay.

 Marilee's Memo _____

In certain limited circumstances, Medicare will pay for services during a short-term need for care, if you meet their requirements (see Chapter 10). But claims lasting less than 90 days will not be paid under most long-term policies being sold today. And remember, even with a claim expected to last more than 90 days, you must pay for your own care to satisfy the elimination period on most policies. The out-of-pocket expense at claim time can be substantial.

You May Need LTC but Not Trigger a Claim

Most people who buy long-term care insurance count on that coverage paying a benefit if they need assistance. But needing assistance is not the same as meeting the definition of needing long-term care. If you have a tax-qualified policy, certain standard language is included, as well as a description of how benefits are *triggered* (qualified for). Your policy, whether tax-qualified or nontax-qualified, should clearly explain how you can trigger benefits.

Let's consider a widow with a typical, tax-qualified LTC insurance policy. Her benefit triggers are two out of six ADLs, and cognitive impairment. Most people living in nursing homes have no difficulty qualifying for LTC insurance benefits. Half of the people living in nursing homes have limitations with *five* activities of daily living! But it's a different story when we look at living in our own home or in an assisted living facility.

Let's recap the six ADLs in a standard long-term care contract. The policy cited in the widow example above, since it's a TQ policy, must include at least five of these six in its contract:

◆ Bathing

◆ Continence

◆ Dressing

◆ Eating

◆ Toileting

◆ Transferring

The widow, who is 80 years old, is starting to fail. Although she is able to do everything on the preceding list, she is nervous stepping in and out of her bathtub to take a shower. She's also tired of cooking for one. Keeping up her apartment has become a burden, and so she has a housecleaner come in once a week. Her children know she isn't eating well, and since her last automobile accident she's stopped driving. She's upset that she can't go shopping or to church on her own anymore. The kids are nervous that she may fall, or even be taken advantage of by a con man.

Her children encourage her to apply for the next space at the assisted living facility in her town. An apartment opens up, and she moves in. Will she qualify for long-term care benefits? Well, let's see. Cognitively, her memory has slowed, but other than that, she's fine, so there's no claim there. Although she's frail, the only ADL she needs help with so far is bathing. So, right now, we're waiting for another ADL impairment or a cognitive problem before the insurance will pay. The care she's receiving is on her own dime.

Remember that I mentioned that the woman is nervous stepping in and out of her bathtub to shower? Well, when we take a look at her insurance policy, that fear doesn't qualify as difficulty with bathing. You see, contrary to how you or I would define bathing, in some long-term care insurance policies, "bathing" is defined as "washing oneself by sponge bath; or in either a tub or shower ...." So as long as she can give herself a sponge bath, she has not satisfied the bathing ADL trigger.

Often before someone needs help with ADLs, they need help with IADLs (instrumental activities of daily living). These include activities such as ...

- Using the telephone.
- Getting to places beyond walking distance.
- Grocery shopping.
- Preparing meals.
- Doing housework or handyman work.
- Doing laundry.
- Taking medications.
- Managing money.

Someone could need help with these activities, but not trigger benefits on a long-term care insurance policy. When doing your long-term care planning, keep in mind that there will likely be a period of time when assistance may be needed, but before LTC insurance benefits would be triggered.

You can see how some frail elders, who can no longer live on their own safely, sometimes would not qualify for long-term care insurance benefits. They may have to wait to collect—until they lose another ADL or become cognitively impaired.

The Least You Need to Know

- Care outside the United States is not covered by most long-term care policies.
- Care by family members or unlicensed providers is not covered by most LTC policies.
- Frail older people may not be able to live by themselves anymore, yet may not qualify for long-term care insurance benefits.
- Long-term care insurance is expensive, and the premium is not guaranteed level.
- If you need long-term care, you can't beat long-term care insurance. The return on insurance versus your savings can be eight times higher—or even more!

Part  5

A Buyer's Guide to LTC Insurance

You could have a long-term care insurance policy from one of the best insurance companies in the world, but if it's not designed properly, it may not do the job. Buying long-term care insurance can be like buying a mattress: Often the differences are hidden from view and not apparent to the consumer. It's tough to make an informed choice between policies. Because you're not an insurance expert, it's hard to know if you're comparing apples to apples, or apples to oranges (or even celery!).

This part gives you insight into the important differences between policies. If you want to know how to design an LTC policy correctly and what to look for in a policy, read on.

18

Comparing Apples to Oranges

In This Chapter

- ◆ The ways policies may differ
- ◆ Home sweet home-care coverage
- ◆ It may be customary, but, is it reasonable?

When you buy auto insurance, the policy form is standard in your state, and you choose from limits and contracts that do not vary from insurance company to insurance company. Same with Medicare supplement policies. And although there are a variety of different types of life insurance, we all know how to collect.

Long-term care insurance isn't that simple. Although policies share certain standard requirements, they can vary quite a bit.

Here are some of the ways that long-term care insurance policies that appear to be the same can vary. Reading this chapter, along with Chapters 19 and 20, will give you the information you need to know to be a savvy consumer.

Benefits vs. Pricing

Before we get into some of the ways that policies differ, we should talk for a moment about how, when it comes to insurance, there is no free lunch. Similar to other things we buy, whether a car or a vacation, there is usually a relationship between price and benefit. But, with long-term care insurance, the relationship between price and benefits is particularly important. Since all full-pay LTC policies are guaranteed renewable, the premium can be raised in the future, with permission of the state insurance department. It's important that consumers select policies wisely. If it looks too good to be true, it probably is. The department of insurance in your state (see Appendix A) can give you information on how to choose a policy. Your insurance agent is also an excellent information source.

Marilee's Memo _____

A full-pay long-term care insurance policy is a policy that you pay the premium for until the coverage is no longer wanted or needed (if you are collecting a benefit on claim, most policies won't require you to pay any more). Compare this to a limited-pay policy, which is designed to be paid for a stated number of years. With a limited-pay policy, you pay a higher premium over a shorter number of years.

There is a tension between the following components of a LTC insurance policy. If one is out of whack, beware—it may mean that the policy premium is too good to be true, and can't be maintained over the long run (and a premium increase is likely down the road).

Long-term care policies must balance ...

♦ Expenses (including claims payments, reserves set up, agent commissions, customer service, management expenses, and profits).

♦ Contractual benefits (how easy is it to collect?).

♦ Underwriting standards (how tough a company's health requirements are directly affect the amount paid out in claims).

♦ Premium being charged (if underwriting requirements are easy and/or contractual benefits are rich, the premium must be higher than otherwise).

Inflation Protection

Inflation protection is perhaps the most important decision that you will make on your policy. It is also a decision that many people overlook. The 50-year-old who purchases a $200 daily benefit policy with no built-in inflation protection may be rudely awakened at age 80, when his cost of care is $864 per day (based on 5 percent compound inflation), but his policy only pays a $200 daily benefit!

Inflation protection is one way that policies may differ substantially. The younger you are when you purchase insurance, the more important differences in inflation protection become. This is because we know that the cost of long-term care will increase each year. If the policy you own does not increase along with the cost of care, you are left paying for the shortfall with your own money. Worst case, you don't have the money to cover the shortfall, and you end up on an assistance program, without private-pay choices, even though your have a long-term care benefit!

At a very basic level, there are two different types of inflation protection in policies. The more expensive, built-in protection automatically increases your daily benefit amount each year, without an increase in your premium. Built-in inflation protection is very expensive; it can increase your premium anywhere from 40 percent to 120 percent—depending primarily on your age when you buy the policy! This is an expensive option because it does so much for you—doubling, tripling, and even quadrupling your benefit before, during and after claim.

Wisdom of the Aged

One of the best ways to find out if you are comparing apples to apples or apples to oranges with LTC insurance policies, is to ask your agent how the contracts differ, or request a copy of the outline of coverage or a specimen (sample) policy. Be sure to ask for a specimen of any riders (optional benefits) that you are considering. Do not count on marketing literature to highlight the differences between contracts.

The other choice, which is much less expensive at first, is inflation protection in the form of options. Options allow you the opportunity to purchase additional coverage at future dates, with no medical questions asked. When you use an option, you pay for the additional insurance based on your current age, which is older than when you bought the policy. You lose future options if you turn them down a certain number of times; and most policies stop options once you are on claim. This means that if you have a policy with options, once you are on claim, your daily benefit is frozen at that level.

Some insurance companies base their option amounts on the change in the U.S. CPI (Consumer Price Index). Others base it on the change in the medical component of the CPI. This can be three to four times higher than the overall CPI. Other policies may offer options based on a standard amount, such as 5 percent each year.

With options, your premium is increased each time that you increase your benefit. Over the long run, a policy with options could cost you much more than if you bit the bullet and bought built-in inflation protection up front. Options should not be considered a good strategy for people who are concerned about increasing premiums. They are certainly better than nothing for people who should buy, but will not buy, built-in inflation protection. They are also a reasonable option for wealthy people who can choose how much of the cost of long-term care to self-insure.

So, if you know that inflation protection is included in your long-term care insurance or a policy that you are considering, it is very important that you understand which type is included (built-in protection or options to purchase more insurance), and how it works.

LTC Lowdown

Built-in inflation protection is an expensive option. Depending on your age and the insurer, inflation protection can double the cost of your LTC insurance policy. Have you ever heard that "you get what you pay for?" Inflation protection is vital for almost everyone purchasing this insurance. Those who do not buy it need to be confident that they can write personal checks for the shortfall (the part of the future long-term care bill not covered by insurance).

A typical built-in inflation protection increases your daily benefit by 5 percent, compound each year. However, some policies limit the effectiveness of their built-in inflation protection by placing a cap on it. The cap may mean that, once you turn age 80, your benefit is frozen. Or once your daily benefit has doubled, your benefit is frozen.

Let's take a look at the benefit of a 45-year-old, who purchases a policy with a cap that kicks in once his benefit is doubled, and compare that policy to one without a cap. Both individuals purchased a $100 daily benefit, which we will assume is equal to the average cost of care in their area:

Year	Age	With Cap	No Cap
Year 1	Age 47	$100	$100
Year 2	Age 48	$105	$105
Year 3	Age 49	$110	$110

Year	Age	With Cap	No Cap
Year 4	Age 50	$116	$116
Year 5	Age 51	$122	$122
Year 6	Age 52	$128	$128
Year 7	Age 53	$134	$134
Year 8	Age 54	$141	$141
Year 9	Age 55	$148	$148
Year 10	Age 56	$155	$155
Year 11	Age 57	$163	$163
Year 12	Age 58	$171	$171
Year 13	Age 59	$180	$180
Year 14	Age 60	$189	$189
Year 15	Age 61	$198	$198
Year 16	Age 62	$200	$200
Year 17	Age 63	$200	$218
Year 18	Age 64	$200	$229
Year 19	Age 65	$200	$240
Year 20	Age 66	$200	$252
Year 21	Age 67	$200	$265
Year 22	Age 68	$200	$278
Year 23	Age 69	$200	$292
Year 24	Age 70	$200	$307
...			
Year 35	Age 80	$200	$500

By age 65, the daily benefit on the policy with no cap has grown to $240. The capped policy's benefit is only $200. By age 80, which is the average age that many carriers report for long-term care claims, the daily benefit of the policy without a cap is almost $500! Compare this to the daily benefit of the capped policy at $200. If the average cost of long-term care increased 5 percent per year, from the time the policies were bought, the person without the policy cap would have, at age 80, a daily benefit of $500, which gives her the same buying power that her original $100 policy had. The person with the capped policy has an entirely different situation. If costs increased at 5 percent per year, and now, at age 80, long-term care costs $500 per day, that policyholder (whose benefit was capped at $200 in year 16) would have to pay the $300 difference out of his or her own pocket!

Some people argue that the medical component of the CPI is a better measure, but I don't think so. The long-term care inflation rate (which is not tracked by the U.S. government) will vary depending on the type of care discussed (home care, facility care), the location of the care, and the supply and demand in any given geography. Of course, the cost of real estate and labor are also important.

How big a mistake is it, exactly, for someone not to buy inflation protection? LTCi Decision Systems, Inc., in Tustin California (www.ltcia.com) provides software designed to assist advisors and clients in making decisions about long-term care insurance. Here's how their analysis answers the question: Should I buy coverage at today's care cost and self-insure inflation? They call this scenario "a $750,000 bad decision."

Here are their assumptions:

- A 50-year-old person (current local cost of care $150 per day).

- The person doesn't need long-term care until age 76 (care cost increases at 5 percent compound interest, and then costs $508 per day).

- The person needs five years of care.

- Policy design analyzed: 30-day elimination, $150 daily benefit, 6 percent compound inflation protection built-in.

- Unlimited benefit period.

- Yearly premium: $836 with no inflation protection; $1,658 with 5 percent built-in.

	5 Percent Compound Inflation	No Inflation
Cumulative premium paid	$41,450	$20,900
Cost of Care	$1,024,467	$1,024,467
Insurance Claims Paid	$1,009,228	$269,250
Out of pocket/self insurance	$15,239	$755,217

The person who chose a policy with no inflation protection would have only $269,250 of their $1,024,467 LTC claim cost paid.

Read Chapter 20 for more guidance on choosing inflation protection for a LTC insurance policy.

Premium Waiver

Premium waiver provides that, once you are collecting benefits, you do not have to pay premiums. This is a common benefit that is included in almost all long-term care policies. However, not all policies work the same when it comes to waiving premium.

Some policies waive the premium for nursing home claims only. With a policy like this, if you were collecting for home care, you would still need to pay your premium. Is that a horrible thing? Not necessarily. Usually the amount that you would be collecting would far exceed your premium payments. A policy that requires you to pay premiums during home care should have lower premiums from day one. Some policies waive premiums for both insured spouses when one spouse is on claim.

Home-Care Considerations

Some people who are on an LTC claim at home need a variety of services. These may include *chore care*, such as grocery shopping, cutting the lawn, and shoveling the driveway. When we think of needing long-term care and we are planning to stay in our home, we need to consider the extra expenses involved. Some policies cover this kind of care, but many don't.

Home-Care Details

Most LTC insurance policies will cover home health care provided by a nurse or a licensed home health aide (nurses' aide) hired through a licensed agency. Agencies provide a level of oversight that can be helpful, but they also add to the cost of care. Agencies also provide employee benefits, bonding, and worker's compensation to take care of on-the-job injuries.

Other policies allow you to hire a freelancer—someone who is licensed by your state, but not employed through an agency. These people are generally less expensive to hire.

We could debate for pages the pluses and minuses of utilizing agencies vs. hiring directly. What you need to anticipate is how your LTC insurance policy works when you are hiring home health care.

Clarifying the Elimination Period

Elimination period, sometimes called waiting period, is like a deductible. It is the number of days that must be waited before a policy's benefit starts. How elimination-period days are satisfied varies between contracts. Most contracts require that for a day to count towards your elimination period, not only must care be received that day, but you must pay for that care.

This is consistent with the concept of a deductible, as in traditional health insurance or auto insurance. But there's one big difference between a LTC deductible and other deductibles you are used to: The LTC deductible is not met by a specific amount of spending, but by paying for care for a number of days. Therefore, a 90-day deductible could cost you $18,000 if you met the deductible in a nursing home that cost $200 per day. If, instead, you received home care costing $80 a day, the same deductible would cost you only $7,200.

Other policies credit seven days toward the elimination period when only one day of care is paid for in a week. This gives people who are receiving home health care the opportunity to manage their out-of-pocket expense. Often, especially at the beginning of a LTC claim, there are many friends and relatives willing to help out. If the insured pays for one day of professional home care a week, and has friends and relatives provide the other six days of care, out-of-pocket expense to satisfy a deductible of this type can be minimal.

Let's imagine that you are receiving professional care at home every other day, and you qualify for benefits under your policy. If you have a 90-day elimination period with a typical policy, it will take you 180 days, or about 6 months before your policy would start paying. If you had a policy which credited seven days toward the elimination period if professional care was received for at least one day during that week, your benefit would become payable after only 90 calendar days.

LTC Lowdown

LTC policies that have different ways of satisfying the elimination period are only different when you are receiving your care at home on an intermittent basis. Once you are receiving care in a facility, you are paying for care every day, and the differences in crediting days toward your elimination period are no longer meaningful.

Some policies limit the number of days in which the elimination period must be met (for example, you have 180 days in which to accumulate 90 days of paid care).

Many policies have a lifetime elimination period; once met, it does not have to be satisfied again in the event of future claims. Under these policies, once you have a claim paid, if you get better and go off claim, the next long-term care claim that you have will be covered from the first day (if your policy is TQ, the 90-day precertification paperwork would have to be signed).

CAUTION

Truth & Consequences

If you have a policy with a 90-day elimination period, it's not unusual to be able to line up unpaid, informal help at the beginning of a claim. Neighbors may offer to help; children may take unpaid leaves from their jobs. Since unpaid help does not satisfy the elimination period in most contracts, by accepting this help you may unwittingly be *delaying* the start of insurance benefits.

Reasonable and Customary Benefit Limitations

A small number of insurers are adding reasonable and customary (R&C) limitations to some of their contracts. It's sometimes called "prevailing charge" language. So if you bought a policy that paid $250 per day so that you could go to the most exclusive nursing home in the nicest section of town, a policy with R&C language would limit your benefit to the average cost of nursing homes in your area.

This kind of language is common in dental insurance. But, in my opinion, it doesn't belong in LTC insurance. You have paid for a specific daily benefit and you are entitled to collect that benefit, in my mind. R&C penalizes you for choosing high-cost options—the ability to choose high-cost options is likely one of the reasons that you bought LTC insurance in the first place!

The Least You Need to Know

- Most long-term care policies require that the covered person pay for professional care for a day to count towards satisfying the elimination period.

- Premiums for similar policies between comparably rated insurance companies vary widely.

- Reasonable and customary language allows companies to limit benefits for high-cost care options.

- Caps limit the effectiveness of inflation protection.

- A delicate balance exists between the richness of policy benefits, ease of underwriting, premium price, and insurer expenses.

- If a policy looks too good to be true, it probably is. Too low premiums and too good policy benefits will eventually necessitate premium increases.

Chapter 19

Understanding the Structure of Your Insurance Policy

In This Chapter

- ◆ Who has the best policy?
- ◆ How level does your premium grow?
- ◆ Home care only and nursing home only policies
- ◆ Policies that spouses can share

The type of long-term care insurance policy that you buy can make a big difference in the premiums that you pay, how you access benefits, and how these benefits are paid to you.

I've already discussed the subject of tax-qualified versus non-tax-qualified policies (see Chapter 12), and group vs. individual policies (see Chapter 14). In this chapter, I take a look at some other considerations when looking at LTC insurance.

Which Policy Is Best?

Let's start with the question on everyone's mind. Which policy should I buy? Or, you may ask, "Marilee, what policy do *you* have?" If it would do you any good to tell you, I would. But, the truth is, the policies are changing so quickly, the prices are so competitive, and the health underwriting is so different now than when I bought my policy, that it wouldn't help you.

As I explained in Chapter 13, the underwriting requirements and level of health required vary company to company. If you have a health problem, make sure that you read Chapter 13. The presence of a health condition can greatly impact your plan choices.

Did you know that premiums vary quite a bit between different insurance companies? Here are annual premium quotes from five different insurance companies, each offering a 60-year-old person $100 of daily benefit, starting after 90 days, for a 3-year benefit period. Five percent compound inflation protection is included, as is 100 percent home health care in addition to facility care. I requested quotes for five different, highly rated companies.

Company #1:	$1,344
Company #2:	$1,138
Company #3:	$1,390
Company #4:	$1,070
Company #5:	$897

(Source: StrateCision, Inc., Needham, Massachusetts, www.ltca.com)

Did you also know that most insurance companies sell more than one type of long-term care insurance policy? Insurers call these different *policy forms*. One insurance company may sell, for example, five different policy forms. Some are basic policies that cover nursing home care only. Another form may cover home care just like nursing home care, with additional benefits such as only one elimination period per lifetime.

Here are quotes for five different long-term care insurance policy forms, issued by the same insurance company, on the same person, with the same basic policy design (daily benefit, home care, elimination period, benefit period):

Policy 1:	$1,210
Policy 2:	$1,089

Policy 3:	$1,074
Policy 4:	$981
Policy 5:	$959

(Source: StrateCision, Inc., Needham, Massachusetts, www.ltca.com)

Marilee's Memo

Policy forms are different forms of the same type of insurance offered by the same insurer. One LTC policy form, for example, may have the home health-care benefit always equal to the nursing home benefit. Another policy form may have the maximum home health care benefit limited to 80 percent of the nursing home benefit.

So you see, when someone tells you that he or she has a policy from a company that you are considering, but that policy costs 30 percent less than what you were quoted, this *is* possible—even if the policy design is the same, and even if the person is the same age and health as you are. When people tell me what insurance company they have a policy through, and then ask me if they have a good policy, I can't answer the question without knowing which policy form they have. Also, keep in mind that someone could have the "best" policy form in the world, but if the policy design wasn't right for him or her, it may not accomplish their goals, either (see Chapter 20 for details).

Per Diem vs. Reimbursement Policies

By far, most LTC policies are reimbursement policies. These work similar to old-fashioned health insurance. The insured spends money for covered services, and the insurance company reimburses them instead for their out-of-pocket expense, up to the policy limit. In a long-term care policy, this limit is usually a daily amount, and only covered types of services would be eligible for reimbursement. Of course, for any policy to pay a benefit, benefit triggers must be met (through the loss of ADLs or a cognitive impairment, for most policies). Tax-qualified policies have an additional 90-day precertification requirement.

Truth & Consequences

The benefit paid from a tax-qualified per diem/indemnity contract could be taxable, if the benefit paid exceeds your actual cost of qualified long-term care services, and is more than $210 per day (2002 figure). The taxation on benefits from a non-TQ policy of any type is unclear (see Chapter 12). Ask your tax preparer for more information.

The other type of LTC policy is a per diem policy. These policies are sometimes referred to as indemnity policies. This type of policy, which in its purest form is extremely rare, pays a flat benefit to the insureds when they are receiving LTC—even if the insured have no out-of-pocket expenses for their care (if family and friends were providing the care). Like reimbursement policies, benefit triggers must be met, and TQ policies must have the 90-day care precertification.

The more common variety of per diem/indemnity policies work this way: They pay the insured their full daily benefit, only if they paid out-of-pocket for professional care services on that day. I call these policies hybrid per diem/indemnity policies. They are paid the full daily benefit amount regardless of the amount of their care bill. For example, someone who has a $180 daily benefit, and who had a short visit by a home health aide costing $45, would receive the full $180 daily benefit. With what I am calling the "pure form" per diem/indemnity policy, they would collect the full $180 even if they received no paid care that day.

Here's another example: A woman with severe arthritis is legally blind. She needs help with bathing, dressing, and eating. She lives with her spouse who helps her every day. If she had a "pure" per diem/indemnity contract, she would collect the full daily benefit each day. If she had a reimbursement policy, with most policies she would receive nothing, because she is not paying for professional, licensed care through an agency (in addition, almost all reimbursement policies have an exclusion for paying family members, even if they are licensed caregivers). If you are purchasing a hybrid per diem policy, check to make sure that you understand exactly what kind of care is required for you to be paid your daily benefit.

Because most LTC policies are reimbursement policies, this means that you first must spend the money on care, and then be reimbursed. Here's how it would work. If you have a policy with a 30-day elimination period, and you have met all the policy's requirements for payment, you would pay for your care during the 30-day elimination period. Now, the clock starts on your care, which is eligible to be reimbursed. You would pay for your care for the second month. Then you would put in a claim to be reimbursed for the second month's care. You are always "out" the expense of one month's care, until your claim ends and you are reimbursed for the last month of care.

LTC Lowdown

True per diem/indemnity contracts give you cash benefits to use as you'd like. You can use the benefit to pay a grandchild to take care of you, or even to hire a landscaper and someone to balance your checkbook!

If You Want Premium Guarantees

As you know, level premiums are not guaranteed with almost all long-term care insurance policies. The best protection against potential premium increases is to buy a policy from a reputable company that has priced the contract correctly (read more in Chapter 17). Here are some alternative options that can insulate you against potential future premium increases.

- ◆ **Full-pay policies.** Most LTC policies are full-pay policies. You pay until you have a claim, or as long as you want coverage in force. Most companies waive your premium when you have a claim. Some full-pay policies are guaranteeing that their premium will not increase for a certain length of time, such as 3 years, or 10 years.

- ◆ **Limited-Pay Policies.** Some companies offer what is called at limited-pay policy. Similar to limited-pay life insurance policies, you pay a higher premium so that, after paying premiums for a certain number of years (or to a certain age), no more premiums are due. A typical limited-pay policy might be a "10-pay" or "to age 65."

  Not all limited-pay policies are the same, and not all are guaranteed-limited pay. At the end of the limited-pay period, is the policy guaranteed paid up, or does the company retain the contractual right to ask for additional payments if the insurance department in your state grants a premium increase to other policy-holders?

- ◆ **Long-term care riders.** Some insurance companies that offer long-term care riders on their life insurance policies (or annuities) guarantee that the premium for these riders will not increase. And if the base policy is a limited pay, they guarantee that when the base life insurance is paid up (no more premium is due), the same is true for the long-term care rider—it's also paid up. For more details on riders, please refer to Chapter 7.

Home Health-Care Coverage

Since most people want to receive their long-term care at home, it's important that our long-term care insurance help us in that goal—to stay at home forever, or for at least as long as possible.

Is the Home Care Benefit Limited?

Some policies cover home health care differently than nursing home or facility care. Home health care may be covered at 80 percent of actual charges, to the maximum daily benefit. Or it may be covered at 100 percent, up to 80 percent of the daily benefit. Do you see the difference?

Truth & Consequences

Most long-term care insurance policies cover assisted living facility care under their nursing home or facility benefit. Others cover it under their home care benefit. If your policy doesn't include the same benefit amount for both home care and facility care, make sure that you know how an assisted living facility stay would be treated.

Let's say that I have a policy that pays $150 per day for nursing home care, and that my home health care costs $120 per day. If my home care is covered at 80 percent of actual charges, up to the maximum daily benefit, my home care would be covered at $96 (80 percent of $120). The balance, or $24 per day, would be paid by me. However, if my home health care was covered at 100 percent, up to 80 percent of the daily benefit, $120 would be covered, up to a maximum of $120 (80 percent of $150). I would have no out-of-pocket expense. So when you hear that home health care is covered at 80 percent, ask: 80 percent of what? You'll recall from Chapter 2 that extensive home health care can cost much more than even nursing home care.

Home Health Care Only

Some long-term care insurance policies cover home health care only. Some people like these policies, usually for two reasons: They are less expensive than comprehensive policies that also cover care in institutional settings; and the person doesn't want to ever leave their home anyway. Why pay for a benefit that you don't want?

Here's why. No one knows the nature of the health problem that may cause them to need long-term care. It's also hard to imagine that, years in the future, the joys of home ownership and maintenance may become a tremendous burden to you—especially when you need long-term care. The best option for you may be the nicest nursing home in town—or even in another state—closer to your family. Your home health care only policy won't be a bit of help in that situation. Also, consider that assisted living facilities are normally not covered in a home health care only policy.

By the way, just as there are home care only policies, there are also nursing home only policies. Just as I don't recommend home health care only policies, I don't recommend nursing home only policies. One of the huge benefits to having comprehensive long-term care insurance is that it buys you extra choices and flexibility. Who knows what the nature of our need to care will be, and whether we will want to be living in our own home or in the nicest nursing home in our region? The person who bought a home care only policy twenty years ago could not have imagined that, twenty years later, he or she would want to move to the assisted living facility that just opened up in their town last year—but their policy doesn't cover it.

Home Care Is Usually Not for a Single Person

Long-term care in your own home is a great goal, but, if you are living by yourself, it is often unrealistic. Why? It's tough to coordinate, often tough to find caregivers, and, depending on the amount of care that you need, can be extremely expensive. If home care is your goal, and you live alone, make sure that the long-term care policy that you are buying is high enough.

Home health care is very realistic if you live with someone; perhaps a spouse or a child. For most couples, the first spouse to need long-term care is cared for in the home, and, if they enter a facility at all, it is normally at the tail end of their life, when their need for care has overwhelmed their spouse. Often the spouse has ruined her (or his) own health being the caregiver. A home care benefit from a long-term care policy can literally be a lifesaver for the caregiver spouse.

LTC Lowdown

In 1990, 63 percent of long-term care insurance policies purchased were nursing home only plans. In 2000, this percentage had dropped to 14 percent. Also in 2000, 77 percent of policies were comprehensive covering both home health care and nursing home care.

Daily or Monthly Benefit?

When purchasing a long-term care policy, you will notice that most policies state a maximum daily benefit, while some state a maximum monthly benefit. What's the difference? In a nursing home or facility-based claim, there is little or no difference, because you are charged each day for care. But in a long-term care claim at home, your care may be less predictable, with care on some days consisting of a two-hour visit, while other days requiring 3 shifts (24 hours) of home health aides.

If a policy has what I call a true monthly benefit, you would collect for the covered services that you paid for, up to the monthly benefit maximum. But many monthly benefit policies don't act like monthly benefits; they limit your reimbursement for care on any calendar day to 1/30th of your monthly benefit. That's no different than a policy with a daily benefit.

Some policies are more flexible. They allow you to exceed your daily benefit on any given day for home health care services, as long as you keep within a weekly maximum. For example, if your daily benefit was $150, and you had 2 days of home health care in one week, at a cost of $250 per day, a flexible policy would pay you $500 ($250 per day × 2 days), since the amount doesn't exceed your weekly benefit (7 × $150, or $1,050). Remember, with most policies, any amount that you do not use waits there for you, extending your benefit period.

An Alternate Plan of Care

Many people read about a benefit called "alternate plan of care," or something similar to it, and think that this benefit is designed to cover everything the policy doesn't specifically list. Here's how the alternate plan of care works. If you are receiving benefits, you can apply for benefits not expressly given in your policy. A typical request would be for the installation of a ramp at your front door, or the purchase of an emergency alert system. If your doctor and the insurance company agree to the plan, benefits will be paid under the alternate plan of care.

In some cases, it is less expensive for the insurance company to pay for home alterations than to have the insured stay in a facility, for example. Then, they are likely to agree to an alternate plan of care. But remember, your doctor must sign off on the plan. Many physicians are reluctant to sign off on home care for very sick people without evidence of 24-hour-a-day professional care. Your insurance company is not likely to sign off on a plan that will cost it more than a nursing home. A good rule of thumb is this: If it's not guaranteed in your policy, don't count on it.

Pooled Benefits vs. Separate Pools

When you buy a comprehensive long-term care insurance policy, care in virtually any setting (from your home, to an adult day care program, to assisted living facilities or nursing homes) is all covered, up to the daily benefit amount for the benefit period. Some people describe this type of comprehensive policy as integrated—you have bought a pool of money (your daily benefit times the number of days covered), which is paid out as care is received in any of the mentioned settings.

But some policies don't have one, integrated pool. They have two pools. What do I mean? They have one benefit period for home-based benefits, and another benefit period for community-based/facility benefits. So, instead of a six-year benefit that can be used for either home care or facility care, a policy with two separate pools may, for example, cover three years of home care and three years of facility care. If you have a policy like the one in the example, and you've used up your three-year benefit for home care, you are faced with a horrible choice: to either move to the nursing home (to continue having your policy pay for your care), or to pay for your home care out of your own pocket. What if you have a catastrophic health problem, and you go straight to a nursing home, never having received home care? In the policy described, you would collect for three years only, and would never use your home care benefit. Policies that offer one pool of money for benefits give you flexibility, and save you from having your policy determine where you should live in order to collect.

Sharing Care

Because the first spouse in a couple who needs long-term care normally uses much less professional care than the second spouse to need care, many couples have asked if they could buy a policy that could be shared. It makes a lot of sense. Since the odds are that one will take care of the other, at the first claim, the first spouse to need care will likely be able to get along nicely with relatively inexpensive home care—a couple of hours a day, or maybe an eight-hour shift every other day.

It's the second spouse who will need more extensive (and expensive!) professional care, since he or she is normally widowed at that point. But here's the tricky part—no one knows for sure which spouse will need care first. This means that if big, comprehensive policies are purchased on each spouse, one may be effectively "wasted." A shared spousal benefit takes care of this problem.

Wisdom of the Aged

Given a traditional couple, it is usually the man who needs long-term care first, since he is older. Men receive most of their care in their own home. The nursing homes are filled with widows who took care of their own husbands at home. When she needs care, she is normally a widow, too frail to remain in her home. When a couple does long-term care planning, it is truly a gift for the wife. It allows her to hire home care when she's taking care of her husband, and allows her to choose the best facility for her own care.

Policies and how they work vary between carriers, but, essentially here's how it works. Each spouse (or people living together) purchased a policy for long-term care, with a spousal benefit option rider. If either individual runs out of benefits on their policy, they can use the benefits on their spouse's policy. The rider adds approximately one-third to the policy cost, and may be more or less depending on the insurer and the benefit period of the policies. The shared spousal benefit is not available on lifetime benefit periods, since you couldn't run out of a lifetime benefit.

Linking policies this way can be a great option for spouses if lifetime benefits are not affordable. They are a practical solution for spouses who want flexibility, and who are willing to use their assets if their need for long-term care is catastrophic. Here's how their thinking may work. The first spouse who needs care will remain in the home, and their policy will probably not be exhausted by that care. After they die, the surviving spouse has their own policy plus the remaining benefit on the deceased spouse's policy, to pay for his or her care needs. If he or she runs out of benefits and wants to remain in the home, perhaps a reverse mortgage or other asset can be used.

Proceeds from the sale of the home, or other assets and income could be used to pay for facility care.

Compare the benefits and cost of spousal shared care policies to traditional, stand-alone lifetime benefit period policies on each spouse.

The Least You Need to Know

♦ The vast majority of long-term care insurance policies are not guaranteed to have a level premium.

♦ Almost all long-term care policies are reimbursement contracts; they reimburse the insured for covered services they have paid for.

♦ Many per diem/indemnity policies require you to pay for some amount of professional care to collect the daily benefit.

♦ An alternate plan of care benefit may be helpful at claim time, but it should not be counted on to pay a particular type of benefit.

Chapter 20

Designing an LTC Insurance Plan

In This Chapter

◆ How to design the plan that's right for you

◆ How much insurance you really need

◆ The trade-offs you can make to save money

◆ How to avoid common mistakes

Having a high-quality LTC insurance policy from a reputable company isn't enough. If little thought was put into the design, you may either be paying for coverage you don't need, or your policy may be inadequate when you require care.

Long-term care insurance is, without a doubt, the most complicated type of coverage you will ever purchase. In this chapter, I take you step-by-step through designing a policy. My goal is for you to identify the smallest and least expensive policy that meets your needs. You may, of course, decide to "super-size" coverage—to buy more benefits, so that you end up with a policy that exceeds your minimum requirements. If you haven't already read Chapters 18 and 19, check them out for important tips for choosing a long-term care insurance policy.

By stripping the design process down to the basic components, I am hoping that you will not overlook any critical parts of your coverage. When you go to buy a car, for example, it's not necessary that the car has a leather interior; it is necessary that it has an engine and four tires. Many long-term care policies have other optional benefits or riders that you may choose to buy—or not. Following the steps below will help make sure you don't buy a long-term care policy that's the insurance equivalent of a car with only two tires.

Step 1: Choosing a Daily Benefit

The daily benefit is the maximum amount that your policy will pay for long-term care services per day. With most policies you choose from a daily benefit from $50 to $350 per day.

Begin the design of your policy by choosing the minimum amount of daily benefit that you need. Compare your financial situation to the cost of long-term care. If you are already retired, it is easier for you to figure this out. You know what your income is, and you know how you feel about potentially selling assets to pay for long-term care if your policy benefit runs out.

Let's say that nursing home care costs $5,000 per month in your area, and assisted living costs $3,000 per month. You may be thinking that you could handle a monthly bill of $2,000, but any more than that would be a problem. To figure out how much you are willing to pay for care out of your own pocket (if any), think about your monthly budget. Some people have excess retirement income each month, so they don't mind dedicating that to pay for long-term care. Maybe you are willing to use some or all the earnings on your life savings either toward your long-term care costs, or now to buy insurance. Many retirees want to leave their life savings intact, and not have to ever sell assets to pay for long-term care. They may use some of the earnings on their life savings to buy long-term care insurance, so that they never have to liquidate their assets.

LTC Lowdown

What happens to the daily benefit amount that you don't use? For example, your care costs $75 and your daily benefit is $150. With most policies, whatever you don't use waits there for you, extending your benefit period. So if my home health care costs $75 per day, and I have a policy that pays $150 per day for two years, my benefit will actually last four years.

LTC Lowdown

Because the daily benefit that you don't use waits there for you (with most policies), it is better to have a higher daily benefit than a longer benefit period. Any daily benefit that you don't use extends your benefit policy. For example, if my policy pays $200 per day for a two year benefit period, that's better than a policy that would pay $100 per day with a four year benefit period. Even though both have the same maximum policy benefit ($200 per day multiplied by 365 days per year multiplied by two years = $146,000; so does $100 per day multiplied by 365 days per year multiplied by four years). But, if my claim doesn't last four years, I won't use up my benefits on a four year benefit policy; with the two year policy, I will have higher benefits available, and what isn't needed extends the benefit period.

Back to the scenario we just started. If you are designing a long-term care policy to pay for nursing home care, which is your worst-case expense, you would want the insurance to pay at least $3,000 (that's the monthly expense of $5,000 minus the $2,000 that you're willing to pay).

If you're still working and not sure what your retirement income will be, depending on your whole financial situation, you may design a policy to cover the whole cost of long-term care, or less. That's a personal decision that no one except for you can make. For many younger working people, it makes sense to insure for the full cost of care; as you accumulate retirement savings and other assets, any type of insurance should become less critical, since you will have other assets to rely on if you need to. That's one reason that it's so important to review all your insurance at least every five years, or whenever you have a major life change.

Read the story of a special man, who self-insured his wife's Alzheimer's care—even though he had to sell their house to do it. Successful long-term care planning means you will never have to sell a critically important asset to pay for the care you or a loved one needs.

Keep in mind that you don't want your daily benefit to be too low; with an inadequate daily benefit you may find out that you cannot afford the long-term care choices you want at claim time. I have seen too many people with policies that pay a lifetime benefit, with a horribly low daily benefit. That's like a car with one tire.

> **The Devoted Husband**
>
> Don was the primary caregiver of Rose, his wife of 40 years, who had Alzheimer's disease. After five years of caregiving, Don could no longer manage without some help. He needed someone to stay with his wife through the night so that he could get some sleep. Rose spent most of her days and nights awake and extremely agitated. Neither spouse had long-term care insurance. After sitting down with his insurance agent and going over the cost of home care, Don decided his only option was his biggest nightmare … a nursing home. His only income was his social security and the small amount of equity left in his home. Rose qualified for Medi-Cal (California's Medicaid). The nursing home where he wanted Rose to be, close to the home where they had raised their family, had no Medi-Cal beds available. So, he sold the house and began private paying for a room. Over the next two and half years he spent day and night with Rose, renting an apartment across the street. The local newspaper did a story on him and his devotion to his wife. He spent his time caring for all her personal needs and made sure that she never had to be restrained when she became belligerent and agitated. Two months before he would have run out of money, Rose died of pneumonia. Don's insurance agent finishes the story: "I hadn't seen Don since. One day he came to my office. We sat down and he got me up-to-date, sharing his favorite memories. I thought he just needed someone to talk to, but then he said he needed a favor. He needed a job. He had no money left to his name, and wanted to offer a family his services in exchange for room and board. In one of those coincidences that I guess you could call a miracle, my phone rang that afternoon. A woman was looking for a companion for her elderly widowed father, who was living alone in a huge house. Don moved in within the week. The last I heard from Don was a note in the mail, thanking me and saying how well everything was going."

Step 2: Choosing Inflation Protection

Now that you've chosen your minimum daily benefit, the next decision to make is inflation protection. This may surprise you: I'm saying that you should choose inflation protection before we even discuss benefit period or deductible! That's right. Inflation protection is the one of the most important—and most ignored—parts of designing a long-term care insurance policy. Continuing the car analogy, without the proper inflation protection, your beautiful new car may look perfect, with an engine and four tires, but it will run out of gas before you have a claim.

Here are some guidelines for inflation protection, tied in to the age that you purchase your LTC insurance. (For more information on the importance of inflation protection, read Chapter 18.)

Building In for Inflation

Optimally, every purchaser should have compound built-in inflation protection. Every year your daily benefit automatically increases, even when you are on claim. Most policies offer a 5 percent inflation interest rate, and give you the option of choosing simple or compound interest. Purchasers under age 60 should choose compound interest, which increases your current daily benefit by 5 percent each year. This is an expensive option, adding from 40 to 120 percent to the cost of your policy.

A Simple Option

Sometimes simple inflation protection instead of compound is recommended for purchasers over age 65. The daily benefit grows slower under this option, since it increases each year by 5 percent of the *original*, not current, daily benefit. Over a 10-year time horizon, there is not a huge difference between simple and compound inflation, as shown in the following table. But, if you don't need care within the next 10 years, in the years after that, the difference between simple inflation and compound inflation protection can really add up. And remember, any shortfall in benefits comes right out of your own wallet, when private paying for long-term care. Policyholders are always best served by compound inflation protection, but simple inflation can be a reasonable compromise, as long as you understand what risk you are running.

Daily Benefit	No Inflation	5 Percent Simple	5 Percent Compound
Policy year 1	$100	$100	$100
Policy year 10	$100	$145	$155
Policy year 20	$100	$190	$253

Building In Your Own Inflation

Purchasers over age 70 might consider building in their own inflation protection by purchasing a much bigger daily benefit than they need right now. Look into what your insurance would cost with built-in inflation, then have the policy quoted at the same premium, with no inflation. This will show you how much bigger a daily benefit you could buy if you build in your own inflation protection. If you have a claim sooner rather than later, this strategy can serve you well. Of course, if you are like my grandmother, who didn't need care until age 89, a policy bought without inflation protection could leave you paying quite a bit of money out of your own pocket.

LTC Lowdown

Only 41 percent of people who purchased individual LTC policies in the year 2000 bought inflation protection. This means that, every year, as the cost of long-term care increases, the value of their policy declines.

Truth & Consequences

Review your long-term care policy every two to five years. Check the current local costs of care against your policy. Make sure that the design is still right for you. You may need to apply for more coverage, or ask the insurance company to reduce your coverage, if your situation has changed a lot.

You may also want to have future purchase inflation options on your policy. Options allow someone to purchase additional coverage in the future, with no medical questions. This can be an expensive way to buy coverage, since the additional benefit is purchased based on your age when you use the option. Once you are on claim, or have declined to use the options a number of times, they are no longer available. Some company's options are a stated dollar amount, but most are tied to the Consumer Price Index.

Options should not be considered a smart strategy for people who are worried about their ability to pay increasing premiums. Whenever an option is used, the premium increases.

Options and/or building in your own inflation by overbuying the daily benefit do not make sense when you have a lifetime benefit. Purchasing a lifetime benefit, by definition, would mean that you are worried about a catastrophic claim that lasted longer than five or six years. If you are healthy enough today to qualify for long-term care insurance, a claim is unlikely to happen soon. Add to your possible claim date the more than six years that you are worried a claim could last, and the purchasing power of your daily benefit has been severely eroded—that is, unless you have made plans for keeping up with inflation.

Step 3: Choosing an Elimination Period

The elimination period (sometimes called a waiting period) is the number of days that you pay for your long-term care before the insurance kicks in. Most insurance policies have elimination periods of between 20 and 100 days. Some have shorter or longer elimination periods available.

Don't confuse the elimination period with the 90-day precertification requirement on tax-qualified policies. If you have a tax-qualified policy and your need for care is expected to be less than 90 days, your claim will not be approved for payment, even if you have satisfied your elimination period. Read Chapter 12 for more information about how this works.

A 90- or 100-day elimination period is the most popular choice, and is probably where you should start. If we increase the elimination period beyond 90 or 100 days, the resulting savings in premium cost are usually not enough for someone to elect this option. So, start with 90 or 100. If you do not have the money to pay for care while you wait for policy benefits to begin, you will need to choose a shorter elimination period.

Once you've chosen your maximum elimination period, remember that once you've finished designing your policy, you can choose to "super-size" the policy by selecting a shorter elimination period. Compare the additional premium for a shorter elimination period against the money that you'll save at claim time.

Wisdom of the Aged

A benefit period is actually the minimum number of calendar days that a long-term care policy will pay benefits. Let's say that you are receiving long-term care at home, from a home health aide who comes to your home every other day. If your policy benefit period is three years, since you have care only every other day, the policy will actually pay over six calendar years.

Step 4: Choosing a Benefit Period

The *benefit period* is the length of time that your policy will pay benefits. The total amount of money that is available in your LTC policy is determined by multiplying your daily benefit by the number of days in your benefit period. For example, a policy that pays $100 per day, with a three-year benefit, has a value of $109,500 ($100 daily benefit × 3 years × 365 days in a year).

As we've mentioned earlier, any daily benefit that is unused normally extends your benefit period. If you don't receive paid care daily, your benefit period (BP) can extend beyond the original time frame. For example, if you have a BP of two years and receive care in your home every other day, the policy will actually pay for four years.

Marilee's Memo _____

The **benefit period** is the length of time that your policy will pay benefits. Don't confuse the benefit period with the length of time that you have your policy. You could buy a long-term care policy with a three-year benefit period today, and your policy wouldn't expire in three years. You would usually have your policy for many years before a claim occurs. At that point, the insurance company would owe you three years of benefits.

What's the right benefit period? Most policies offer benefit periods between one and six years, and then a lifetime benefit period. Many people choose a three-year benefit, taking their cue from the statistic that the average nursing home stay is two years, nine months (lately there have been reports that this average stay is becoming even shorter!).

Is a three-year benefit the smartest choice, since it covers the average nursing home stay? Many lawyers also recommend a three-year benefit, for a different reason. Current Medicaid rules allow people to give away assets, then wait three years and one day, in order to qualify for Medicaid.

Here are the problems with a three-year benefit. First, the average nursing home stay reflected in these statistics includes the increasing number of people who are entering the nursing home for short-term, rehabilitative stays after a hospital visit. These short stays, when averaged with the people who are using the nursing home in the traditional manner, dramatically bring down the average stay. So although the average stay is less than three years, it includes both people who are there for three months, and people who are there for 10 years. Another problem is that these numbers do not include the care that the people received before they entered the nursing home. Whether in their own home or an assisted living facility, this care must be taken into consideration when planning.

Next, let's look at the Medicaid three-year look-back rule. People who buy LTC insurance to cover this look-back period may be very disappointed if the rule changes. The trend in recent years has been for Medicaid to extend look-back periods. The strategy of having your LTC insurance pay for your care while you give everything away and wait to apply for Medicaid is a risky one (see Chapter 24 for more details).

Often the decision on benefit period comes down to your budget. If you've followed the steps above, you've identified a daily benefit, the correct inflation protection, and an elimination period. Using your answers from steps 1 to 3, take a look at what a lifetime benefit period would cost. If you can afford the cost, buy that design. It offers a benefit that you cannot outlive.

LTC Lowdown

What if you end up receiving your long-term care in a different state from the state where you bought your LTC insurance policy? No problem—the insurance is portable.

If you cannot afford a lifetime benefit period, what benefit period should you buy? I would have to say the answer is this: Buy the longest benefit period that you can comfortably afford. At claim time, there is no such thing as too much benefit. But you shouldn't neglect today's necessities to fund a possible future need for long-term care. In a perfect world, we'd all be driving Cadillacs and Mercedes. But any car that runs is better than walking.

Any long-term care policy will increase the amount of money that you have available for your care. A policy with a three-year benefit period, for example, gives you three years of private-pay options. The choice of benefit period is a personal decision that you make, based on your concerns and your budget.

The Least You Need to Know

- ◆ Identify the basic, minimum design of your long-term care policy to make sure it meets your needs.

- ◆ Be aware that you are on the hook to pay for your care during the policy elimination period.

- ◆ Do not confuse the policy benefit period with the amount of time that you own your policy. The benefit period begins when you are on claim.

- ◆ Built-in inflation protection is an expensive option, but critical for all purchasers under age 70.

- ◆ The policy benefit period is the last decision to be made when considering a policy.

Part 6

The Truth About Medicaid

If you want the government to pay for your long-term care and you want to leave the maximum amount of money to your family, Medicaid planning is a viable option. Many people end up on Medicaid because they didn't plan how to pay for long-term care; in those cases, Medicaid planning becomes their planning of last resort.

If you are planning on Medicaid to pay for your long-term care, you need to understand the program: how it works, and what care it will—and won't—cover. Medicaid regulations, planning techniques, and available services vary widely depending on the state where you live. The information in this part of the book must be supplemented with your state's information; how and where to get state-specific information is covered here. Reading the four chapters in Part 6 will help you decide if Medicaid is the best option for you.

Chapter 21

What Is Medicaid?

In This Chapter

- ◆ Medicaid versus Medicare
- ◆ Who is eligible for Medicaid
- ◆ The kind of care Medicaid pays for
- ◆ When you should seek legal advice

Seventy percent of nursing home residents have their bill paid by Medicaid. To qualify for Medicaid, you must be poor. Are you planning on having Medicaid pay for your long-term care? Then you'd better understand how the program works, to see if you're likely to qualify.

Some middle-class and affluent people choose to have Medicaid pay for their long-term care. They give away assets to qualify for Medicaid. This legal process is called Medicaid planning.

Medicaid eligibility varies state to state. The penalties for certain maneuvers in Medicaid planning, or even mistakes on a Medicaid application, are severe. If you are applying for Medicaid or thinking about Medicaid planning, you should consult with a qualified professional who specializes in Medicaid. In this chapter we'll tell you how to find that kind of help. Consulting with an expert can save you a lot of money and a lot of headaches.

A Closer Look at Medicaid

Medicaid is a joint federal and state government program that pays for health care and for long-term care. It started in 1965 under Title XIX of the Social Security Act. Medicaid is means-tested; in other words, Medicaid looks at an applicant's financial situation, and to qualify for Medicaid financially, you must be what the system rates as "poor."

The Medicaid program is a critical safety net to pay for the health care and long-term care needs of the poor. Each state has its own eligibility requirements. However, all states require that Medicaid recipients for long-term care be at least 65 years old, blind or disabled, and have low income and assets. If you are on public assistance, or welfare, Medicaid provides your health insurance. If you are in a Medicaid-approved nursing home and you run out of money, Medicaid will pay for your nursing home stay.

The vast majority of Medicaid spending for long-term care is on nursing homes. However, Medicaid does cover some community-based long-term care. This coverage is inconsistent across states. For example, 35 percent of Medicaid's spending on home care in the United States in 1995 was spent in one state: New York. In most states, people who are relying on Medicaid to pay for their care do not have the option of home health care. Even if you live in state that has Medicaid-paid home health care, the services may or may not be available in your town.

To qualify for Medicaid, you need to be poor. This requirement is an important one. By contrast, any person who has paid into the Social Security system or the Railroad Retirement system for enough quarters is automatically eligible for Medicare—regardless of his or her financial situation. The retired waitress enjoys the same Medicare plan as the retired millionaire.

Medicare and Social Security are often referred to as entitlement programs. Indi-viduals can see on their payroll stubs that, during their working lives, they paid taxes for Social Security and Medicare. These taxes are paid so that the worker (and his or her family, in some cases) is entitled to receive benefits at retirement. Some benefits under these programs are available before retirement, if disability or death strikes first.

There is no such "bargain" made between the federal government and working citizens for Medicaid. Working men and women do not pay a Medicaid tax so that they are entitled to benefits when they need long-term care. Medicaid is funded as a welfare program through federal and state taxes, not through payroll taxes.

Medicare Is to Medicaid as Apples Are to Bananas

Before we explore what the Medicaid programs is, I'd like to touch upon what Medicaid isn't. Medicaid is not Medicare!

Medicare is the health insurance that most people age 65 and older have in the United States. Medicare is designed to cover the kinds of expenses health insurance covers—doctor's visits, hospital stays, surgery, and lab tests, for example. To learn more about Medicare, read Chapter 10.

Medicaid does not limit the number of days that it will pay for your long-term care. You may be familiar with the Medicare program's 100-day maximum limit on nursing home care in any benefit period. In most cases, unless you benefit from a financial windfall, it is expected that once you are eligible for Medicaid and Medicaid is paying for your care, that you will remain on the program until you either recover or pass away.

Wisdom of the Aged

It's unfortunate that the government's Medicare and Medicaid programs have such similar names. I have heard many reporters and experts mistakenly say one name when they mean the other. (I've even done it myself!) Since both programs tend to benefit the older and sicker population, the verbal mistake is often not caught and corrected, and can have a tragic consequence. Many people mistakenly believe that Medicare pays for extended nursing home care, and they may even have "heard" that it does! Here's how I keep them straight. *Medicare cares* for seniors. *Medicaid aids* the poor.

Medicaid Varies State to State

Because Medicaid is a joint program between the federal government and each state, the program varies state to state. Federally, the program is administered by the Center for Medicare & Medicaid Services (CMS). This agency was known as the Health-Care Financing Administration (HCFA) before its name was changed on July 1, 2001.

The federal government hands down minimum requirements that each state must meet in order to get federal matching funding for its Medicaid program. States are given quite a bit of freedom in defining their Medicaid long-term care benefits. To a large extent, within general guidelines established by federal statutes, regulations, and policies, each state can set eligibility rules, define services, and set the reimbursement rate for those services.

LTC Lowdown

Just because you read or hear that the federal Medicaid program has made new rules, that doesn't mean that your state is going to use the new rules. Many states are very slow to come into compliance with new mandatory rules; some states remain out of compliance for years.

The federal Medicaid regulations don't cover home- or community-based services (HCBS) for those receiving long-term care. However, if a state wants to provide HCBS under Medicaid, the state may request a waiver from the federal government. If approved, that state's Medicaid program would pay for services in the community that otherwise would require the eligible person to live in a facility. Many states have done this, and this is one of the reasons why Medicaid services vary, often significantly, from state to state.

Since the federal government administers Medicaid, you would think that when the federal government changes the rules, that the states must follow the new rules, right? Wrong ... I mean, not always. Although the vast majority of states conform to the current federal rules, not all of them do.

For example, it took Massachusetts until late 1998 to come into compliance with federal regulations issued in 1993.

As of the date this book was written, in early 2002, California has been out of compliance with the Medicaid regulations since 1993, when the Omnibus Budget Reconciliation Act (OBRA) became effective.

As another example, the federal government mandates *estate recovery* when a Medicaid recipient dies, which is the process of recovering money paid for long-term care from the recipient's estate. Georgia is a state where estate recovery is not currently enforced.

At the other end of the spectrum, some other states will force the sale of your home while you are still alive (if a doctor has said you are permanently a resident of the nursing home). It's hard to believe, but the federal government does not hold back funding or otherwise punish states that do not comply with its estate-recovery requirement. No wonder citizens who are trying to figure out how the system works are confused!

Marilee's Memo

An **elder law attorney** is a lawyer who specializes in Medicaid and other legal issues that concern the elderly. A qualified elder law attorney is not usually the same lawyer who handled your last real estate closing, and he or she may not be the lawyer who handled your will.

Like all other national books on Medicaid, the information here must be supplemented with knowledge of your own state's Medicaid program. There are two great sources for this information. The first is your state's Medicaid office. The second is a qualified *elder law attorney*.

Getting Information in Your Area

The first resource is your state's Medicaid office. Although the program is called Medicaid at a national level (and by most people), states often call their programs something else. In California, the program is called Medi-Cal, for example. Every state has a main office, and your state may also have conveniently located satellite offices. Appendix B lists your state's main office.

If you call or visit the Medicaid office to get information on how it pays for long-term care, be sure that you ask for information on Medicaid for *long-term care and nursing homes*. If you are not specific, it will likely send you information on the Medicaid health insurance program in your state instead. Make sure that the information that you get is up-to-date. Sometimes consumers are sent brochures that are old, and the information is no longer accurate. A guide or brochure needs to be updated whenever a change in regulations is made, or a minimum of once a year, when the federal guidelines change. When ordering information, ask when it was last updated, or check the date printed on material.

In many cases your best source of knowledge will be a qualified elder law attorney. Please notice that I wrote "a *qualified* elder law attorney." An elder law attorney is a lawyer who specializes in Medicaid and other areas that impact seniors. A qualified elder law attorney is a specialist. Later in this chapter I give you tips on how to find a qualified lawyer that you would want to work with. For more information, refer to Appendix E.

LTC Lowdown _____

Medicaid is an ever-changing program. You don't want to be the one to pay an inexperienced attorney to get up to speed in this area of the law. You also don't want your case to be the first (or second) time that the lawyer has sent in a Medicaid application or filed a Medicaid appeal. Like many areas of modern life, the more you know about Medicaid, the more apparent the opportunity for missteps, and the more obvious the need for a specialist.

I have had the good fortune to meet and even have dinner with some of the leading elder law attorneys in the country. I noticed that when discussing strategy, recommendations, and future likely changes in Medicaid that they sometimes disagreed almost as often as they agreed. It's a similar outcome to the one I experienced having dinner with some of the top medical researchers, or with some leading insurance agents.

Here's what I learned by listening to some of the top legal minds: Given the intricacies of Medicaid and the size of the stakes, heaven help you if you don't have an expert on your side. Anyone who thinks that Medicaid planning can be practiced on an occasional basis is foolhardy.

A mistake on a Medicaid application—or in the timing of the application—can cost tens of thousands of dollars that could've been protected, or more. If you, a friend, or family member needs long-term care now, and you don't have the money to pay for care privately or a plan in place to pay for your care, run—don't walk—to a qualified elder law attorney. At the end of this chapter is information on how to find an elder law attorney.

Who Pays for Medicaid?

The funding for Medicaid comes from both the federal government and each state. That's why, as taxpayers, we should be interested in how the program works. In times when tax receipts are down, such as during a recession, Medicaid funding and programs can be vulnerable to funding cuts as a result of political realities. There is a direct relationship between Medicaid spending and our tax bills, which is one reason that Medicaid can be such an emotional topic.

> **Truth & Consequences** _____
>
> If you are on your way to qualifying for Medicaid, or already on Medicaid, make sure that you are not named as a beneficiary on any life insurance policies, or lined up for a *bequest* in someone's will. Any financial windfalls, such as a bequest, which is something that you are left through a will, can temporarily knock you right off Medicaid. You will be expected to private pay for your care using the windfall.

How Do I Become Eligible for Medicaid?

Most people tend to focus on the amount of money that you can keep and still qualify for Medicaid (the asset limit). In addition to nonfinancial eligibility such as citizenship requirements, there are both income and asset tests to meet before you are eligible for Medicaid. Let's start by taking a look at the income limits.

Income Limits of Medicaid

How much income are you allowed to keep and still qualify for Medicaid? The answer depends on two factors: what state you are a resident of, and whether or not you are married.

Let's start out with the simpler example of a single person. Keep in mind that when I use the word "single," this includes widows and widowers, as well as divorced people and people who are not legally married.

If you live in an income-cap state, you are not eligible for Medicaid if your income exceeds the cap limit in your state. The cap limit is $1,635 per month for 2002, and increases each year.

States that impose cap limits are:

Alabama	Alaska	Arizona
Arkansas	Colorado	Delaware
Florida	Idaho	Iowa
Louisiana	Mississippi	Nevada
New Mexico	Oklahoma	Oregon
South Carolina	South Dakota	Texas
Wyoming		

What if you live in an income-cap state, your monthly income is $3,000, and your long-term care costs $5,000 per month? Assume that you have no assets to supplement your income. Here's your dilemma: Your income is not high enough to pay for your long-term care, but it's too high to qualify for Medicaid in your state. What do you do?

The U.S. Supreme Court ruled that individuals in exactly that situation can qualify for Medicaid by using a special type of trust. This trust is called a Miller trust in honor of the person whose case was debated. It allows someone who otherwise qualifies for Medicaid to put excess income into the trust; they retain in their name only income below the state's cap amount. Upon their death, the full amount in the Miller trust is paid to the state, to help recover the cost of the long-term care that was provided.

Most states, however, are not cap states. In a noncap state, you generally qualify for Medicaid from an income point of view if your income is less than your cost of care.

By the way, don't think that the *personal-needs allowance* is revised upward every year. The amounts are set by each state on an ad hoc basis. Sometimes the amount of allowed personal needs allowance is actually cut from prior levels!

Marilee's Memo

The amount of money that someone on Medicaid is allowed to keep each month from his or her income is called the **personal-needs allowance.** It varies state to state, but is generally around $30 to $60 per month. All other income, with some exceptions (health insurance premiums and income paid to support a healthy spouse), must be paid to the nursing home. The nursing home then bills the state Medicaid program for the shortfall.

What If I'm Married?

If you are married and on Medicaid, the program has provisions to allow some of your income to be paid to support your spouse, if it's needed. Congress passed the Medicare Catastrophic Coverage Act (MCCA) so that healthy spouses still living in the community, called *community spouses,* would have enough to live. In this book, the phrase "healthy spouse" is sometimes used instead of "community spouse." In the past, if the household income was primarily in the name of the spouse needing nursing home care, the spouse at home was often impoverished. Restating the honorable intention of this act, this bill is often referred to as the "Spousal Anti-Impoverishment Act."

Marilee's Memo

A **community spouse** is the spouse who is not applying for Medicaid, and is still living in the community. Sometimes he or she is referred to as the "healthy spouse."

The amount of the nursing home spouse's (Medicaid recipient) income that a healthy spouse can keep to live on is called the Minimum Monthly Maintenance Needs Allowance, or MMMNA. To divert some or all the nursing home spouse's income to the community spouse, the healthy spouse applies by filling out a worksheet which lists the costs of supporting himself or herself. This worksheet takes into consideration shelter costs such as property-tax payments, heating oil, and insurance.

LTC Lowdown _____

If you are married, whose income does Medicaid look at to determine whether or not you qualify? Medicaid generally follows the "name on the check" rule. Any income in the name of the spouse receiving long-term care is taken into account to determine Medicaid eligibility. If your state follows the "name on the check" rule, Medicaid doesn't care about income in the other spouse's name in terms of Medicaid eligibility.

The minimum MMMNA that a spouse can keep is $1,493, and the maximum is $2,232 (figures are as of July 2002, increased annually). These amounts are set by the states, but the minimum amount must be at least 150 percent of the federal poverty level. Let's take a look at an example.

Mr. Jones is living in the nursing home. He worked hard his whole life, and his combined Social Security and pension is $4,000 per month. His wife never worked outside the home. Mr. Jones's state Medicaid Departments allows him to keep $50 a month (of the $4,000) as his personal-needs allowance. He can also pay his Medicare supplement premium of $250 per month. That leaves $3,700. His wife is entitled to keep $1,493 (the minimum of the MMMNA). If her living expenses are less than $1,493, she still gets to keep the MMMNA of $1,493. The rest of the $3,700, $2,207 per month ($3,700 minus $1,493), is paid to the nursing home. The amount paid to the nursing home is called the patient-paid amount. The nursing home is reimbursed by the state Medicaid office up to the Medicaid reimbursement rate.

What if Mrs. Jones needed $2,000 a month to maintain her household? She would fill out the worksheet Medicaid provided to justify keeping more than the MMMNA of $1,493. Since her requested amount is less than the maximum MMMNA, her request to keep $2,000 per month would be approved.

But what if Mrs. Jones needed $3,000 a month to live on? Because the maximum MMMNA is $2,232, to keep any more of her husband's income above $2,232, she would have to file an appeal with the Medicaid office. She may or may not win the appeal. It's important to keep in mind that Medicaid beneficiaries have the opportunity to appeal decisions about their case. This is another reason that you are well advised to seek out advice early in the process. Sometimes a lawyer will recognize a situation when you should appeal that would not be known to you. For example, someone with low income but assets above the standard allowable limits would often, upon appeal, be allowed to keep some assets that would otherwise have to be spent down.

LTC Lowdown _____

If a couple's income is very low and doesn't equal the minimum MMMNA (the amount any community spouse is allowed to keep), the healthy spouse would be entitled to keep all the income in the nursing home spouse's name. Otherwise, it would go to the nursing home. If the couple had good advice before exhausting their assets, they may have been able to keep more assets than the guidelines allow, in an effort to generate income to the minimum MMMNA level.

Medicaid and Assets

In most states, if you are single, in order to qualify for Medicaid you must have no more than $2,000 in countable assets. Some states have different maximum asset levels, from a low of $999 (Missouri) to a high of $4,000 (Rhode Island).

The rules are very different for married couples. The applicant spouse (the spouse in the nursing home) is allowed to keep the amount of countable assets that a single person can keep (usually $2,000). The community spouse is allowed to keep countable assets up to what is called the Community Spouse Resource Allowance of $89,280 (2002 figure, but it increases on January 1 each year). It's important to note that, although Medicaid looks at income based on whose name is on the check, there is no such rule for assets.

Medicaid considers assets in either spouse's name to be fair game for Medicaid *spend-down* purposes. Medicaid has an unlimited spousal obligation, which means that each spouse is obligated to exhaust assets, until the combined assets equal a maximum of about $90,000.

Marilee's Memo _____

To **spend down** means to liquidate and then spend the proceeds, preferably on your long-term care, until you are down to the qualifying asset levels for Medicaid. Assets held in either spouse's name are subject to spending down. Medicaid makes no exception for assets which have surrender penalties, early-withdrawal penalties, or substantial capital gains taxes or income tax bills or penalties, such as highly appreciated assets, 401(k)s, or IRAs.

When you apply for Medicaid, you need to recreate financially the day the spouse entered the nursing home. This is called your snapshot day. In most states, the community spouse is allowed to keep 50 percent of their combined assets on snapshot day, to a maximum of $89,280 (2002 number). Keep in mind that this snapshot day does not necessarily have anything to do with the day you apply for Medicaid. Your snapshot day may be tomorrow, and you may not apply for Medicaid for many months or even years.

Seek advice before your snapshot day. Sometimes it makes sense to do things such as paying off a mortgage with cash, so that the cash does not have to spent down. You will also want to have good financial records of that day. It can be burdensome to recreate your financial situation on snapshot day, down the road, when you are applying for Medicaid.

In some states, Medicaid allows the community spouse to keep 100 percent of combined countable assets, to a maximum of $89,280. A small number of states have their own floors—amounts that the community spouse can keep as a minimum. For example, a state may allow the community spouse to keep a minimum of $25,000 of countable assets, if the couple has that much. No matter what your state's formula, the maximum amount of countable assets that the community spouse can keep is always the federal figure of $89,280 (as of 2002).

Let's look at the example of a couple with $102,000 in countable assets. The nursing home spouse can keep $2,000. In a state where the community spouse can keep 50 percent of the remaining $100,000, she keeps $50,000 (because this is less than $89,280). If she lives in a state that allows her to keep 100 percent up to $89,280, she would not have to spend down $50,000, but would have to spend down, or liquidate, only $10,720 in countable assets. This would allow her to keep $89,280.

By the way, the federal government sets the Community Spouse Resource Allowance each year. It is a standard number for the whole country. There is no variation based on regional costs of living.

Wisdom of the Aged

People often ask, why is a single person only allowed to keep $2,000 in most states, and a married couple can keep over $90,000? There's an important reason for this apparent discrimination against single people. Imagine for a moment the 65-year-old woman whose 70-year-old husband is in a nursing home on Medicaid. This woman may live another 20 to 30 years, and the spousal allowance is her only nest egg (besides the house, which may have a Medicaid lien on it). Congress passed the bill creating the Community Spouse Resource Allowance so that healthy spouses weren't left impoverished when their spouse needed long-term care.

What Doesn't Count

Countable assets are assets that count in terms of qualifying for Medicaid. *Noncountable assets*, sometimes called excludable assets, do not count. Owning noncountable assets will not affect your Medicaid eligibility.

By far the biggest noncountable asset that most of us own is our house, or primary residence. Our house is not countable in any state. Examples of assets considered noncountable in most states include …

- ◆ A primary residence, of any value.

- ◆ Burial plot, for the applicant and family members.

- ◆ A prepaid irrevocable funeral and burial contract.

- ◆ Income-producing assets, such as a business (the income may count on the income side).

- ◆ A life insurance contract with a death benefit of $1,500 or less.

- ◆ Automobile (value may be subject to a limit, unless the applicant or a family member can establish a need to own a car).

- ◆ Household items and personal belongings, such as furniture and jewelry.

What Does Count

Assets that count against the Medicaid limits include almost everything else that you can think of. Here's a partial list:

- ◆ Stocks, bonds, and mutual funds

- ◆ Bank accounts, including certificates of deposit

- ◆ Jointly titled assets (the applicant is deemed in some cases to be the sole owner, unless it can be proved otherwise)

- ◆ Vacation homes or second homes (rental properties may be noncountable)

- ◆ 401(k)s, IRAs, or other qualified plans

- ◆ Assets in either spouse's name that are not noncountable and can be liquidated, even at a horrible loss

- ◆ Assets held in any revocable trust (such as a living trust, for example)

- ◆ An annuity which is still in the form of a lump sum (it has not been turned into a stream of income yet)

> **CAUTION**
>
> **Truth & Consequences** _____
>
> Just because an asset is noncountable, don't think that Medicaid doesn't care about it at all. Noncountable means its value is not included in when determining whether or not you qualify for Medicaid. Once you are on Medicaid, however, there may be a lien placed against the noncountable asset. This lien makes it easier for the state to do estate recovery after you've died. Your home or primary residence is the perfect example of a noncountable asset that is often subject to estate recovery.

The Income-First Rule

If the community spouse's income is less than her MMMNA, the income-first rule says that some states require her to look to her husband's income to make up the shortfall. The alternative has been to apply to Medicaid for the ability to keep assets above the spousal resource allowance, to generate more income.

When the state Medicaid office authorizes an increase in the spousal resource allowance to generate income, the nursing home spouse's income would all go to the nursing home, and the community spouse would have more assets to keep forever. Once the nursing home spouse passes away, the community spouse benefits from having assets above the typical required limit of about $90,000.

As of the time this book was written, there is a trend for states to require income be used first before a couple can ask for additional assets to provide income. This means that couples with low-income community spouses will be less able to shelter assets for the healthy spouse from the ravages of Medicaid's spend-down.

The Look-Back Penalty

When you apply for Medicaid, the forms ask you to list any transfers or gifts that you have made to an individual (like a son or a daughter) in the last 36 months, or three years. Any funding of a trust is requested going back 60 months, or five years. If a transfer is discovered during these *look-back periods* (how long the government looks back), the market value of your transfer is divided by the average cost of care in your region or state, according to Medicaid, to determine your number of months of ineligibility for Medicaid.

So, for example, if four years ago you gave away $500,000 to one of your children, and Medicaid says the cost of care in your state is $5,000 per month, you would be ineligible for Medicaid for 100 months, or more than eight years, if you applied for

Medicaid within 36 months of the date you gave the money away. If, instead, you had waited 37 months to apply, you would not have to disclose the transfer, and the transfer would not trigger any period of ineligibility. There's more about the look-back periods in the next two chapters.

By now, you should have an appreciation of the complexities of Medicaid, and the benefits of working with someone who is up-to-date on your state's situation. Keep reading to find out how to choose the right legal advisor.

How to Find a Qualified Elder Law Attorney

Finding a qualified *elder law attorney* is not as easy as finding other kinds of attorneys. You may rely on a friend or your real estate agent to recommend a real estate lawyer. But if your friend hasn't been through a Medicaid–funded long-term care experience, it's not likely he or she will be of help. State bar associations can be of some value, but be aware that sometimes they do not recognize elder law as a separate specialty. Instead of sending you a list of elder law attorneys, they may instead send you a list of estate-planning attorneys.

Marilee's Memo

An **elder law attorney** is a lawyer who specializes in legal matters for seniors, and is usually an expert in applying for Medicaid and in Medicaid planning. Some elder law attorneys also do planning for disabled children and adults. They may practice in other areas such as Social Security, Medicare, and even age-discrimination lawsuits.

My favorite resource is the National Academy of Elder Law Attorneys, or NAELA. It maintains a website that allows you to search for an NAELA member by your state or even your ZIP code. NAELA is the nationwide professional association of lawyers who specialize in elder law. It's like what the American Medical Association is to doctors, or the American Library Association is to librarians. Check Appendix E for their contact information, as well as other useful sources.

The one question that I always ask if someone is an elder law attorney is this: Are you a member of NAELA? Since that is the professional industry organization for elder law attorneys, I figure that if he or she doesn't belong to the organization, it's unlikely that elder law is a big part of the business.

Does a membership in NAELA prove competence? Absolutely not! But it's a first question, and a great screen to separate the serious elder law lawyers from those who only occasionally practice this specialty.

Wisdom of the Aged

If a consumer hires a lawyer who describes his or her practice of law as a specialty (such as elder law), the consumer has more protection than if the same kind of advice came from a general practitioner. If the consumer feels that he or she was given bad advice, and sues the lawyer for malpractice, in the court proceedings the specialist lawyer is held to a higher standard.

A general practitioner is held to the following standard: Given the level of knowledge that a general practitioner would have about Medicaid, did he or she do something wrong?

Those who describe themselves as elder law attorneys (in their advertising or their business card, for example) are held accountable for knowing more than a general practitioner. A specialist could be found guilty to malpractice when, under the same set of facts, a general practitioner might not be.

Other sources of elder law attorneys include the same list of people that you ask for information about long-term care services and resources in your area:

◆ The director of your local Council on Aging

◆ The discharge planner or social worker at your hospital

◆ Local support groups (like those sponsored by the Alzheimer's Association)

Be sure to tell them that you are looking for referral to a Medicaid elder law attorney, not just to any attorney.

Here are some other trusted sources for information or recommendations concerning an elder law attorney:

◆ Your doctor

◆ Your insurance agent or financial advisor

◆ Your (general practice) lawyer

◆ Your tax preparer or accountant

 LTC Lowdown

Some lawyers hold seminars to attract new clients. These can be a nice, low-pressure way to check out a potential lawyer. Come ready to ask a question, and see how they do. Keep in mind that a professional will not want to answer a personal, specific legal question in a seminar room filled with people.

When choosing a lawyer, you may want to check their reputation with others, such as the people listed above. You may also ask for a biography listing the professional accomplishments of the person, and/or a list of clients who have agreed to be listed as referral sources.

Once you have a list of elder law attorneys, you need to decide who to work with. I recommend that you interview each candidate until you find a good match. Request a 10- to 15-minute in-person consultation, and ask when you make the appointment what the charge will be. Most attorneys will give you this initial consultation free of charge. It is up to you to decide whether or not to pay if an attorney does not give free consultation.

Some attorneys are so busy that they do not have to look for new business, and don't meet for free. Whether the consultation is free or not, the initial meeting to determine whether you want to work together should not take any more than 20 minutes. Here's some questions that you may want to ask:

- *Where did you go to law school?*

- *What is the profile of a typical client served by your firm?*

   The closer it matches your situation, the better.

- *How do you charge for your services?*

   Make sure that you absolutely understand the answer.

- *What do you think my case will cost in total?*

   They will ask you questions before they can answer this question, and may answer with a dollar figure range.

- If you are seeking help about an immediate need to qualify for Medicaid, ask: *How many Medicaid applications do you handle each month?*

   The more, the better.

- If you are healthy today, ask: *Is there any Medicaid planning that you can do for me that will guarantee that when I need long-term care, I will qualify for Medicaid?*

   This answer should be, "No—no one can guarantee, because the regulations can change."

- *Why do people pick you instead of other attorneys?*

   Here you will learn his or her perceived strengths, and also it's a great question to test your basic compatibility and ability to work together well. Two alternate questions would be: How long have you been practicing elder law? How did you decide to get into this area of law?

- *Will you explain to me the pluses and minuses of any strategy that you recommend?*

   If you sense the answer is no, run!

Does it matter if you choose a lawyer from a referral or from the NAELA's list of names? Not really. Just like a single person looking for a spouse, some couples meet at concerts and others are fixed up by friends. Overall, you should feel good about your attorney. If you feel unnecessarily rushed or intimidated; keep looking.

That said, these are busy professionals, and often the better they are, the less time they have! I guess you should be suspect of any professional who has all the time in the world! Remember, you are trading your money for the lawyer's knowledge, experience, and perspective. You don't have to be best buddies, but you have every right to feel appreciated and valued as a client. Report improper or insulting behavior formally to the bar association; it's the only way to protect others from the same situation!

The Least You Need to Know

- Medicaid is a joint federal and state government program for the poor. There are both income and asset tests to qualify for Medicaid.

- Medicaid planning is the legal practice of rearranging your finances so that the program pays for your nursing home care.

- Medicaid does a great job of paying for nursing homes. In most areas, Medicaid does not pay for home care or assisted living facility care.

- In order to qualify for Medicaid, any countable assets, in either spouse's name, in excess of the allowable limit must be liquidated, or spent down.

- If you apply to Medicaid after giving away money or funding a trust, but before the applicable look-back period has expired, you trigger a period of Medicaid ineligibility; the duration depends on the amount transferred and the Medicaid cost of care.

- Hire a specialist in Medicaid planning, an elder law attorney, if you are considering Medicaid planning or are ready to apply for Medicaid.

Chapter 22

When Medicaid Planning Makes Sense

In This Chapter

♦ Why people may or may not consider Medicaid planning

♦ Medicaid and nursing homes

♦ Class warfare and long-term care planning

♦ The HIPAA Act and the future of Medicaid

There was a time in the 1980s when animal-rights activists were extremely brazen in their effort to stop people from wearing fur coats. Do you remember? They simply walked up to the offending fur wearer, brought out a spray paint can, and marked the fur with the paint. The painting was destructive and ugly—and illegal. Buying and wearing a fur coat was perfectly legal. Still is, to the best of my knowledge!

When I speak to groups about Medicaid planning, sometimes I feel like the person in the fur coat. You see, there are few topics that engage (or should I say enrage?) people as emotionally as Medicaid planning.

Medicaid is one of the largest payers of long-term care in this country, but it doesn't pay a cent for your care unless you meet the Medicaid definition of poor. But there are certain allowable transfers, legal moves, and financial moves that allow someone to meet the Medicaid definition of poor while sheltering thousands of dollars, even millions of dollars, for the use of their healthy spouse or their heirs. And that's where the controversy comes in.

What's the story? Read on.

Who Should Consider Medicaid Planning?

Before I answer the question above, let me make it clear that if you are considering Medicaid planning, please make sure that you go on to read every chapter in this section. It's especially crucial that you know the importance of seeking qualified help in your own state, where the regulations may differ from the standard regulations described in this book.

In my opinion, there are a few situations where you would be well advised to consider Medicaid planning. By the way, if you are already poor, there is no need to do Medicaid planning. You will qualify for Medicaid quickly (read about Medicaid eligibility in Chapter 21).

When I talk about Medicaid planning, I am talking about people making financial and perhaps legal moves in order to qualify for Medicaid, when they otherwise would have too much money to qualify. In order to make an informed decision about whether or not to do Medicaid planning, you need to know the pluses and minuses. The tremendous upside of Medicaid planning is it allows you to preserve assets. The downside is that it's a welfare program, and once you are on Medicaid you do not have as much control over your assets or where you receive that care.

In the following three situations, I am assuming that preserving assets is more important to the person considering Medicaid planning than preserving their choice of care. I am also assuming that he or she doesn't mind being on a public-assistance program. (For more information on problems with Medicaid planning, please refer to Chapter 24.)

Medicaid planning makes sense, if your desire to preserve assets is very strong, and ...

- You are already receiving care in a Medicaid-approved nursing home.

- Your health is compromised, you cannot purchase long-term care insurance, and your finances (income, home, savings, and life insurance) are not enough to pay for long-term care.

- You have low to moderate income and assets, meaning that you cannot afford to pay for long-term care from your finances, and you cannot afford long-term care insurance (at an average premium of about $1,700 a year).

With any of these situations, it's important that you understand that Medicaid is a public assistance program that lawmakers can change at any time. Because the current program favors care in nursing homes, you may be limiting the choice of where you'll receive your care.

As soon as you or a loved one is aware that long-term care will be needed, and you are not sure how to pay for the care, it is smart to seek out a qualified elder law attorney immediately. Putting a strategy in place as soon as possible will give you peace of mind. Many people wait too long to apply, and spend assets that otherwise could've been legally preserved.

Does Medicaid Always Equal Nursing Home?

We live in a time when the government is proposing major changes in Social Security, Medicare, and Medicaid. I think it's important that we realize that the Medicaid program for funding long-term care 10 years from now is likely to be a very different program than the one we have today.

While there have been moves in many states to broaden the services covered (especially community-based services and assisted living facilities), knowledgeable observers question whether this kind of reform is sustainable. Considering the aging population and taxpayers' aversion to broad-based tax increases, a broadening of Medicaid services is not in the cards in most states.

Since home-based services and assisted living facilities often cost much less than nursing home care, families wonder why these services aren't uniformly covered nationwide. The answer is easy. It's based on something called the "woodwork effect."

Most people do not want to go to a nursing home, and they will spend their own money and rely on family caregivers until the point that there is not choice but to enter the nursing home. This aversion to nursing home care has been described by many as the government's ultimate cost-containment method!

If more attractive options, such as home health care and assisted living facilities, were routinely covered by Medicaid, people would rush to Medicaid. They would enter the program earlier and stay longer. This would result in an overall increase in spending. So you see, even though community-based care is less expensive on a case-by-case basis, overall spending would rise if these services were uniformly covered. Many

LTC Lowdown

The vast majority of Medicaid long-term care funding is for skilled-nursing facility (nursing home) care. Although there are some community-based programs, these programs are not available in many states.

people would argue that this would be money well spent. The reality is that Medicaid has been struggling to contain the cost of providing long-term care for many years, and an expansion of services seems unlikely.

The Future of Medicaid Nursing Homes

As it stands now, many states are routinely paying nursing homes less than their actual cost to take care of a Medicaid patient. As a result, in 2001, about half of the nursing homes in Massachusetts were losing money, and about 20 percent were bankrupt. Massachusetts is not alone in this problem. Numbers like this aren't sustainable over the long run.

Stories of abuse and inspection deficiencies are rampant. It's the predictable outcome of nursing homes housing older, sicker patients, and not being able to pay competitive wages for high-stress jobs that are physically and emotionally demanding.

More nursing homes will be bankrupted because they will lose lawsuits brought on by family members of residents who received substandard care. There are already reports that some nursing homes are not able to afford the skyrocketing premium of liability insurance.

LTC Lowdown

The nursing home industry in this country is in crisis, as evidenced by the bankruptcy of some prominent national nursing home chains. Nursing homes can't afford to recruit, train, and keep quality employees when they are financially on the ropes.

Nursing home operators are stuck. They are not being paid enough by Medicaid to provide the level of care they would like, and we would like. Such a small percentage of their residents are private pay that they cannot possibly make up the difference by charging even higher rates to their private payers. Most people entering a nursing home are already on Medicaid.

Medicaid and Nursing Home Residents

The pay for a nurse's aide in a nursing home is notoriously low. With finances the way they are, the nursing homes can't pay more! Imagine if you were offered a job at $9 an hour, with no health insurance coverage, to dress, bathe, and change the diapers of your neighbor's 80-year-old parent. This is a typical nurse's aide position.

With some notable exceptions, this is the job that the person with no choice takes, usually temporarily. The special people who enjoy this work find that they can't afford to stay. They do the work of angels in one of the most demanding worksites on Earth.

There is a tremendous shortage of workers to attend to the personal needs of nursing home residents. America's nursing homes are in crisis, and I'm afraid things are likely to get worse before they get better.

Wisdom of the Aged

In most states, newspapers explain Medicaid spending increases in the context of providing health care to poor adults and children. The reality is that the Medicaid funding for health insurance is a much smaller number than the amount that is paid for the long-term care needs of the elderly. As our population ages and life spans increase, it's only common sense that additional tax dollars will be needed to support Medicaid.

Meanwhile, I believe that more and more nursing home operators will do what a small number have done so far: Just say no. What I mean by that is these nursing homes have gone cold turkey off Medicaid, and are exclusively private pay. There have always been a certain number of exclusive private-pay facilities at the very high end of nursing homes. You could call them the "Ritz Carltons" of nursing homes. But now, we are seeing facilities geared toward middle-class and upper-middle-class families embracing private pay.

Here's the surprise: These facilities are often described as the most desirable in their area (they'd have to be—otherwise why would you pay with your own money?), *and* their prices are *much less* than nursing homes that accept Medicaid. They can make a bigger profit charging less for private-pay residents, since those private payers are not subsidizing Medicaid residents.

I believe that we are seeing the beginnings of a revolution in nursing home care. My prediction is that, over the next 10 to 20 years, there will be two kinds of nursing homes. Private-pay nursing homes will be open for business to serve residents with the ability to private pay with cash or insurance. Public facilities will accept Medicaid.

Truth & Consequences

Twenty years ago, if you needed long-term care, you had few choices: were either able to stay in your own home or you went to a nursing home or rest home. But today, private-pay residents have more attractive options, such as assisted living facilities and private home care.

My crystal ball tells me that this trend will continue, leaving the private-pay person with many more attractive options than the Medicaid recipient.

Medicaid-planning attorneys report that more and more clients want the ability to choose private-pay options, and many elder law attorneys are now recommending long-term care insurance as the preferred method of funding care.

My personal hope is that people who have the ability to private pay for their care, either out of pocket or through long-term care insurance, do so. That'd reduce the burden on all taxpayers and bring money into the long-term care industry, giving all care recipients a higher quality product. Otherwise, in my opinion, we're headed to a two-tier system.

I've included all this commentary because we can be fairly certain that if you are healthy today, the Medicaid system and its choices will be very different by the time you are ready to collect. Decisions that you make today about how to fund your long-term care in the future cannot be made by looking at dollars and cents only.

What's Your Medicaid Time Horizon?

Since most of the people reading this book will not be needing long-term care for many years, it's important to try to get our arms around how Medicaid will work in the future. It's also important to look at this topic from both a qualification and a services-offered point of view. When you plan on Medicaid to pay your future long-term care costs, you should consider not only how Medicaid works now, but how it may work when you need care.

 **LTC Lowdown**

If your need for long-term care is just around the corner (or you already are receiving care), don't be worried about future trends in Medicaid eligibility. You can find out very quickly what can be done in your situation to preserve assets, and what being on Medicaid would mean to your care choices. But if you're healthy today, it's important to look at the history of Medicaid to try and guess what the future holds.

What if you're a disabled 65-year-old with a solid pension and half a million dollars in the bank, but you just don't want to use your own money to pay for long-term care? Should you consider giving everything away so that you can have the government (Medicaid) pay for your care?

The decision to do Medicaid planning sounds very selfish to many people. There's no doubt that in some cases the motive is selfishness. But let's look at it another way.

No one faults the taxpayer who invests in a tax-favored financial product for selfish reasons. I believe that if we as a society cannot afford to have people do Medicaid planning, then the loopholes should be closed. Period.

But when we close those loopholes we send a message. The message is this: If you need long-term care and you're not rich, paying for this care will likely make you poor. Therefore, you must buy long-term care insurance the same way that you must buy homeowners insurance to protect yourself financially against fire, theft, and other risks.

By closing the loopholes, Congress would send an obvious message. Although the tax deduction that went into effect in 1997 for long-term care insurance (explained in Chapter 12) was a strong hint that there was not going to be a meaningful new program to provide for long-term care, people haven't rushed to buy the insurance. A big part of the reason, I think, is that with 70 percent of nursing home occupants' bills paid by Medicaid, people know they can get onto that system. They may have seen their parents, grandparents, and neighbors get onto Medicaid.

Closing the Medicaid loopholes is a tough-love kind of message that I'm not sure our country is ready for. I saw well-respected attorney Alexander A. Bove Jr. speak many years ago at a local AARP meeting in downtown Boston. He described a glaring problem that exists to this day for seniors. Although they have great coverage through Medicare for acute situations such as heart attacks and hip replacements, Bove described how they were out of luck if they got the "wrong illness," something like Alzheimer's disease or severe rheumatoid arthritis. (Remember, Medicare is the health insurance most retirees have, and Medicaid has a benefit to pay for long-term care for the poor.)

Bove went on to explain how Medicare would pay tens of thousands of dollars on up for surgeons and hospitals and such, but the senior who needed help bathing and dressing because he or she had the "wrong illness" would have to spend most of his or her life savings before the Medicaid program would help.

It's hard to think of the Medicare beneficiary who needs two new hips after quadruple-bypass heart surgery as lucky while the Alzheimer's patient is out of luck, but, financially, it's true. Our health-care system discriminates against people whose care needs are custodial. They often need just a few hours a day of personal care, not the latest whiz-bang medical device.

People who confront the reality of needing years of custodial care can find it very easy to justify doing Medicaid planning when they see that their neighbor's medical bills are being paid by Medicare, while they write personal checks for tens of thousands of dollars and up. Who are we to blame them?

Josepha the Seamstress's Story

In some circles, there is a stigma to being on Medicaid. In this chapter we discuss in more detail the topic of morality as it relates to Medicaid planning.

My grandmother had a real aversion to welfare, or what she called "charity." My grandmother, who I called Nanny, died at age 99 after spending 10 years in a nursing home. Over the course of those 10 years, she spent her whole life savings and qualified for Medicaid. Her daughters managed her checkbook and completed the Medicaid application when her money ran out; they didn't tell her.

Every once in a while, Nanny would ask, "Am I still paying my way or am I on charity?" To minimize her distress, her daughters would assure her that she was still private paying. The reality was this: Her money was long gone. One day, after getting the usual reassurances from her daughters, Nanny insisted, "Show me the bank statement!"

Nanny knew that she must be out of money, and that's when they finally had to tell her she was on Medicaid. It meant a lot to Nanny to be private pay. No matter what we said, going onto Medicaid in her mind meant that she had outlived her usefulness and that she was a burden.

In my mind, Nanny was exactly who the Medicaid long-term care benefit was designed for: an old person who needed care and had outlived his or her resources. Medicaid is the ultimate safety net.

Medicaid Shatters Seniors' Security and Dignity

Is it right that someone who worked hard her whole life can see the fruits of this labor disappear because of an extended need for long-term care? The Medicaid spend-down process breaks the spirit of our seniors. One woman, whose mother had Alzheimer's disease, explains how her mother was obsessed even before the disease with never being a burden. "She had all everything in place, from a durable power of attorney, to the will, to the health-care proxy. She had planned for problems," the daughter says. Using her mom's life savings to pay for nursing home care, the daughter said that she "used to do the math constantly. I really believed that Mom's money would run out." Her mom had enough funds to pay for eight years of nursing home care, and died before her money ran out.

The Future of Medicaid Reimbursements

How does the federal government view Medicaid? A review of recent history can clearly see the direction that Medicaid qualification is taking.

The 1993 Omnibus Budget Reconciliation Act (OBRA) made sweeping changes to Medicaid. Guess what direction the reforms went towards? That's right, OBRA made it tougher and less palatable to do Medicaid planning. It's important to highlight these changes, since many families have gone through the Medicaid qualification process before 1993, and they may be under the mistaken impression that these rules remain unchanged. A few highlights are listed below. You must check with your state's Medicaid office or a qualified elder law attorney to see how these changes affect Medicaid eligibility in your state:

♦ OBRA '93 extended the look-back periods from 30 months to 36 months for transfers to an individual, and 60 months for transfers involving a trust. Among other consequences, this change extends the private-pay period for those who want to do last-minute asset transfers and Medicaid planning.

♦ OBRA '93 shot down the ability of someone on Medicaid to maintain eligibility by disclaiming (refusing) any inherited money that might come his or her way. The change means that now, even if a disclaimer is made, the Medicaid program considers that the assets were received and then given away, with the result that the person has made a "disqualifying transfer," and so temporarily can't qualify for Medicaid.

Wisdom of the Aged

Let's imagine that your spouse goes into the nursing home, and he qualifies for Medicaid. Later, you purchase a lottery ticket that's a big winner. Guess what? Even though your assets were combined for the purposes of qualifying for Medicaid, once the application is approved, your individual assets aren't looked at again. However, if it was your spouse who won the lottery, the winnings could knock him off Medicaid.

If this happens, I'm hoping your first call is not to your state lottery office, but to a qualified Medicaid attorney. He or she will help you with questions such as: Should I take the lump sum or multiyear payout, and what will be the effect to my spouse on Medicaid? Only an elder law attorney is qualified to both represent your best interests and interpret how your state's Medicaid program will treat your good news!

♦ OBRA '93 obligates states to do aggressive estate *recovery*. Recovery is a process by which the government tries to recover costs paid for your care when you pass away after having been on Medicaid. States have traditionally only pursued recovery with a lien on the primary residence, or perhaps going after the part of the estate which goes through probate. OBRA '93 gave each state the ability to extend the definition of estate to include all assets, even those which do not go through probate. Examples would be property held jointly and life estates, to the extent of the Medicaid recipient's interest at death.

- On the plus side, OBRA '93 made provisions to allow parents to establish trusts for the benefit of disabled children, and not delay Medicaid eligibility.

- Another important aspect of OBRA '93 is that it allows people who transferred assets (starting a period of Medicaid disqualification) to cure the transfer by taking it back. This can be a lifesaver for those who make a mistake or got bad advice, and cut themselves off from Medicaid without other funds to pay for care. Prior to OBRA '93, those people were generally out of luck.

The 1996 HIPAA Act

The Health Insurance Portability and Accountability Act (HIPAA), sponsored by senators Kennedy and Kassenbaum, was signed into law August 21, 1996. It included broad new protections for those covered by employer-sponsored health insurance, tried to eliminate Medicaid planning by making it illegal to do transfers to qualify for Medicaid, and imposed a gag rule on attorneys and others who made a living giving this kind of advice. HIPAA also had many items pertaining to long-term care insurance.

Effective January 1, 1997, HIPAA mandated criteria for a new class of long-term care insurance (called tax-qualified). It also included the first tax deduction for long-term care insurance. These aspects of long-term care insurance are discussed in Chapter 12.

You may have heard about the "Granny Goes to Jail" law. This was a part of HIPAA. This law made it illegal for someone to transfer assets to qualify for Medicaid. It also made it illegal for someone (like a lawyer) to charge a fee to instruct someone how to transfer assets to qualify for Medicaid.

The public outcry was tremendous. The law was changed in the Balanced Budget Act of 1997 so that people who transferred assets to get onto Medicaid could not be criminally charged. However, the provision which makes it illegal to advise someone how to make lawful transfers to qualify for Medicaid is still on the books.

On March 11, 1998, Attorney General Janet Reno told Congress that the Department of Justice would not enforce HIPAA's criminal provisions. In the case of the New York State Bar Association versus Janet Reno (N.D.N.Y. No. 97-CV-1760, April 7, 1998), a chief judge of the U.S. District court issued a preliminary injunction, citing the "chilling effect that unconstitutional burdens on free speech may occasion." Although the law as it stands now is widely considered unconstitutional, it's still the law. Any lawyer or other advisor practicing Medicaid planning in an area not under the jurisdiction of the District Court for the northern district of New York has no assurance he or she will not be prosecuted.

Tougher measures have been proposed but have not passed, including legislation to dramatically extend the look-back period. Most observers expect that future legislative action will make it tougher for people to accomplish Medicaid planning.

The Least You Need to Know

- ◆ With a number of changes since the 1980s, Congress has toughened up existing rules and broadened penalties to make Medicaid planning less desirable.

- ◆ OBRA '93 extended the look-back periods from 30 months to 36 months for transfers to an individual, and 60 months for transfers involving a trust.

- ◆ There are certain allowable transfers and purchases, legal and financial moves that allow someone to meet the Medicaid definition of poor while sheltering thousands, even millions, of dollars for the use of their healthy spouse or their heirs.

- ◆ You should consider Medicaid planning if your desire to preserve assets is very strong and you are already receiving care in a Medicaid-approved nursing home, or your need for care is imminent.

- ◆ If you have low to moderate income and assets and you cannot afford long-term care insurance, then you may want to consider Medicaid planning.

- ◆ It's important that people who plan to rely on Medicaid understand that it is a public assistance program, and as such its benefits and availability depends on the current political climate.

Chapter 23

Medicaid-Planning Techniques

In This Chapter

- Why you may want to give up your money
- The Medicaid-and-LTC-combo platter
- How to have your Medi-*cake* and eat it, too
- The assets that became income
- How to save the house

Long ago, in a galaxy far, far away … or was it four score and seven years ago … wait a minute, Medicaid's only been around since 1965! Before the regulations changed, Medicaid planning was a heck of a lot easier.

We could go to a lawyer and establish a trust that let us invade *principal* and name trustees, but—*poof!*—once one of us was in a nursing home, the trust would morph into the kind of trust that allowed us to qualify for Medicaid. Those trusts don't work anymore.

Or, we could put hundreds of thousands of dollars into a trust, and only have to wait two years and one day to apply for Medicaid, not the five years and one day now required.

In this chapter, I look at the most popular Medicaid-planning techniques. The goal of Medicaid planning is to have the applicant's assets and income be below the allowable limits (read Chapter 21 for an introduction to Medicaid). Remember, most states still allow these Medicaid-planning techniques, but some don't. Don't do Medicaid planning without consulting with a qualified advisor. The stakes are too high for errors.

Medicaid and Timing

Before 1993, the maximum look-back and penalty period for transfers to anyone, or any trust, was only 30 months, or two and a half years. Now, some look-backs are as long as five years, and citizens lacking Medicaid savvy can find themselves with penalty periods that may last longer than they do!

 Marilee's Memo

Principal is the value of an asset. Normally, an asset such as cash or a marketable security would earn income, in the form of interest or dividends. If the income were taken out, the principal would remain unchanged. If the income were reinvested, the amount would increase the principal. Many people like to live off the interest from their life savings, and hope to pass along the principal to their heirs.

If you were to compare the modern Medicaid planner to a dentist, his number of instruments is shrinking and his painkiller is gone. His patients have fewer options, and the penalty for a wrong move is very painful.

In Chapter 22, I mentioned that there are certain allowable transfers, legal moves, and financial moves that allow someone to qualify for Medicaid while sheltering assets. I hope that you'll consult with a qualified elder law attorney before you make any decisions. Not all these techniques work in every state. Let's take a look at some of the most popular Medicaid-planning techniques.

Giving Away Your Money

In an earlier chapter, I mentioned that the federal Medicaid program requires that individuals be eligible for the program financially. This means that a person must be poor from both an asset and an income point of view. The Medicaid-planning techniques described here allow assets that would otherwise have to be spent down by the person needing long-term care to instead be preserved for someone else, such as the healthy spouse.

In order to be approved for Medicaid, the applicant has to be down to only about $2,000 in countable assets. If married, the spouse of the applicant is allowed to keep $89,280 (2002 figure) in countable assets (some states allow the spouse to keep only half of total countable assets, or $89,280, whichever is less). But what if, well before applying for Medicaid, the assets have been given away, or gifted? What happens then?

Have you ever heard the phrase "can't get blood from a stone"? If the applicable look-back period has expired and the Medicaid applicant, or his spouse, do not own the asset, it can't be used to deny Medicaid approval.

Here's a list of the top seven mistakes people make with Medicaid (courtesy of Harry Margolis, elder law attorney and founder of Elderlawanswers.com):

1. Thinking it's too late to plan. It's almost never too late to take planning steps, even after a senior has moved to a nursing home.

2. Giving away assets too early.

3. Putting your security at risk by putting it in the hands of your children. Make sure you take care of yourself first. Precipitous transfers can cause difficult tax and Medicaid problems as well.

4. Ignoring ample protections in the law for the spouse of a nursing home resident, and safe harbors for transfers to other family members.

5. Applying for Medicaid too early.

6. Applying for Medicaid too late.

7. Not getting expert help.

Here Ya Go: Gifting to a Person

Why not just give away your assets to the person you were planning to leave them to after you died? Giving away, or gifting, assets before you apply for Medicaid can be an effective strategy. It allows you to make sure that assets are left to a person or an institution such as a charity, even if you require long-term care and end up on Medicaid.

After all, if you leave someone money in your will and you end up needing Medicaid to pay for your long-term care, the money you wanted to leave to your friend or relative won't be there. It would need to be spent down before you could qualify for Medicaid.

When you give away an asset to someone besides your spouse, the transfer is subject to the scrutiny of the 36-month look-back period. There are some important exceptions to the transfer penalty. For example, you can give anything to a permanently and totally disabled child, a blind child, or into trust for the sole benefit of any disabled person under age 65.

Let's return to the situation where you are giving away an asset to someone besides your spouse. If the market value of the asset you are giving away is substantial, you may have to plan on private paying for your care to get past the look-back period. Here, by substantial I mean equal to 36 multiplied by the number that Medicaid in your state uses as the average cost of monthly care.

What if you are giving away a more modest amount? Let's say the average cost of care in your state is $4,000 per month, according to Medicaid. You are a single person with $42,000 in countable assets. You give $40,000 to your sister. Because this is a transfer to an individual, it triggers a 36-month look-back period. Do you need to wait 37 months before you apply for Medicaid? Absolutely not!

If you move to the nursing home 12 months after giving away the $40,000, and apply for Medicaid immediately, Medicaid will tell you that the transfer means you are not eligible for Medicaid for 10 months from the date of transfer. This is because the gift ($40,000) divided by the cost of care per month ($4,000), is ten. The period of ineligibility starts the day that you made the transfer, not the day you apply for Medicaid. In this example, since you make the transfer 11 months ago, you have already satisfied the ineligibility period, and are approved for Medicaid benefit immediately.

It's usually only necessary to wait 37 months to apply for Medicaid if the amount that you have transferred is worth more than 36 times the Medicaid monthly cost of care number.

Truth & Consequences _____

When you transfer an asset, be aware that any penalty period of ineligibility for Medicaid starts on the day you did the transfer, *not* the date that you apply for Medicaid. Also, if you give away a small amount, your penalty period may be less than the 36- or 50-month look-back periods. Seek expert help to make sure that you apply for Medicaid at the right time. Applying either too early or too late could be a very costly mistake!

The downsides of this strategy, as well as others, are discussed in Chapter 24. Consider these downsides as you contemplate how much to give away, and whether to use a trust or an outright gift.

Examples of Gifting

Let's take the example of Mr. and Mrs. Lane, a married couple in their 70s. They both have health problems, and believe that it's likely they will eventually need long-term care. They have $500,000 in the stock market that they are hoping to leave their children. Meanwhile, their income is enough for them to live comfortably in the house that they own.

Like many retirees, their income is enough for them to live comfortably, but not enough for them to pay for long-term care without dipping into their life savings. If they wanted to make sure that the stock was not used up by long-term care costs, they could give away the stock (worth $500,000) to whomever they'd like. As long as neither one of them applies for Medicaid during the look-back period (which is now three years for transfers to individuals, five years for transfers to trust), the fact that they gave away stock with a value of $500,000 will have no effect on their ability to have Medicaid pay for their long-term care.

Wisdom of the Aged

If you give away an asset and apply for Medicaid within the look-back periods, you're penalized for the transfer. In figuring the penalty, Medicaid uses the value of the asset on transfer day. Let's say you bought a vacation house 40 years ago for $40,000, and today it's worth $300,000. If you were to retitle the house in your child's name, then apply for Medicaid within three years, the valuation of the house would be $300,000. Don't think you can get around this high valuation by selling the house for a ridiculously low amount (say $100) instead of giving it away. Since Medicaid considers sales for less than fair market value a gift, selling the home for $100 does nothing in terms of helping you qualify for Medicaid. In this case, since the house was sold for less than fair market value, Medicaid values the transfer at $299,900, to account for the $100 that was paid.

What happens if Mr. and/or Mrs. Lane need long-term care meanwhile? Since they will not want to apply for Medicaid until the look-back period has expired, they will use other assets to pay for their care in the meantime. That's why many elder law attorneys would recommend that they keep enough life savings available to fund their care over the 36 months following the stock transfer.

Just a reminder that transfers of assets between spouses is allowed at any time without a penalty period. This is because Medicaid considers any asset in either spouse's name one and the same. It's called the unlimited spousal obligation. So, retitling an asset out of the name of the spouse who needs long-term care into the healthy spouse's name generally accomplishes nothing.

There is an exception in the case of the home, or primary residence, where it is usually a good idea to have it titled in the healthy spouse's name. You may recall from Chapter 21, that the house is not considered in qualifying for Medicaid. But the house is subject to Medicaid recovery, when the state tries to get back the money that was paid on your care after you die. The house (primary residence) is a special asset. Later in this chapter, we look into some strategies for saving the house from Medicaid.

Trust Me!

There are many smart reasons why someone may choose to put his or her money in a *trust* for Medicaid-eligibility purposes. Gifting money to an individual has turned into a huge mistake in many families; these problems are discussed in the next chapter.

Many seniors have revocable, living trusts (these are sometimes called "loving trusts"), set up to avoid probate and perhaps to allow for the easy sale of property in the event of incapacity. If you only remember one thing in this chapter, have it be this: Revocable trusts offer you no protection from Medicaid spend-down.

To be a safe harbor from Medicaid spend-down, a trust must be irrevocable (that means you can't change it), and it must be properly drafted. Some trusts which used to be effective in protecting assets from Medicaid are effective no longer. For example, a law that went into effect in 1986 made Medicaid Qualifying Trusts, often known as MQTs useless overnight. The important lesson here is that Congress did not grandfather existing trusts. To read more about what can go wrong with Medicaid planning, see the next chapter.

If you know of a trust that was drafted before June 1, 1986, I urge you to bring it to a competent elder law attorney for review. As you do your long-term care planning, it may not be a bad idea to pick up the phone and request a sanity-check review of any trust drafted anytime.

Marilee's Memo

A **trust** is a legal instrument that can own property. Property that can be held in trust includes cash, stocks, and even homes. If your goal is to qualify for Medicaid and you are setting up a trust, it has to be the right kind of trust.

These days, attorneys usually recommend either irrevocable, income-only trusts or irrevocable, nonretained-interest trusts to protect assets against Medicaid spend-down. When money is put into a trust, you have triggered a five-year look-back period, so this is not the kind of Medicaid planning that is usually done at the last minute.

Truth & Consequences

Although Medicaid-planning strategies are effective for getting onto Medicaid, they may be at odds with income tax planning, gift-tax planning, and estate planning. Depending on your desires, the plans of your heirs, the numbers, and your other financing options, Medicaid planning may be a very expensive way to pay for your long-term care! Consult with your elder law attorney and/or tax advisor to understand all the trade-offs involved with any suggested Medicaid-planning technique.

By outright giving a child a house, stock, or other highly appreciated asset (something worth much more now than what you paid for it), your child may pay much more in taxes than is necessary. The use of a life estate or trust can take care of this problem. Before you give away a highly appreciated asset, consult with tax and legal advisors. The capital gains tax savings can be significant.

Combining Medicaid Planning with LTC Insurance

One of the biggest drawbacks to Medicaid planning is that it requires the person doing the planning to give up control of assets. People are understandably quite reluctant to willingly give up control of their life savings if they are healthy today in order to do contingency planning for a worst-case future scenario.

That's why many Medicaid planners are recommending their healthier clients take a hybrid approach, combining traditional Medicaid-planning techniques with long-term care insurance.

In the prior example, we met the Lanes, who were ready to give away the $500,000 that they had in the stock market. They were in their 70s, and felt strongly that they wanted to leave the stock to their children. But what if the Lanes were not in their 70s, but were in their 60s and were healthy? Let's imagine that, although they wanted to leave the money to their children, they were concerned that they might actually need the money to supplement their retirement income. What then?

Traditionally, we might tell the Lanes to keep enough of the $500,000 to pay for 3 years of long-term care in an account, and give the rest away to their kids. Of course, if you're a pessimist, you'd keep enough aside to pay for three years of long-term care for each member of the couple, though that scenario is unlikely!

But by considering the use of long-term care insurance, we gain a lot of flexibility. Instead of giving anything to the kids today, the Lanes purchase long-term care policies with three-year benefit periods on both the husband and wife. In order to save the maximum amount of assets, the policies should cover the full cost of nursing

LTC Lowdown

Many people think that once their loved one has entered the nursing home, it's too late to do Medicaid planning. This is not true at all. Often, planning techniques such as half-a-loaf or Medicaid annuities (both discussed later in this chapter) are not done until someone is already in the nursing home.

home care. These policies allow them to delay transferring assets until the last possible moment, when they are at the doorstep of long-term care in the nursing home.

If someone is already experiencing health problems, of course the long-term care insurance is probably not an option. Under current Medicaid rules, a LTC policy with a three year benefit period would allow someone to transfer assets to an individual and then allow the LTC insurance to pay for care during the look-back period.

When one of the Lanes is moving into the nursing home, they apply for their long-term care insurance benefit, and, at that point, they take a look at their assets. How many assets need to be spent down, or liquidated, before the sick Lane qualifies for Medicaid? Subtracting from this number the amount of assets that they need to pay for long-term care during the policy elimination period, they give away the rest to their children or favorite charity. They have kept the total of the following assets:

♦ The amount that the healthy spouse is allowed to keep (spousal resource allowance)

♦ The amount that they will pay out of pocket for the sick Lane's long-term care during the LTC policy elimination period (deductible), and for any daily shortfall (actual cost of care minus what the policy pays) for the duration of the look-back period

The long-term care insurance policy will pay the long-term care bill for three years. Assuming no change in Medicaid rules, once it's been three years and one day past the date that the Lanes gave away their assets, they are free and clear to apply to Medicaid. They don't have to reveal that they gave away $500,000, since they are beyond the look-back period.

Truth & Consequences

If you are considering buying long-term care insurance to allow for a last-minute transfer of assets, consider buying a benefit period longer than three years. Here's one reason why. When a claim begins, you may not be sure how much care you need. You may want the type of care not covered by Medicaid in your area. A longer benefit period buys you time to access your situation without the pressure of seeing either your assets depleted or considering the premature transfer of assets.

Making the Best of a Bad Situation

Okay, you've decided to consider Medicaid planning. Maybe you're already in the nursing home, and want to save assets for your family. Perhaps your health prohibits you from buying long-term care insurance, or you can't afford it. You've heard that there are legal ways that you can preserve assets. It's true. In most states (though not all), the techniques listed below will get you onto Medicaid without having to spend down to the program asset limits. As I've said before, consult with a qualified elder law attorney before you do anything: They will help you choose the best option given your situation and Medicaid program in your state.

Turning Countable Assets into Noncountable Assets

You can protect assets that need to be spent down before you are Medicaid eligible by liquidating and spending them on noncountable assets. Good examples would be paying off a mortgage, purchasing family burial plots, replacing an old automobile with a new one, replacing a furnace or roof, and updating appliances and rugs. When faced with a Medicaid spend-down situation, the healthy spouse should not be reluctant to spend money on his or her home and care.

This type of planning can be critical for the financial well-being of the spouse still living at home. If the healthy spouse stays in the home, repairs and upgrades now will reduce home-maintenance costs in the future. If the house will be sold eventually, the work done now will increase the selling price.

Turning Assets into "Invisible" Income

Do you remember that all assets held by either a husband or wife are lumped together for purposes of qualifying for Medicaid? Well, income is different. Medicaid considers the income of the sick spouse, and most of his income must go to the nursing home (unless his spouse needs to keep income to get her Minimum Monthly Maintenance Needs Allowance, or MMMNA—the amount she gets to keep based on the worksheet she filled out with the Medicaid application). But guess what? Medicaid doesn't look at the income in the healthy spouse's name only. You read correctly. If their combined assets meet the asset limits (around $90,000) and his income meets the income limit, she can have monthly income of any amount (for example, $20,000), and it doesn't matter. She can keep it all.

This is good news for couples where the "right" (read "low-income") spouse needs care, and horrible news if the "wrong" (read "high-income") spouse needs care. Let's look at an example. Ricky and Lucy's life has mirrored many of their contemporaries, dubbed the "greatest generation." Lucy's last day of work outside the home ended the day Ricky returned from WWII.

Ricky retired 10 years ago, collecting a strong pension. The couple has life savings of $200,000. All the couple's retirement income is in Ricky's name. If Ricky needs long-term care and wants Medicaid to pay the bill, the results can be financially devastating to Lucy.

He is allowed to keep $2,000 in assets; she is allowed to keep what is called the Community Spouse Resource Allowance of $89,280 (this is the 2002 figure, but it increases each year). To reach the combined limit of $91,280, *they must spend down $108,730 dollars of their life savings.*

What if the money is in a CD that has premature surrender penalties? Sorry. What if the money is in the stock market, which happens to be at a low point? Sorry. That's the way the system works. Their application will not be approved until their combined countable assets are $91,280.

By the way, the federal government sets the Community Spouse Resource Allowance each year. It is a standard number for the whole country. Although the allowance does increase each year to reflect increases in the Consumer Price Index, there is no variation based on regional costs of living

What if, instead of spending down the $108,730, they transfer this amount into Lucy's name? This is allowed, since transfers of assets between spouses are okay. Lucy then purchases a Medicaid-friendly annuity that will pay her an income for the rest of her life.

She has succeeded in turning a countable asset into income that Medicaid doesn't consider. If the money were left as an asset, it would all have to be spent before Medicaid would start paying. Now Ricky qualifies for Medicaid quickly, and Lucy's income is boosted.

Not just any annuity will work for this technique. For the purchase of an annuity to not be considered an asset transfer, it needs to be actuarially sound, according to life-expectancy tables which are published in your state's Medicaid manuals. It is important, for example, that any guaranteed income be paid only for a period that doesn't exceed life expectancy. Many lawyers recommend an annuity that pays for the life of an individual, with a guaranteed payment period that is shorter than his or her life expectancy. For example, if the spouse's life expectancy is 12 years, she may purchase a life-payable annuity that pays for a minimum duration (term certain) of 10 years.

The Half-a-Loaf Technique

The half-a-loaf technique is extremely powerful. It allows people who are planning to go onto Medicaid to save approximately half of their money (countable assets), even if they are already in the nursing home and even if they do not have a spouse!

Here's how it works. Let's imagine that you are single parent who qualifies for Medicaid from an income point of view. You are already in a nursing home that accepts Medicaid payments, and you have $302,000 in countable assets. You can keep $2,000 and qualify for Medicaid.

You'd like to leave your $300,000 to your adult child, and you have no long-term care insurance or other money to pay for your care. You know that, if you don't do anything, the full $300,000 will go to the nursing home. Your nursing home costs $5,000 per month, and that's the same amount that Medicaid uses for average cost of care in your state.

To avoid having your life savings go to the nursing home, you give half of your life savings ($150,000) to your child. You keep the other half, to allow you to private pay for your care during your ineligibility period for Medicaid. You apply for Medicaid, and must disclose the $150,000 transfer. Medicaid divides the $150,000 by $5,000, and tells you that you are ineligible for Medicaid for 30 months. You private pay with the money you've kept.

In most states, the private-pay nursing home rate is not the same as the Medicaid average cost-of-care number. When these numbers are different, and you are using the half-a-loaf technique, the amount that you can give away is going to be some amount less or greater than exactly half of the money. For instance, in the example above, if the Medicaid number were $4,000 per month, the period of ineligibility would be 37.5 months—which would be a problem, since the Medicaid applicant had only reserved enough money to private pay for 30 months. In that case, less than $150,000 could be transferred and more would have to be kept in reserve to pay.

Wisdom of the Aged

Let's say that you have taken a good look at your long-term care planning options, have consulted with a qualified professional, and have decided to do Medicaid planning. Will you use the half-a-loaf technique or will you purchase a Medicaid annuity? In most cases, to a large extent the decision depends on your marital status. In most states, if you are single, the half-a-loaf technique will be recommended. If you're married, the Medicaid annuity to boost your healthy spouse's income is usually recommended.

Whether you are best to give away "half a loaf" and apply for Medicaid sooner, or give away assets and delay applying for Medicaid until the look-back period has expired, depends on the amount of money you have, the Medicaid cost-of-care number in your state, and the private-pay cost for your nursing home.

Does Half a Loaf Work for Small Amounts?

It may be useful to look into a smaller example of half a loaf. Janice, age 50, has one child, 25-year-old Steven, and is in a wheelchair as a result of multiple sclerosis. She has $37,000 to her name, and qualifies for Medicaid from an income point of view. Her state Medicaid office says that the average cost of care in her state is $3,000 per month, but the nursing home where she lives has a private rate of $4,000 per month.

Janice is allowed to have $2,000 and still qualify for Medicaid from an asset point of view. From her $37,000, she gives $15,000 to Steven, keeps $22,000, and then applies to Medicaid. The Medicaid caseworker, seeing that Janice gave away $15,000 in the last three years, divides this number by $3,000, and tells her that she is ineligible for Medicaid for five months from the date she gave the money away. That's OK with Janice, because she kept enough money to private pay for five months at $4,000. She private pays for five months of care ($20,000 total), and has $2,000 left over. If she hadn't given the $15,000 to Steven, she would've had to spend down the whole $35,000 before qualifying for Medicaid.

These examples were given to illustrate the half-a-loaf technique simply. When it comes to half-a-loaf planning, the amount that you can give away and the amount that you must keep to private pay during the ineligibility period may not be split 50/50, for half a loaf. The split can vary dramatically, because the numbers are calculated based on the amount of money you are trying to save, how much your care costs, your income and other expenses, and your state's rules. If too much is transferred, it may be possible to fix the situation by doing what is called a partial cure (taking back some assets). Don't try this yourself—seek out a competent professional. A mistake can be very costly.

LTC Lowdown

What happens if you give away your money and do not reserve enough money to pay privately through the ineligibility period? Then you are in a tough situation. You will need to ask your child or whomever you gave the money to for some of it back in order to pay your own bill.

The "D" Word: D-I-V-O-R-C-E

What if your spouse is in need of long-term care in the nursing home, and you have a lot of countable assets that can't easily be sold? It may be tough to use the half-a-loaf method or the Medicaid annuity method if your money is tough to get at. Perhaps it's tied up in a vacation home, a 401(k), or other assets that you don't want to have to liquidate.

What if this is your second marriage, and you are the one who brought all the money to this marriage? Your spouse needs nursing home care, and, although you had agreed that your money would be left to your children from a prior marriage when you died, you are seeing your life savings used to pay for your spouse's care (the good ol' unlimited spousal obligation).

Some Medicaid planners recommend a divorce. That's right. If you're divorced, there can be no unlimited spousal obligation to support. The divorce can save assets that would otherwise have to be used to pay for the nursing home spouse's care.

Wisdom of the Aged

Sometimes divorce is recommended, not to save assets, but for income-preservation purposes. If the nursing home spouse has high unearned income, after paying the healthy spouse the amount of alimony she qualifies for, most of this high income will be paid to the nursing home. If, as a result of a divorce, the nursing home spouse was required to pay half of his income to his ex-wife, she would likely have higher income (and the nursing home would be paid less) than if they remained married. In other words, it's possible that a court order of support can be used to give the healthy community spouse more income than would've been allowed if she were still married to the nursing home spouse.

Divorce is not a preferred method of accomplishing Medicaid planning. In fact, on its face, it is highly distasteful. For a couple who have been married anywhere from 20 to 60 years to get divorced when one spouse is ill, in order to save assets, is an example of an incredible lack of planning. Imagine the heartache of the person whose spouse suffers from Alzheimer's disease, who must go to court to argue for the divorce, since the sick spouse is legally incompetent.

While a divorce can be used to preserve assets in the healthy spouse's name, it can also be used in situations where the sick spouse has high income. If the spouse who needs nursing home care has high income and the community spouse wants to keep more income than the Medicaid regulations allow, a divorce can sometimes be a solution. A court order of support to a former spouse can sometimes allow more of the sick

LTC Lowdown

By the way, most people describe Medicaid-motivated divorces as divorces on paper only. The couple can continue to live together, although no longer legally married. What a mess our long-term care financing system is in to even have to mention the option of divorce!

spouse's income to be paid to the community spouse than the Medicaid regulations permit.

The ability to get this kind of divorce varies. In some areas, a judge will not go along with this. On the other hand, in other states, the Medicaid office has supported the right of a person to simply refuse to support his or her spouse in a nursing home, without even needing a legal divorce! This technique is called spousal refusal planning.

House-Keeping Tips

The primary residence, or home, has always been a special asset. In most states, it's not counted when figuring your eligibility for Medicaid, but it's the one asset that is most vulnerable to estate recovery after you've been on Medicaid and died.

In order for your house to not be counted in terms of qualifying for Medicaid, some states require a single person to show that he or she is likely to return home within six months. Otherwise, the house must be sold.

Since the value of your house is not counted in terms of whether or not you qualify for Medicaid, the house is called a noncountable, or exempt, asset. But exempt assets can still be subject to estate recovery at your death. This means that, in most states, the day your Medicaid application is approved is the day that a Medicaid lien is placed against your house.

As Medicaid pays for your care in the nursing home, it keeps a tab of what was paid. If you want to leave the house to someone, like your children or a favorite charity, they will not get the title of your house until they have paid back the Medicaid lien.

There are some circumstances where Medicaid allows you to leave your house to someone, without having to worry about estate recovery. There are also some ways of titling the house so that it is not usually considered part of your estate. If an asset is not part of your estate, Medicaid cannot try to recover money spent on your care through that asset.

LTC Lowdown

The amount of Medicaid lien against your house is not based on the private-pay rate of the nursing home you are living in, it's based on the rate that Medicaid pays. In many places, that is much less than the private-pay rate. So even if you end up having to pay for your nursing home care with the equity in your home, you may be getting a bargain, since you paid at Medicaid, not private-pay, rates. This same thing holds true for any recovery made from your estate—your heirs would benefit from a lower recovery due to Medicaid rates.

Take My House ... Please!

Some of the most common situations where Medicaid allows you to transfer your house free and clear to someone, even if you are on Medicaid, are if ...

◆ Your child is under age 21.

◆ Your siblings are on the title and have lived in the home for at least a year before you entered the nursing home.

◆ Your "caretaker child" has lived in the home with you for at least two years immediately before you entered the nursing home, and if the child provided care which allowed you to stay in the home instead of moving to the nursing home.

◆ You are a disabled person under age 65.

Before you get your hopes up too high, though, you should get some expert legal advice to see if any of the above situations, or perhaps even others, are legally recognized in your state.

If You Have a Spouse ...

What if your situation doesn't include anyone on the laundry list of special people that Medicaid allows you to give your house to?

Many planners recommend that, when one spouse needs long-term care, that his or her name be taken off the title. Then the title of the house would be in the healthy spouse's name only. Remember, transfers of assets between spouses up until (and even after) Medicaid eligibility are allowed with no penalty.

Here's why it usually makes sense to have the healthy spouse alone on the title. Most couples own their home jointly. Once the nursing home spouse is on Medicaid, if the community spouse were to die, a house held in joint names would pass to the spouse on Medicaid.

> **Truth & Consequences** _____
>
> Many people give away their homes, usually to a child, for Medicaid-planning purposes. This may have unintended adverse tax consequences. If people give away their home, they are missing the residential capital gains exclusion that they may have qualified for. And now they are passing along a tax time bomb. When an asset is given away instead of left in a will, the capital gains taxes that are paid when it is sold are normally much higher.

If instead of gifting, an asset is left to someone in a will, there is a favorable tax treatment called a *stepped-up basis*. For purposes of capital gains taxes due on the eventual sale, the cost basis is the market value of the asset on the day the owner passed away. When an asset is given away, there is no stepped-up basis. Figure in this potential extra cost when evaluating long-term care planning options.

In some places, if a doctor says that the nursing home occupant is not likely to be able to return home, Medicaid will force the sale of the house. The proceeds will be used for the nursing home care. Even if the sale was not forced, a house in the name of the now-single nursing home occupant would likely have a Medicaid lien placed against the property. If, instead, the title were in the name of the community spouse only and the nursing home spouse died, in many cases the house could be left free and clear to a child, other individual, or charity.

Life Estates

Many people use a simple alternative to a trust for protecting the home against Medicaid. This alternative, called a life estate, gives the house away—but not until the homeowner's death. The homeowner reserves the right to live in the home for the rest of his or her life. A life estate can give the children who are left the house a stepped-up basis, saving significant capital gains taxes. This can also be accomplished through the use of a proper trust. Transferring the deed of the house into a life estate can trigger the 36-month look-back. In some states, life estates are under fire, and may leave the house vulnerable to estate recovery.

The Least You Need to Know

◆ There are some circumstances where Medicaid allows you to transfer your house to someone, without having to worry about triggering a penalty period—for example, to a disabled individual or caretaker child.

◆ In most states, the day your Medicaid application is approved is the day that there is a Medicaid lien placed against your house.

◆ Obtaining a divorce is sometimes recommended to save assets that would otherwise have to be used to pay for the nursing home spouse's care.

◆ Your primary residence is not counted when figuring your eligibility for Medicaid, but it's the one asset that is most vulnerable to estate recovery after you've been on Medicaid and died.

◆ The half-a-loaf technique allows people who are planning to go onto Medicaid to save approximately half of their money (countable assets) from Medicaid.

◆ Contrary to popular belief, it is not too late to do Medicaid planning once you are already in the nursing home!

Chapter 24

The Top Five Problems with Medicaid Planning

In This Chapter

◆ Beware of whom you trust

◆ The risks of relying on an unreliable system

◆ Why you should seek professional advice

◆ The true cost of transferring your assets

◆ Don't outsmart yourself

As I discussed in the last chapter, although Medicaid serves needy people, middle-class and affluent citizens sometimes access benefits by doing what is called Medicaid planning. This type of planning preserves assets by making it invisible to Medicaid, so that the person qualifies for Medicaid without spending his or her assets on care.

Some Americans embrace Medicaid planning as a way of paying for long-term care without depleting their life savings. Others are repulsed by the idea of Medicaid planning, and do everything they can specifically so that they never need Medicaid to pay for their long-term care.

Thoughtfully considering your choices in the light of day, without an immediate crisis, is your best shot at coming up with a decision you can live happily with. In Chapter 23, I discussed Medicaid-planning techniques that, as of the writing of this book, work in most states. In this chapter, I highlight some of the problems with Medicaid planning. I also take a good look at what you should consider if your plan is to rely on Medicaid.

#1: You Really Can't Own It!

To save money from being spent on your long-term care, and also to spare assets from Medicaid estate recovery, the assets cannot be in your name if you are planning on having Medicaid pay. It's that simple ... and that hard. You can simply make sure that nothing is in your name, and you won't have to worry about it being used for your care. However, when you transfer assets out of your name, you give up control.

The fact is, when your name is no longer on the asset, you cannot count on it being available for you or control what happens to it. In many families, when Mom and/or Dad do Medicaid planning, they give their assets away to trusted family members, with an understanding: Even though the money has been given away on paper, it's still considered Mom or Dad's. If they need the money, they can just pick up the phone, and a check will be sent right away.

Or will it?

Family Transfers

Whenever I speak to public groups on long-term care planning, people come up to me afterwards and tell me what went wrong in their family with long-term care. If I passed along some of the stories I heard, you would think I had made them up. The truth is, when you have aging parents, their children and their spouses, failing health, and a pile of money, the stage is set for trouble.

If the stories weren't true, they could be funny: the son-in-law who gambled away his wife's parents' life savings. The story about the widow who gave her life savings to her daughter, who lost half of Mom's money when she divorced her husband five years later. The story about the son who raided his dad's life savings when he lost his job. The story about the granddaughter who lost her grandma's life savings when it was awarded to a plaintiff as the result of an automobile-accident lawsuit.

Money or other assets held by a relative or friend are vulnerable. As described above, they can be gambled away, lost in a divorce settlement, spent in times of economic need, or awarded as compensation in a lawsuit. If the person holding your money dies before you do, where will the money go? It will probably be left to someone who feels less of an obligation to you. If it's left to you, the windfall will likely knock you off Medicaid.

Wisdom of the Aged

There are many stories of relatives and trusted friends who take advantage of the vulnerable senior. Remember, when most of us need long-term care, we are at the most vulnerable point of our adult lives. As a healthy 50-, 60-, or even 70-year-old, it is hard to imagine relying on others to help us with our bathing ... and banking! What if the assets are misused by the person you trusted? It happens every day, even among close family members! There are many things that can go wrong when a senior gives up his or her life savings.

Many seniors are very reluctant to give up control of their assets. This is an instinct that serves them well. Whoever holds the money holds the power. But if you are going to keep your assets in your name, and you do not want to use these assets to pay for long-term care, figure out how you will pay for your long-term care now—otherwise, your assets are vulnerable if you need care.

Professional Trustees

Seniors who know that they want to shelter assets while not subjecting the assets to the problems highlighted above should consider using a properly drafted irrevocable Medicaid trust, with a professional trustee. The trustee may be an entity such as a bank or trust company.

Hiring a professional trustee takes the day-to-day management of the money out of the hands of friends or family members, and avoids a laundry list of problems. Professional trustees can protect your assets from the whims of friends and relatives, and keep your assets out of a lot of family maneuvering and in-fighting. They are not usually a realistic option for very modest estates. Ask your banker or family lawyer if this is something that makes sense for you.

If you are a bargain shopper, you may not like the idea of hiring a professional trustee. They charge fees that a family member most likely wouldn't. However, I have been told by many people that they wish they had not been penny-wise and pound-foolish, and spent the money to hire a professional trustee. How much is peace of mind and family harmony worth to you?

Of course, keep in mind that transfers to a Medicaid trust subject the applicant to a potential five-year look-back period.

#2: The System Is a Moving Target

Healthy people who do Medicaid planning are especially vulnerable to program changes. That's because the Medicaid eligibility requirements and the Medicaid look-back periods may change at any time. So, if you are relatively young (young can be under age 70!) and healthy today, you run a bigger risk that the Medicaid program may change than someone who is already sick and entering a nursing home. If the rules change before you apply for Medicaid, you may find that you are not eligible under the new rules.

What could change? Suppose the look-back period for transfers to an individual is increased from 36 months (three years) to 120 months (10 years) in the year 2010. But, in 2009, let's say that you gave away a very large amount of money (a million dollars) for Medicaid-planning purposes. Keep in mind that if Medicaid saw that huge transfer on an application during a look-back period, the disqualification penalty would be a very long time. If Medicaid figured the average cost of care in your state was $5,000, your disqualification period would be more than 16 years!

Under the old 36-month look-back, you could have applied for benefits 37 months after the date you gave away the money in 2009—so you'd be eligible for Medicaid in 2012. But if the rules changed in 2010, and your state was enforcing the new rules, you would now have to wait until 2019 before applying for Medicaid, or seven more years than before. During this time, if you needed long-term care, you would need to pay privately.

I spoke on long-term care planning to a group of businesspeople in the early 1990s. After I spoke, I joined a table to eat. To my right was a man who introduced himself as a partner in the biggest law firm in town. He said, "I'm so glad that you're out talking about the topic of long-term care planning. My firm drafted dozens of trusts for Medicaid-planning purposes that don't work anymore." He continued, "We don't know how to notify everyone, or what to do. They think their assets are protected, but they aren't protected at all anymore." He went on to explain, "A lot of these people are very old now, and couldn't buy long-term care insurance now because of their health. But back when we did the trusts, some could have qualified." *The important lesson here is that Congress did not grandfather (that is, make an exception for) existing trusts.*

LTC Lowdown

To avoid being stuck with an irrevocable trust that doesn't work anymore, most lawyers recommend that special language is included in the trust, allowing modifications if Medicaid regulations change. This language may allow you to amend the trust to comply with new regulations.

And remember, these trusts were irrevocable! Irrevocable is an ancient word meaning "Don't even *think* about changing this!" Just kidding—sort of. You can't just go back and change an irrevocable trust.

The chance that laws change and render your planning ineffective is a very real risk. That's why many Medicaid planners are reluctant to do Medicaid planning for healthy, younger individuals who may not need Medicaid for years, and may never need long-term care!

#3: It's Complicated

If you've read the rest of this section on Medicaid, you are probably painfully aware of how complicated the system is. Rules change at unpredictable times, and even the experts sometimes disagree about the best course of action.

The Medicaid application process is not designed to encourage Medicaid planning, and the consumer who tries to go it alone can find it almost impossible to get advice on how to proceed.

People who don't have a lot of money are naturally reluctant to hire a lawyer. If they are faced with a loved one needing long-term care they are often trying to minimize their expenses, not take on new ones. But a mistake in timing on a Medicaid application or a mistake on the application can have horrible consequences.

Imagine the couple who has lived together for 20 years, but are not married. The house is in the name of the person who needs to go to the nursing home. On the Medicaid application, there is a question about whether the person moving to the nursing home is planning on returning to the house. In most cases, a lawyer will advise you to always check off "yes," since this prevents Medicaid forcing the sale of the house until the nursing home spouse passes away. But this couple didn't know that, and, thinking that it's unlikely the sick person will return home, they check off "no." Medicaid moves immediately to require the sale of the house, forcing the other member of the unmarried couple to either buy the home at market price or move. If the couple were married, Medicaid would not force the sale of the house, in order to preserve housing for the spouse.

Get professional, competent advice!

#4: Medicaid Planning Can Be Expensive

If you were doing Medicaid planning to minimize your out-of-pocket expense in paying for long-term care, wouldn't you want to know if by transferring assets you were setting up for a huge tax bill? Depending on the amount of the tax bill, it could make

Medicaid planning a lot less attractive, right? Well, that's exactly what's happening right now to many families. While they are saving assets from Medicaid, their surviving family members are being set up to spend a lot of money in taxes that could've been avoided.

Imagine that you give your second home to your daughter, to save it from having to be spent down (sold) if you ever need nursing home care and want to qualify for Medicaid. It's now her vacation home. You bought the vacation house years ago, for only $50,000, but today it's worth $250,000. Six months later you die in your sleep, never having needed long-term care. Your daughter sells the home for $250,000.

Because you gave her the house when you were alive, her income tax cost basis is the same as yours, $50,000. So when she sells the house for $250,000, she has a taxable gain of $200,000. If, instead, you had left her the house in your will and made other arrangements to pay for long-term care, at your death, your daughter inherits the vacation home with a cost basis equal to its market value that day. That favorable tax treatment is called a stepped-up basis. If you had left her the house in that manner, and she sold the house then, she would have no taxable capital gain.

However, since you have left her the house while you were alive, she's writing out a check to the federal government for capital gains taxes of about $40,000, just because you did Medicaid planning.

In many families, seniors are giving away highly appreciated assets such as homes and stocks. By transferring title while you are alive, you are preserving the low cost basis of the asset. This results in a much bigger tax bill when the person you gave it to eventually sells the asset. You are well advised to take a close look at the true cost of transferring highly appreciated assets in evaluating the attractiveness of this strategy. In many families, the extra taxes that will be paid could've purchased a lifetime of private long-term care insurance, maximizing the inheritance to the children and minimizing the tax bill.

The True Cost of Having a Child Hold Your Assets

If your life savings are being held by your child, besides the risk of having the money disappear that we talked about earlier, there are two other financial considerations. Any earnings on the money will be taxed at your child's income-tax rate. This is often higher than your income-tax rate in retirement, so more is being paid in taxes than if you were still holding the assets.

> **Truth & Consequences** _____
>
>   If your child is holding your life savings for Medicaid-planning purposes, that may be a problem when your grandchildren apply for college financial aid. Your life savings would appear available to pay for their college expenses, and could reduce or eliminate their ability to obtain financial aid.

The True Cost of Having a Trust Hold Your Assets

If your life savings are being held in trust, for Medicaid-planning purposes, the trust will likely pay more in income taxes than you would as an individual. That's because any earnings on money held in trust is taxed at a higher income tax rate than the same earnings in an individual's name. Consider this additional cost when looking at the pros and cons of Medicaid planning.

#5: I Didn't Plan on *This!*

Many people who are focusing on Medicaid planning are thinking about the significant upside: Their hard-earned life savings can be protected against the cost of nursing home care. In many cases, they are not considering what they give up in the bargain.

In most areas of the country, Medicaid will indeed pay for your nursing home care, but it will not pay for your home care, or for you to move into one of those nice new assisted living facilities.

And if you are leaving the hospital to go to the nursing home, do not make the mistake of thinking that you will have your choice of the most desirable nursing homes. You will be given a short list of nursing homes (maybe only one or two) that have Medicaid beds available. In the nursing home, Medicaid recipients are often sharing a room with two or even three roommates, while their private-pay counterparts have private or semiprivate rooms.

Our capitalistic society will find creative ways to meet the increasing demand for long-term care services. Since facilities that rely on government reimbursements have proven to be disappointing investments, investors will instead invest in private-pay options. These private-pay options will meet market demand and be more attractive than the facilities that the government programs fund.

Wisdom of the Aged

I recently toured a new assisted living facility. I was particularly interested in seeing this place because I had heard that it was one of the very few assisted living facilities that accepted Medicaid. I saw the sunny, private apartments, with kitchenettes and private baths. At the end of the tour, the director asked "Would you like to see the Medicaid units?" I remember being surprised and thinking, "Oh, they're different?" She took me down to the ground floor (or, as real estate agents prefer to describe it, "garden level"), on the north, dark side of the building. Even though the Medicaid unit was for two people (the private-pay unit was for one), it was smaller than the private-pay.

We are already seeing the marketplace come up with private-pay long-term care at a variety of price points. Some business are offering different types of assisted living facilities. The prices are designed to meet different budgets. One facility may offer buffet-style meals served in a casual homestyle atmosphere, while another facility served restaurant-type meals in a formal dining room with private tables.

The Teacher's Mother: Eileen's Story

Eileen told me an amazing story the other day.

Her mother had received five years of long-term care in Eileen's home. She stayed at their house until she wasn't able to see and had incontinence. She started becoming forgetful. If Eileen and her husband had to leave the house, they had to hire a sitter. It was time for the next move.

All the kids wanted Mom in a comfortable, nice place. They chose a local assisted living facility. Like most assisted living facilities, it did not accept Medicaid. Eileen's mom had lived there for two years when she had almost run out of her modest life savings.

The kids talked to each other: How will we come up with the $3,500 per month to keep Mom in the place she now called home? The alternative was to put Mom on Medicaid and move her out of the assisted living facility. Eileen's husband had just retired from teaching. He was looking into taking money out of his qualified retirement plan to pay for his own mother's care.

The children had gut-wrenching discussions: "Will we put ourselves in the poorhouse to pay for Mom?"

She was almost out of money, but the kids hadn't told her. They would work something out. They had planned a catered party of over 100 guests for her ninetieth birthday.

Mom went to sleep and died one week before her ninetieth birthday, and just before running out of money. "It was like she knew," Eileen said.

The family went ahead and had the party.

To those people who are considering Medicaid planning but who have the option of private paying instead, the writing is on the wall: Private payers have more attractive options than those on Medicaid.

If you do Medicaid planning so that the program will pay for your long-term care, do you know that the same care that's covered today will be paid for in the future?

Money Talks, and It Screams for Long-Term Care

Have you ever heard the phrase "Money talks"? In this capitalist, consumer-driven culture, you can't help but know this. However, you may not be aware of this sentiment in relation to planning for long-term care.

Weigh these five big problems with Medicaid planning with all the other information you collect as you do long-term care planning.

The Least You Need to Know

- ◆ By sheltering assets to get onto Medicaid, we no longer have care options that private-pay people have.

- ◆ Because Medicaid is a fast-changing program, healthy people who plan today do not know what the program will be like when they need long-term care.

- ◆ Relying on others to hold money for us leaves the money vulnerable to lawsuit judgments, divorce, and just plain mismanagement.

State Insurance Departments

ALABAMA DEPARTMENT OF INSURANCE
201 Monroe Street
Montgomery, AL 36130
334-269-3550
www.aldoi.org

ALASKA DIVISION OF INSURANCE
333 Willoughby Avenue, 9th Floor
Juneau, AK 99801
907-465-2515
1-800-467-8725 (in state)
www.dced.state.ak.us/insurance

ARIZONA DEPARTMENT OF INSURANCE
2910 North 44th Street, #210
Phoenix, AZ 85018
602-912-8444
1-800-325-2548 (in state)
www.state.az.us/id

ARKANSAS DEPARTMENT OF INSURANCE
1200 West Third Street
Little Rock, AR 72201-1904
501-371-2600
www.state.ar.us/insurance

CALIFORNIA DEPARTMENT
OF INSURANCE
300 South Spring Street,
9th Floor
Los Angeles, CA 90013
213-897-8921
1-800-927-HELP (in state)
www.insurance.ca.gov

COLORADO DIVISION OF
INSURANCE
1560 Broadway, #850
Denver, CO 80202
303-894-7499
1-800-930-3745 (in state)
www.dora.state.co.us/insurance

CONNECTICUT
DEPARTMENT OF
INSURANCE
P.O. Box 816
Hartford, CT 06142-0816
860-297-3802 or 860-297-3800
1-800-203-3447 (in state)
www.state.ct.us/cid

DELAWARE DEPARTMENT OF
INSURANCE
Carvell Building
820 North French Street
Wilmington, DE 19801
302-739-4251
1-800-282-8611 (in state)
www.state.de.us/inscom

DISTRICT OF COLUMBIA
DEPARTMENT OF
INSURANCE
810 First Street NE, #701
Washington, DC 20002
202-727-8000
www.disr.washingtondc.gov

FLORIDA DEPARTMENT OF
INSURANCE
200 East Gaines Street,
Larson Building
Tallahassee, FL 32399
850-413-3100
1-800-342-2762 (in state)
www.doi.state.fl.us

GEORGIA INSURANCE FIRE
SAFETY COMMISSION
2 Martin L. King Jr. Drive (716 West
Tower)
Atlanta, GA 30334
404-656-2056
1-800-656-2298 (in state)
www.gainsurance.org

HAWAII INSURANCE
COMMISSIONER
250 South King Street, 5th Floor
Honolulu, HI 96813
808-586-2790
www.state.hi.us/dcca/ins

IDAHO DEPARTMENT OF
INSURANCE
700 West State Street, 3rd Floor
Boise, ID 83720-0043
208-334-4250
1-800-721-3272
www.doi.state.id.us

ILLINOIS DEPARTMENT OF
INSURANCE
320 West Washington Street,
4th Floor
Springfield, IL 62767-0001
217-782-4515
1-866-445-5364 (in state)
www.state.il.us/ins

INDIANA DEPARTMENT OF
INSURANCE
311 West Washington Street, #300
Indianapolis, IN 46204-2787
317-232-2385
1-800-622-4461 (in state)
www.in.gov/idoi

IOWA INSURANCE DIVISION
330 Maple Street
Des Moines, IA 50319
515-281-6867
1-800-351-4664 (in state)
www.iid.state.ia.us

KANSAS INSURANCE
DEPARTMENT
420 SW Ninth Street
Topeka, KS 66612-1678
785-296-3071
1-800-432-2484 (in state)
www.ksinsurance.org

KENTUCKY DEPARTMENT OF
INSURANCE
215 West Main Street
Frankfort, KY 40601
502-564-3630
1-800-595-6053 (in state)
www.doi.state.ky.us

LOUISIANA DEPARTMENT OF
INSURANCE
950 North Fifth Street
Baton Rouge, LA 70804-9214
504-342-5900
1-800-259-5300 (in state)
1-800-259-5301 (in state)
www.ldi.state.la.us

MAINE BUREAU OF
INSURANCE
34 State House Station
Augusta, ME 04333
207-624-8475
1-800-300-5000 (in state)
www.maineinsurancereg.org

MARYLAND INSURANCE
ADMININTRATION
525 St. Paul Place
Baltimore, MD 21202-2272
410-468-2000
1-800-492-6116 (in state)
www.mdinsurance.state.md.us

MASSACHUSETTS DIVISION
OF INSURANCE
1 South Station
Boston, MA 02110
617-521-7794
www.state.ma.us/doi

MICHIGAN INSURANCE
BUREAU
611 West Ottawa Street, 2nd Floor
Lansing, MI 48933
517-373-0220
1-877-999-6442 (any state)
www.cis.state.mi.us/ofis

MINNESOTA DIVISION OF
INSURANCE
85 Seventh Place East, Suite 500
St. Paul, MN 55101
651-296-4026
1-800-657-3602
www.commerce.state.mn.us

MISSISSIPPI INSURANCE
DEPARTMENT
501 NW Street, #1001
Jackson, MS 39201
601-359-3569
1-800-562-2957 (in state)
www.doi.state.ms.us

MISSOURI DEPARTMENT OF
INSURANCE
P.O. Box 690
Jefferson City, MO 65102-0690
573-751-2640
1-800-726-7390 (in state)
www.insurance.state.mo.us

MONTANA DEPARTMENT OF
INSURANCE
840 Helena Avenue
Helena, MT 59601
406-444-2040
1-800-332-6148 (in state)
www.sao.state.mt.us

NEBRASKA DEPARTMENT OF
INSURANCE
941 O Street #400
Lincoln, NE 68508-3639
402-471-2203
1-800-833-0920 (in state)
1-800-234-7119 (any state)
www.nol.org/home/ndoi

NEVADA DEPARTMENT OF
INSURANCE
78 Fairview Drive
Carson City, NV 89710
775-687-4270
1-800-992-0900 (in state)
www.doi.state.nv.us

NEW HAMPSHIRE INSURANCE
DEPARTMENT
56 Old Suncook Road
Concord, NH 03301-5151
603-271-2261
1-800-852-3416 (in state)
www.state.nh.us/insurance

NEW JERSEY DEPARTMENT
OF BANKING INSURANCE
20 West State Street
Trenton, NJ 08625
609-292-5363
1-800-792-8820 (in state)
609-984-5273 (fax)
www.state.nj.us/dobi/insmnu.htm

NEW MEXICO INSURANCE
DIVISION
P.O. Drawer 1269
Santa Fe, NM 87504-1269
505-827-4601
1-800-947-4722 (in state)
www.nmprc.state.nm.us/inshm.htm

NEW YORK DEPARTMENT OF
INSURANCE
Empire State Plaza, Agency
Bldg. #1
Albany, NY 12257
518-474-6600
1-800-342-3736 (in state)
www.ins.state.ny.us

NORTH CAROLINA
DEPARTMENT OF INSURANCE
P.O. Box 26387
Raleigh, NC 27611
919-733-7343
1-800-546-5664 (in state)
www.ncdoi.com

NORTH DAKOTA
DEPARTMENT OF INSURANCE
600 East Boulevard
Bismarck, ND 58505-0320
701-328-2440
1-800-247-0560 (in state)
www.state.nd.us/ndins

OHIO DEPARTMENT OF
INSURANCE
2100 Stella Court
Columbus, OH 43215-1067
614-644-2658
1-800-686-1526 (any state)
www.ohioinsurance.gov

OKLAHOMA DEPARTMENT OF
INSURANCE
2401 NW 23rd Street, Suite 28
Oklahoma City, OK 73107
405-521-2828
1-800-522-0071 (in state)
www.oid.state.ok.us

OREGON INSURANCE
DIVISION
350 Winter Street NE, Room 440
Salem, OR 97301-3883
503-947-7984
www.oregoninsurance.org

PENNSYLVANIA DEPARTMENT
OF INSURANCE
1321 Strawberry Square
Harrisburg, PA 17120
717-787-2317
1-877-881-6388 (in state)
www.insurance.state.pa.us

RHODE ISLAND INSURANCE
DEPARTMENT
233 Richmond Street, #233
Providence, RI 02903-4233
401-222-2223
www.dbr.state.ri.us

SOUTH CAROLINA
DEPARTMENT OF INSURANCE
P.O. Box 100105
Columbia, SC 29202-3105
803-737-6180
1-800-768-3467 (in state)
www.state.sc.us/doi

SOUTH DAKOTA INSURANCE
DIVISION
118 West Capital
Pierre, SD 57501
605-773-3563
www.state.sd.us/insurance

TENNESSEE DEPARTMENT OF
COMMERCE & INSURANCE
500 James Robertson Parkway
Nashville, TN 37243-0565
615-741-2218
1-800-342-4029 (in state)
www.state.tn.us/commerce

TEXAS DEPARTMENT OF
INSURANCE
P.O. Box 149104
Austin, TX 78714-9104
512-463-6515
1-800-252-3439 (any state)
www.tdi.state.tx.us

UTAH INSURANCE
DEPARTMENT
3110 State Office Building
Salt Lake City, UT 84114
801-538-3800
1-800-439-3805 (in state)
www.insurance.state.ut.us/

VERMONT INSURANCE
DIVISION
89 Main Street, Drawer 20
Montpelier, VT 05620-3101
802-828-2900
www.bishca.state.vt.us

VIRGINIA BUREAU OF
INSURANCE
P.O. Box 1157
Richmond, VA 23218
804-371-9741
1-800-552-7945 (in state)
www.state.va.us/scc

WASHINGTON INSURANCE
COMMISSION
P.O. Box 40255
Olympia, WA 98504-0255
360-753-3613
1-800-562-6900 (in state)
www.insurance.wa.gov

WEST VIRGINIA INSURANCE
DEPARTMENT
P.O. Box 50540
Charleston, WV 25305-0540
304-558-3386
1-800-642-9004 (in state)
www.state.wv.us/insurance

WISCONSIN INSURANCE
COMMISSION
P.O. Box 7873
Madison, WI 53707
608-266-3585
1-800-236-8517 (in state)
www.oci.wi.gov

WYOMING INSURANCE
DEPARTMENT
122 West 25th Street,
3rd Floor East
Cheyenne, WY 82002-0440
307-777-7401
1-800-438-5768 (in state)
www.insurance.state.wy.us

State Medicaid Offices

ALABAMA
Alabama Medicaid Agency
501 Dexter Avenue
P.O. Box 5624
Montgomery, AL 36103-5624
334-242-5400
www.medicaid.state.al.us/

ALASKA
Division of Medical Assistance
Department of Health and Social Services
P.O. Box 110660
Juneau, AK 99811
907-562-3671 (out of state, Anchorage)
1-800-211-7470 (in state, except Anchorage)
www.hss.state.ak.us/dma/

ARIZONA
Arizona Health-Care Cost
Containment System (AHCCCS)
801 East Jefferson
Phoenix, AZ 85034
1-800-654-8713
www.ahcccs.state.az.us/

ARKANSAS
Division of Medical Services
Department of Human Services
P.O. Box 1437, Slot S401
700 S. Main
Little Rock, AR 72203
501-682-8292 (will refer to county offices)
www.medicaid.state.ar.us/

CALIFORNIA
Medi-Cal Benefit Branch
Department of Health Services
714 P Street
Sacramento, CA 95814
916-657-1460 (first call 1-800-952-5253 to contact your county social services office and ask about long-term care services)
www.dhs.ca.gov/mcs/

COLORADO
Office of Medical Assistance
Department of Health-Care Policy and Financing
1575 Sherman, 10th Floor
Denver, CO 80203-1714
303-866-3513 (Medicaid Customer Service)
www.chcpf.state.co.us/

CONNECTICUT
Medical Care Administration
Department of Social Services
25 Sigourney Street
Hartford, CT 06106
860-424-5201
www.dss.state.ct.us/svcs/medical.htm

DELAWARE
Division of Social Services
Long-Term Care Sector
Robscott Building
153 Chestnut Hill Road
Newark, DE 19713
302-368-6610
www.state.de.us/dhss/dph/index.htm

DISTRICT OF COLUMBIA
Medical Assistance Administration
Department of Health
825 North Capitol Street NE
Suite 5135
Washington, DC 20002
202-442-9055
dchealth.dc.gov/information/maa_outline.shtm

FLORIDA
Agency for Health-Care Administration
2727 Mahan Drive, Building 3
Tallahassee, FL 32308
850-488-3560
www.fdhc.state.fl.us/Medicaid/index.shtml

GEORGIA
Department of Medical Assistance
Two Peachtree Street, 40th Floor
Atlanta, GA 30303
404-656-3200
404-656-4496
www.communityhealth.state.ga.us/

HAWAII
Department of Human Services
P.O. Box 339
Honolulu, HI 96809-0339
808-692-8050
www.state.hi.us/dhs/

IDAHO
Department of Health and Welfare
Eligibility Office
1720 Westgate Drive, Suite D
Boise, ID 83704
208-334-6700
www.state.id.us/dhw/medicaid/
index.htm

ILLINOIS
Medical Programs
Illinois Department of Public Aid
201 South Grand Avenue, East
Springfield, IL 62763-0001
217-782-5565 (out of state)
1-800-252-8635 (in state)
www.state.il.us/dpa/html/
medicaid_program.htm

INDIANA
Medicaid Policy and Planning
Family and Social Services
Administration
402 West Washington Street,
Room W382
Indianapolis, IN 46204-2739
317-233-4455
www.state.in.us/fssa/servicedisabl/
medicaid/index.html

IOWA
Bureau of Long-Term Services
Department of Human Services
Hoover State Office Building,
5th Floor
Des Moines, IA 50319-0114
515-281-3573 (will refer to county)
www.dhs.state.ia.us/MedicalServices/
MedicalServices.asp

KANSAS
Department of Social and
Rehabilitation Services
500 SW Van Buren
Topeka, KS 66612
785-296-2500
www.srskansas.org/main.html

KENTUCKY
Medicaid Services
Long-Term Care Nursing Facilities
Division
275 East Main Street, 6 West
Frankfort, KY 40621
502-564-5707
chs.state.ky.us/dms/

LOUISIANA
Bureau of Health Services Financing
Department of Health and Hospitals
1201 Capitol Access Road
P.O. Box 91030
Baton Rouge, LA 70821-9030
225-342-0415 (will refer to parish
office)
www.dhh.state.la.us/medicaid/
index.htm

MAINE
Bureau of Medical Services
Department of Human Services
Statehouse Station #11
Building 205, 3rd Floor
Augusta, ME 04333
207-287-3832
www.state.me.us/bms/bmshome.htm

MARYLAND
Department of Health and Mental
Hygiene
Eligibility Services
300 West Preston Street, Room 402
Baltimore, MD 21201
410-767-1463
www.dhmh.state.md.us/

MASSACHUSETTS
Division of Medical Assistance
600 Washington Street
Boston, MA 02111
617-210-5001
www.state.ma.us/dma/

MISSOURI
Division of Family Services
Department of Social Services
615 Howerton Court
P.O. Box 6500
Jefferson City, MO 65102
1-800-392-1261
www.dss.state.mo.us/dms/

MONTANA
Department of Public Health &
Human Services
1400 Broadway
Helena, MT 59601
406-444-4540 (will refer to county
office)
www.dphhs.state.mt.us/hpsd/
index.htm

NEBRASKA
Medicaid Division
Department of Health and Human
Services
P.O. Box 95026
301 Centennial Mall South,
5th Floor
Lincoln, NE 68509-5026
402-471-9147 (will refer to local
office)
www.hhs.state.ne.us/med/
medindex.htm

NEVADA
Division of Health-Care Financing
and Policy
1100 East William Street
Suite 101
Carson City, NV 89701
775-684-3676 (will refer to local city
office)
dhcfp.state.nv.us/

NEW HAMPSHIRE
Medicaid Administration Bureau
Department of Health and Human
Services
Office of the Commissioner
129 Pleasant Street
Concord, NH 03301-6521
603-271-4348
www.dhhs.state.nh.us/CommPublic
Health/medicaid.nsf/ByCat?
Openview

NEW JERSEY
Department of Health and Senior
Services
Division of Consumer Support
Office of Long-Term Care Options
12 D Quaker Bridge Plaza
P.O. Box 722
Trenton, NJ 08625
609-588-2613
www.state.nj.us/humanservices/
dmahs/dhsmed.html

NEW MEXICO
Medical Assistance Division
Department of Human Services
P.O. Box 2348
Santa Fe, NM 87504-2348
505-827-3182
www.state.nm.us/hsd/mad/
Index.html

NEW YORK
Office of Medicaid Management
Department of Health
Empire State Plaza
Room 1466, Corning Tower
Building
Albany, NY 12237
Medicaid Helpline 1-800-541-2831
www.health.state.ny.us/nysdoh/
medicaid/medicaid.htm

SOUTH DAKOTA
Medical Services
Department of Social Services
Kneip Building
700 Governors Drive
Pierre, SD 57501-2291
605-773-3495
www.state.sd.us/social/medical/
index.htm

TENNESSEE
Department of Finance and
Administration
Long-Term Care Unit
706 Church Street, 2nd Floor
Nashville, TN 37247-6501
615-741-0212
www.state.tn.us/tenncare/
longtermcare.html

TEXAS
Health and Human Services
Commission
4900 North Lamar Street, 4th Floor
Austin, TX 78751
512-438-3280
1-800-458-9858
www.hhsc.texas.gov/Medicaid/
index.html

UTAH
Medicaid Information Office
288 North 1460 West
Salt Lake City, UT 84114
801-538-6155 (will refer to local
office)
1-800-662-9651
hlunix.hl.state.ut.us/medicaid/

VERMONT
Department of Prevention,
Assistance, Transition & Health
Access
Office of Health Access
103 South Main Street
Waterbury, VT 05671-1201
802-241-3985 (will refer to district
office)
www.dsw.state.vt.us/districts/ovha/
ovha5.htm

VIRGINIA
Department of Medical Assistance
Services
600 East Broad Street, Suite 1300
Richmond, VA 23219
804-786-6273
www.myvirginia.org/portal/
government/index.htm

WISCONSIN
Department of Health and Family
Services
Division of Health-Care Financing
1 West Wilson Street, Room 350
P.O. Box 309
Madison, WI 53701-0309
608-266-8922
www.dhfs.state.wi.us/medicaid/

WYOMING
Department of Family Services
2300 Capital Avenue
Cheyenne, WY 82002
307-777-6074
wdhfs.state.wy.us/WDH/
medicaid.htm

State Executive Offices of Elder Affairs

This is the place in your state dedicated to serving seniors. If you're not sure who to call about something, this is a great place to start.

ALABAMA
Alabama Department of Senior Services
770 Washington Avenue
Suite 470, RSA Plaza
Montgomery, AL 36130
334-242-5743
1-877-425-2243 (in state)
www.adss.state.al.us

ALASKA
Alaska Commission on Aging
P.O. Box 110209
Juneau, AK 99811-0209
907-269-3666
1-800-478-9996 (in state)
www.alaskaaging.org

ARIZONA
Arizona Aging and Adult
Administration
1789 West Jefferson Street, #950A
Phoenix, AZ 85007
602-542-4446
1-800-432-4040 (any state)
www.de.state.az.us

ARKANSAS
Division of Aging and Adult Services
P.O. Box 1437, Slot S-530
Little Rock, AR 72203-1437
501-682-2441
www.state.ar.us/dhs/aging/facts

CALIFORNIA
California Department of Aging
1600 K Street
Sacramento, CA 95814
916-322-3887
1-800-510-2020 (in state)
916-324-4989 (fax)
www.aging.ca.gov

COLORADO
Division of Aging and Adult Services
Department of Human Services
1575 Sherman Street, Ground Floor
Denver, CO 80203
303-866-2800
1-800-290-4530 (in state)
www.colorado.gov

CONNECTICUT
Elderly Services Division
Department of Human Services
10 Prospect Street
Hartford, CT 06103
860-543-8690
www.ctelderlyservices.state.ct.us/
GreetingsFrm.htm

DELAWARE
Division of Services for Aging and
Adults with Physical Disabilities
Department of Health and Social
Services
1901 North DuPont Highway
2nd Floor Annex Administration
Building.
New Castle, DE 19720
302-577-4791
1-800-223-9074 (in state)
www.dsaapd.com

DISTRICT OF COLUMBIA
Office on Aging
441 Fourth Street, NW
Washington, DC 20001
202-724-5626
www.dcoa.dc.gov

FLORIDA
Department of Elder Affairs
Building B, Suite 315
4040 Esplanade Way
Tallahassee, FL 32399-7000
850-414-2000
1-800-963-5337 (in state)
www.elderaffairs.state.fl.us

GEORGIA
Division of Aging Services
Department of Human Resources
2 Peachtree Street, NW
9-398, 9th Floor
Atlanta, GA 30303
404-657-5258
www.dhr.state.ga.us

HAWAII
Executive Office on Aging
No. 1 Capitol District
250 South Hotel Street, Suite 406
Honolulu, HI 96813-2831
808-586-0100
www.state.hi.us/health/eoa/

IDAHO
Commission on Aging
P.O. Box 83720
Boise, ID 83720-0007
208-334-3833
1-877-471-2777 (any state)
www.idahoaging.com

ILLINOIS
Department on Aging
421 East Capitol Avenue, #100
Springfield, IL 62701-1789
217-785-3356
1-800-252-8966 (in state)
www.state.il.us/aging/

INDIANA
Division of Aging and Home
Services
402 West Washington Street
P.O. Box 7083
Indianapolis, IN 46207-7083
317-232-7020
1-800-545-7763 (any state)
www.in.gov/sic

IOWA
Department of Elder Affairs
200 10th Street, 3rd Floor
Des Moines, IA 50309-3609
515-242-3333
1-800-532-3213 (any state)
www.state.ia.us/elderaffairs

KANSAS
Department on Aging
New England Building
503 South Kansas Avenue
Topeka, KS 66603-3404
785-296-4986
1-800-432-3535 (in state)
www.agingkansas.org

KENTUCKY
Office of Aging Services
Cabinet of Health Service
275 East Main Street, 5 C-D
Frankfort, KY 40621
502-564-6930
ww.chs.state.ky.us/aging/

LOUISIANA
Office of Elderly Affairs
412 North Fourth Street
P.O. Box 80374
Baton Rouge, LA 70898-0374
225-342-7100
www.louisianaaging.org

MAINE
Bureau of Elder and Adult Services
State House, Station 11
Augusta, ME 04333
207-624-5335
1-800-262-2232 (any state)
www.state.me.us/dhs/beas

MARYLAND
Department on Aging
301 West Preston Street,
Room 1007
Baltimore, MD 21202
410-767-1100
1-800-243-3425
www.mdoa.state.md.us

MASSACHUSETTS
Executive Office of Elder Affairs
1 Ashburton Place, 5th Floor
Boston, MA 02108
617-727-7750
1-800-243-4636
www.800ageinfo.com

MICHIGAN
Office of Services to the Aging
P.O. Box 30676
Lansing, MI 48909-8176
517-373-8230
www.miseniors.net

MINNESOTA
Board on Aging
444 Lafayette Road North
St. Paul, MN 55155-3843
651-296-2770
1-800-882-6262 (any state)
www.mnaging.org

MISSISSIPPI
Division of Aging and Adult Services
750 North State Street
Jackson, MS 39202
601-359-5131 or 601-359-4929
1-800-948-3090 (in state)
www.mdhs.state.ms.us

MISSOURI
Department of Health and Senior
Services
P.O. Box 570
615 Howerton Court
Jefferson City, MO 65109
573-751-3082
1-800-235-5503 (in state)
www.dhss.state.mo.us

MONTANA
Senior and Long-Term Care
Division
111 Sanders Street
P.O. Box 4210
Helena, MT 59604
406-444-4077
1-800-332-2272 (in state) or
1-800-551-3191 (in state)
www.dphhs.state.mt.us/sltc

NEBRASKA
Department of Health and Human
Services
Division of Aging
State Office Building
301 Centennial Mall South
Lincoln, NE 68509-5044
402-471-2306
1-800-430-3244 (in state)
www.hhs.state.ne.us

NEVADA
Division for Aging Services
3100 West Sahara Avenue, Suite 103
Las Vegas, NV 89102
702-486-3545
www.nvaging.net

NEW HAMPSHIRE
Department of Health and Human
Services
Division of Elderly and Adult
Services
State Office Park South
129 Pleasant Street
Concord, NH 03301
603-271-4394
1-800-351-1888 (in state)
www.dhhs.state.nh.us

NEW JERSEY
Department of Community Affairs
Division on Aging
101 South Broad Street CN 807
Trenton, NJ 08625-0807
609-292-1876
1-800-792-8820 (in state)

NEW MEXICO
New Mexico State Agency on Aging
La Villa Rivera Building
228 East Palace Avenue
Santa Fe, NM 87501
505-827-7640
1-800-432-2080 (in state)
www.nmaging.state.nm.us

NEW YORK
State Office for the Aging
New York State Plaza Agency
Building #2
Albany, NY 12223-0001
518-474-5731
1-800-342-9871 (in state)
aging.state.ny.us/index.htm

NORTH CAROLINA
Division of Aging
2101 Mail Service Center
Raleigh, NC 27699-2101
919-733-3983
www.dhhs.state.nc.us/aging/home

NORTH DAKOTA
Department of Human Services
Aging Services Division
600 South Second Street, Suite 1C
Bismarck, ND 58504
1-800-451-8693 (any state)
www.state.nd.us/humanservices

OHIO
Department of Aging
50 West Broad Street, 9th Floor
Columbus, OH 43215-3363
614-466-5500
1-800-282-1206 (any state)
www.ohio.gov/age

OKLAHOMA
Department of Human Services
Aging Services Division
312 NE 28th Street
Oklahoma City, OK 73105
405-521-2327
1-800-211-2116 (in state)
www.okdhs.org/aging/

OREGON
Department of Human Services
Senior and People with Disabilities
500 Summer Street NE, EO2
Salem, OR 9730-1073
503-945-5811
1-800-232-3020 (in state) or
1-800-282-8096 (in state)
www.sdsd.hr.state.or.us

PENNSYLVANIA
Department of Aging
"APPRISE" Health Insurance
Counseling and Assistance
400 Market Street
Rachel Carson State Office Building
Harrisburg, PA 17101
1-800-783-7067 (any state)
www.aging.state.pa.us

PUERTO RICO
Governor's Office of Elderly Affairs
P.O. Box 50063
Old San Juan Station
San Juan, PR 00902
787-721-5710 or 787-721-6121
www.aoa.dhhs.gov/RegionsI-II/
stpr.htm

RHODE ISLAND
Department of Elderly Affairs
160 Pine Street
Providence, RI 02903-3708
401-222-2858
www.dea.state.ri.us/

SOUTH CAROLINA
Office of Senior Long-Term Care
Service
Bureau of Senior Service
1801 Main Street
P.O. Box 8206
Columbia, SC 29202-8206
803-898-2850
1-800-868-9095 (in state)
www.dhhs.state.sc.us/offices/
long_term_care/bureau.htm

SOUTH DAKOTA
Office of Adult Services and Aging
700 Governors Drive
Pierre, SD 57501-2291
605-773-3656
1-866-854-5465 (in state)
www.state.sd.us/asa

TENNESSEE
Tennessee Commission on Aging
and Disabilities
Andrew Jackson Building, 9th Floor
500 Deaderick Street
Nashville, TN 37243-0860
615-741-2056
www.state.tn.us/comaging

UTAH
Division of Aging and Adult Services
P.O. Box 45500
Salt Lake City, UT 84145-0500
801-538-3910
1-800-541-7735 (in state)
www.hsdaas.state.ut.us/

VERMONT
Aging and Disabilities
Waterbury State Office Complex
103 South Main Street
Waterbury, VT 05671-2301
802-241-2400
www.dad.state.vt.us

VIRGINIA
Department for the Aging
1600 Forest Avenue
Preston Building, Suite 102
Richmond, VA 23229
804-662-9333
1-800-552-3402 (any state)
www.aging.state.va.us

WASHINGTON
Aging and Adult Services
Administration
Department of Social and Health
Services
P.O. Box 45600
Olympia, WA 98504-5600
360-725-2300
1-800-422-3263 (in state)
www.aasa.dshs.wa.gov

WEST VIRGINIA
Bureau of Senior Services
1900 Kanawha Boulevard,
East Holly Grove
Building 10
Charleston, WV 25305-0160
304-558-3317
www.state.wv.us/seniorservices

WYOMING
WDH Division on Aging
Hathaway Building
6101 Yellowstone Road
Room 259B
Cheyenne, WY 82002-0710
307-777-7986
1-800-442-2766 (any state)

Nursing Home and Home Health-Care Costs

This appendix shows the costs of nursing homes and home health care across the country. The nursing home costs are shown as a daily rate. Nursing home costs indicated with an asterisk (*) reflect a different pricing structure in that market than in others (for example, some didn't differentiate between private and semiprivate rooms, and some showed different care levels). The survey was conducted by MetLife's Mature Market Institute and released in early 2002. Though it includes data from 482 nursing homes, not all ZIP code areas in each state are represented.

Nursing Home Costs

Region	State	Semiprivate High	Semiprivate Low	Semiprivate Average	Private High	Private Low	Private Average
Anchorage	AK	$450.00*	$210.00*	**$321.00**	$450.00*	$210.00*	**$330.60**
Birmingham	AL	$115.00	$101.00	**$109.20**	$150.00	$107.00	**$120.80**
Montgomery	AL	$138.61	$110.42	**$126.94**	$143.50	$116.50	**$133.98**
Little Rock	AR	$105.27	$95.00	**$98.70**	$147.00	$95.00	**$118.32**
Phoenix	AZ	$161.00	$111.00	**$131.00**	$185.00	$145.00	**$162.00**
Tucson	AZ	$148.28	$105.00	**$129.85**	$229.50	$123.50	**$165.71**
Los Angeles	CA	$157.00	$110.00*	**$124.22**	$310.00	$110.00*	**$174.66**
San Diego	CA	$140.00	$132.00	**$135.72**	$280.00	$145.00	**$187.96**
San Francisco	CA	$165.00	$122.00	**$146.80**	$324.00	$150.00	**$249.80**
Colorado Springs	CO	$133.00	$114.50	**$122.30**	$128.00	$122.50	**$125.70**
Denver	CO	$140.00	$118.00	**$130.40**	$150.00	$132.00	**$141.40**
Hartford	CT	$220.00	$210.00	**$214.00**	$245.00	$215.00	**$233.00**
Stamford	CT	$320.00	$252.00	**$273.96**	$504.00	$278.00	**$346.67**
Washington	DC	$241.00*	$160.00*	**$193.20**	$241.00*	$160.00*	**$203.20**
Wilmington	DE	$154.00	$130.00	**$142.26**	$187.96	$145.00	**$160.99**
Jacksonville	FL	$137.00	$102.00	**$121.75**	$150.00	$120.00	**$137.33**
Miami	FL	$175.00	$120.00	**$137.20**	$250.00	$150.00	**$193.40**
Orlando	FL	$131.16	$118.00	**$124.87**	$148.13	$125.00	**$134.24**
Alpharetta	GA	$134.00	$110.00	**$122.00**	$164.00	$129.00	**$141.35**
Atlanta	GA	$130.00	$105.00	**$115.40**	$140.00	$115.00	**$129.76**
Honolulu	HI	$200.00	$144.00	**$172.70**	$376.00	$150.00	**$220.50**
Des Moines	IA	$115.00	$95.00	**$102.80**	$128.00	$101.00	**$116.00**
Boise	ID	$139.00	$130.00	**$134.80**	$157.00	$139.00	**$147.40**
Chicago	IL	$174.00	$100.00	**$124.07**	$185.00	$110.00	**$140.14**
Elgin	IL	$198.00	$114.00	**$160.43**	$205.00	$129.00	**$177.00**
Highland Park	IL	$200.00	$125.00	**$156.92**	$239.00	$145.00	**$197.09**
Peoria	IL	$164.00	$95.00	**$128.00**	$190.00	$125.00	**$160.60**
Ft. Wayne	IN	$129.00	$119.00	**$123.20**	$240.00	$139.00	**$161.40**
Indianapolis	IN	$134.50	$89.00*	**$114.40**	$250.00	$89.00*	**$163.19**
Wichita	KS	$120.00	$99.00	**$108.70**	$130.00	$104.00	**$119.30**

Region	State	Semiprivate High	Semiprivate Low	Semiprivate Average	Private High	Private Low	Private Average
Lexington	KY	$129.00	$118.00	**$123.60**	$152.00	$128.00	**$142.40**
Louisville	KY	$120.00	$106.50	**$114.10**	$135.00	$114.00	**$124.80**
New Orleans	LA	$105.00	$72.00	**$89.37**	$117.50	$80.00	**$94.87**
Shreveport	LA	$88.20	$78.00	**$84.13**	$100.30	$83.00	**$87.95**
Boston	MA	$250.00	$170.00	**$207.00**	$350.00	$200.00	**$243.50**
Worcester	MA	$250.00	$180.00	**$219.60**	$400.00	$205.00	**$269.60**
Baltimore	MD	$184.00*	$120.00	**$150.67**	$184.00*	$130.00	**$159.39**
Silver Spring	MD	$190.00	$130.00	**$158.30**	$215.00	$150.00	**$177.50**
Brunswick	ME	$187.00	$145.00	**$164.40**	$200.00	$175.00	**$183.00**
Detroit	MI	$136.00	$105.00	**$119.20**	$148.00	$110.00	**$125.60**
Grand Rapids	MI	$153.00	$125.00	**$139.28**	$172.50	$127.75	**$154.15**
Minneapolis	MN	$175.00	$83.00	**$130.08**	$240.00	$93.41	**$167.60**
St. Paul	MN	$170.00	$120.00	**$137.00**	$340.00	$120.50	**$197.60**
Kansas City	MO	$104.00	$70.00	**$95.55**	$206.00	$125.75	**$147.35**
St. Louis	MO	$120.00	$100.00	**$109.75**	$220.50	$105.00	**$147.78**
Jackson	MS	$106.00	$85.00	**$100.30**	$208.34	$95.00	**$125.98**
Billings	MT	$133.00	$118.00	**$123.70**	$151.00	$128.00	**$135.37**
Charlotte	NC	$166.00	$108.00	**$135.40**	$169.00	$120.00	**$148.40**
Raleigh	NC	$132.50	$115.00	**$124.50**	$155.00	$134.00	**$142.40**
Fargo	ND	$165.50*	$148.50*	**$155.50**	$165.50*	$148.50*	**$155.50**
Omaha	NE	$165.00	$112.70*	**$133.67**	$330.00	$112.70*	**$207.00**
Manchester	NH	$191.00	$160.00	**$173.40**	$211.00	$174.00	**$187.60**
Bridgewater	NJ	$246.00	$179.00	**$209.20**	$268.00	$185.00	**$227.60**
Cherry Hill	NJ	$198.00	$165.00	**$188.07**	$235.00	$181.00	**$205.75**
Albuquerque	NM	$135.44	$118.00	**$126.26**	$180.00	$136.00	**$154.26**
Las Vegas	NV	$140.00	$106.00	**$129.40**	$280.00	$111.25	**$198.65**
New York	NY	$330.00*	$230.00*	**$269.00**	$330.00*	$230.00*	**$274.00**
Rochester	NY	$215.00	$189.00	**$200.00**	$220.00	$198.00	**$208.80**
Syracuse	NY	$215.00	$180.00	**$201.00**	$216.00	$190.00	**$207.00**
Akron	OH	$160.00	$121.00	**$138.60**	$320.00	$142.00	**$185.80**
Cleveland	OH	$155.00	$145.00*	**$151.25**	$310.00	$145.00*	**$230.25**
Columbus	OH	$160.00	$134.00	**$144.60**	$177.00	$135.00	**$158.80**

continues

Nursing Home Costs   (continued)

Region	State	Semiprivate High	Semiprivate Low	Semiprivate Average	Private High	Private Low	Private Average
Oklahoma City	OK	$107.00	$92.50	**$96.70**	$172.00	$94.00	**$125.20**
Tulsa	OK	$110.00	$74.00	**$96.60**	$155.00	$78.00	**$130.60**
Eugene	OR	$139.00	$110.00	**$118.20**	$170.00	$115.00	**$143.00**
Portland	OR	$131.00	$115.00	**$122.00**	$165.00	$120.00	**$143.60**
Philadelphia	PA	$217.00*	$145.00	**$178.83**	$217.00*	$165.00	**$188.83**
Pittsburgh	PA	$177.00	$135.00	**$153.80**	$200.00	$148.00	**$164.40**
Scranton	PA	$170.00	$110.00	**$138.40**	$195.00	$115.00	**$151.60**
Providence	RI	$205.00	$145.00	**$170.00**	$250.00	$145.00	**$181.00**
Charleston	SC	$125.00	$98.00	**$111.60**	$145.00	$108.00	**$125.60**
Columbia	SC	$158.00	$115.00	**$125.20**	$170.50	$125.00	**$136.50**
Dell Rapids	SD	$120.50*	$105.00	**$112.43**	$125.50*	$110.00	**$116.43**
Memphis	TN	$120.00	$98.00	**$111.00**	$156.00	$110.00	**$133.20**
Nashville	TN	$120.50	$109.00	**$113.70**	$137.50	$114.00	**$127.00**
Dallas	TX	$119.00	$80.00	**$102.00**	$160.00	$125.00	**$143.00**
Fort Worth	TX	$108.53	$80.00	**$92.11**	$170.00	$116.57	**$143.11**
Houston	TX	$111.50	$84.00	**$90.90**	$170.00	$106.00	**$143.20**
Salt Lake City	UT	$128.00	$102.00	**$111.80**	$204.00	$110.00	**$148.80**
Alexandria	VA	$168.00	$148.00	**$155.60**	$184.00	$172.00	**$176.80**
Arlington	VA	$187.00	$180.00	**$183.60**	$214.50	$200.00	**$205.10**
Richmond	VA	$153.00	$115.00	**$127.60**	$147.50	$136.00	**$140.38**
Rutland	VT	$216.50	$155.00	**$186.23**	$235.00	$160.67	**$200.93**
Seattle	WA	$184.00	$158.00*	**$169.08**	$326.00	$158.00*	**$203.90**
Spokane	WA	$170.00	$130.00	**$148.73**	$180.00	$151.33	**$160.06**
Madison	WI	$155.00	$138.00	**$147.20**	$186.50	$150.00	**$166.63**
Milwaukee	WI	$192.00	$135.00	**$164.64**	$202.50	$140.00	**$178.07**
Martinsburg	WV	$237.50	$120.00*	**$154.43**	$242.50	$120.00*	**$163.12**
Worland	WY	$115.00	$110.00	**$113.00**	$145.00	$117.00	**$125.80**
Average				**$142.56**			**$167.82**

Source: MetLife Market Survey on Nursing Home and Home Care Costs 2002

Home Health-Care Costs

The home health-care costs quoted here are hourly, through a licensed agency. The survey was conducted by MetLife's Mature Market Institute and released in early 2002. HHA means home-health aide. LPN means licensed practical nurse. Although the survey includes data from 521 home health care agencies, not all ZIP codes in each state are represented.

Region	State	HHA High	HHA Low	HHA Average	LPN High	LPN Low	LPN Average
Anchorage	AK	$40.00	$21.00	**$26.60**	$80.00	$28.00	**$65.60**
Birmingham	AL	$15.50	$12.50	**$13.82**	$27.00	$22.00	**$24.71**
Montgomery	AL	$13.50	$10.50	**$11.70**	$25.00	$18.00	**$21.50**
Little Rock	AR	$16.00	$10.00	**$13.75**	$30.00	$25.00	**$26.90**
Phoenix	AZ	$24.00	$17.00	**$19.39**	$39.60	$30.00	**$33.95**
Tucson	AZ	$16.75	$15.00	**$15.62**	$120.00	$23.95	**$50.69**
San Francisco	CA	$25.00	$17.50	**$20.45**	$50.00	$35.00	**$44.00**
San Diego	CA	$24.00	$15.45	**$17.78**	$39.00	$29.00	**$34.17**
Los Angeles	CA	$18.00	$9.75	**$14.75**	$35.00	$24.00	**$30.35**
Colorado Springs	CO	$30.00	$17.87	**$22.37**	$120.00	$30.00	**$57.00**
Denver	CO	$25.00	$17.25	**$20.65**	$62.50	$33.50	**$41.20**
Hartford	CT	$28.00	$19.50	**$23.70**	$50.00	$37.75	**$42.67**
Stamford	CT	$27.26	$13.00	**$21.89**	$50.00	$35.00	**$43.39**
Washington	DC	$17.00	$15.00	**$16.30**	$90.00	$30.00	**$54.00**
Wilmington	DE	$20.45	$16.50	**$18.89**	$57.50	$32.00	**$40.49**
Orlando	FL	$19.00	$14.50	**$16.65**	$56.00	$26.00	**$40.40**
Jacksonville	FL	$16.50	$14.50	**$15.50**	$30.00	$26.00	**$28.00**
Miami	FL	$20.00	$9.00	**$13.15**	$32.00	$18.00	**$29.53**
Atlanta	GA	$19.00	$15.50	**$16.90**	$40.00	$29.00	**$33.80**
Alpharetta	GA	$20.28	$15.25	**$16.81**	$33.95	$26.25	**$29.04**
Honolulu	HI	$19.75	$17.05	**$19.15**	$37.00	$25.78	**$30.03**
Des Moines	IA	$22.00	$15.50	**$17.95**	$32.00	$20.00	**$27.60**
Boise	ID	$17.00	$16.00	**$16.40**	$38.00	$30.00	**$33.40**
Chicago	IL	$25.00	$14.00	**$18.87**	$40.00	$31.00	**$36.47**
Elgin	IL	$19.00	$16.75	**$18.15**	$38.00	$23.00	**$31.20**

continues

continued

Region	State	HHA High	HHA Low	HHA Average	LPN High	LPN Low	LPN Average
Highland Park	IL	$25.00	$15.00	**$18.13**	$40.00	$30.00	**$34.24**
Peoria	IL	$19.00	$16.00	**$17.76**	$49.00	$28.00	**$36.60**
Indianapolis	IN	$25.00	$15.00	**$20.00**	$40.00	$16.00	**$32.50**
Ft. Wayne	IN	$20.00	$16.50	**$17.70**	$44.50	$23.00	**$30.55**
Wichita	KS	$17.95	$16.25	**$16.99**	$30.00	$21.50	**$26.50**
Louisville	KY	$38.00	$15.00	**$23.25**	$75.00	$30.00	**$56.00**
Lexington	KY	$16.00	$14.50	**$15.65**	$35.00	$26.25	**$30.97**
New Orleans	LA	$20.00	$10.00	**$13.75**	$35.00	$13.50	**$25.25**
Shreveport	LA	$14.00	$12.00	**$12.80**	$29.00	$26.00	**$27.50**
Worcester	MA	$25.95	$19.50	**$22.67**	$46.45	$32.00	**$38.10**
Boston	MA	$22.00	$15.50	**$19.05**	$40.00	$34.00	**$35.83**
Silver Spring	MD	$18.00	$13.50	**$15.08**	$39.50	$17.00	**$32.20**
Baltimore	MD	$18.00	$12.00	**$14.85**	$37.00	$33.00	**$34.50**
Brunswick	ME	$20.00	$16.00	**$18.30**	$32.00	$17.50	**$27.16**
Detroit	MI	$20.50	$15.00	**$17.40**	$36.00	$27.50	**$33.20**
Grand Rapids	MI	$17.66	$15.00	**$16.43**	$32.50	$18.00	**$27.07**
St. Paul	MN	$26.00	$21.50	**$23.60**	$42.00	$31.00	**$35.80**
Minneapolis	MN	$24.00	$20.00	**$21.16**	$38.00	$25.00	**$27.58**
Kansas City	MO	$19.99	$13.50	**$16.95**	$30.00	$19.00	**$25.25**
St. Louis	MO	$18.00	$15.13	**$16.73**	$60.00	$26.50	**$36.14**
Jackson	MS	$25.00	$9.25	**$12.95**	$45.00	$19.95	**$26.39**
Billings	MT	$17.00	$13.85	**$15.34**	$33.50	$20.00	**$25.30**
Charlotte	NC	$17.75	$15.50	**$16.59**	$38.00	$31.00	**$35.40**
Raleigh	NC	$18.33	$14.00	**$16.47**	$38.00	$15.00	**$30.70**
Fargo	ND	$19.00	$17.00	**$18.00**	$45.00	$40.00	**$42.80**
Omaha	NE	$20.00	$18.00	**$18.55**	$90.00	$27.00	**$47.60**
Manchester	NH	$22.00	$19.00	**$20.60**	$36.00	$32.00	**$33.40**
Bridgewater	NJ	$23.00	$17.00	**$18.83**	$51.00	$35.00	**$39.70**
Cherry Hill	NJ	$20.00	$15.50	**$17.30**	$40.00	$25.00	**$33.70**
Albuquerque	NM	$19.00	$14.40	**$16.78**	$35.00	$30.00	**$32.80**
Las Vegas	NV	$21.50	$18.00	**$19.88**	$85.00	$30.00	**$46.21**
Syracuse	NY	$26.25	$15.50	**$17.82**	$53.50	$26.00	**$32.20**

Region	State	HHA High	HHA Low	HHA Average	LPN High	LPN Low	LPN Average
Rochester	NY	$17.50	$15.50	**$16.87**	$30.00	$24.20	**$27.04**
New York	NY	$16.50	$13.50	**$14.92**	$85.00	$32.00	**$41.78**
Columbus	OH	$18.00	$16.75	**$17.75**	$40.00	$20.00	**$28.70**
Akron	OH	$16.00	$15.00	**$15.80**	$28.00	$24.00	**$25.80**
Cleveland	OH	$16.00	$13.00	**$15.23**	$30.75	$23.00	**$26.60**
Oklahoma City	OK	$19.17	$13.00	**$16.43**	$65.00	$22.00	**$39.80**
Tulsa	OK	$16.00	$15.25	**$15.85**	$27.00	$25.00	**$26.20**
Portland	OR	$19.95	$18.13	**$18.82**	$120.00	$43.00	**$73.60**
Eugene	OR	$18.95	$14.50	**$15.89**	$110.00	$23.50	**$50.20**
Philadelphia	PA	$24.00	$17.00	**$19.60**	$46.00	$35.00	**$39.60**
Scranton	PA	$19.95	$16.80	**$18.38**	$30.00	$25.33	**$27.56**
Pittsburgh	PA	$17.00	$16.00	**$16.40**	$35.00	$26.00	**$30.20**
Providence	RI	$21.66	$18.00	**$19.92**	$37.00	$32.00	**$34.40**
Charleston	SC	$17.75	$14.50	**$15.65**	$40.00	$23.50	**$27.72**
Columbia	SC	$14.37	$12.95	**$13.76**	$30.00	$23.45	**$25.58**
Nashville	TN	$18.00	$14.50	**$15.79**	$30.50	$15.00	**$25.49**
Memphis	TN	$16.00	$14.00	**$14.88**	$30.00	$28.00	**$29.00**
Houston	TX	$29.00	$14.00	**$19.50**	$80.00	$25.00	**$43.40**
Fort Worth	TX	$20.00	$15.00	**$17.00**	$40.00	$20.00	**$26.00**
Dallas	TX	$20.00	$14.00	**$16.71**	$40.00	$27.00	**$33.71**
Salt Lake City	UT	$23.00	$13.50	**$19.55**	$70.00	$17.50	**$36.95**
Arlington	VA	$18.00	$15.50	**$17.00**	$120.00	$40.00	**$61.20**
Alexandria	VA	$18.00	$15.50	**$16.30**	$34.95	$30.00	**$32.59**
Richmond	VA	$18.00	$14.00	**$16.10**	$60.00	$22.00	**$32.47**
Seattle	WA	$24.00	$21.75	**$22.55**	$150.00	$33.50	**$94.85**
Spokane	WA	$15.50	$14.00	**$14.89**	$30.00	$22.50	**$25.90**
Madison	WI	$32.50	$17.40	**$22.88**	$120.00	$29.50	**$54.48**
Milwaukee	WI	$21.00	$14.00	**$18.95**	$110.00	$68.00	**$95.60**
Martinsburg	WV	$17.25	$12.50	**$16.05**	$35.00	$26.00	**$32.80**
Average				**$17.60**			**$36.73**

Source: MetLife Market Survey on Nursing Home and Home Care Costs 2002

Appendix **E**

Resources

Want even more information? The web sites, phone numbers, and other resources listed here are ready to help you in your long-term care planning. Combined with the state-specific resources in Appendices A, B, and C, you're well prepared.

Long-Term Care Planning

- **Long-Term Care Learning Institute**
  www.LongTermCareLearning.com
  The Long-Term Care Learning Institute website offers objective information about all aspects of LTC planning.

- **The National Association of Professional Geriatric Care Managers**
  1604 North Country Club Road
  Tucson, AZ 85716-3102
  520-881-8008
  www.CareManager.org
  A professional geriatric care manager (GCM) works with older people and their families to help them find the best solutions to their long-term care challenges. The listing above is for their nonprofit industry association. They have consumer information, and can also refer you to member GCMs in your area. GCM's often are trained as nurses, social workers, gerontologists, or counselors.

♦ **The National Eldercare Locator**
www.eldercare.gov
The Eldercare Locator, is a nationwide toll-free telephone service to help older adults and their caregivers find local services for seniors. The U.S. Administration on Aging now makes some of the service available at the website listed.

You can also call toll free 1-800-677-1116 for more information, Monday through Friday, 9 A.M. to 8 P.M., Eastern time.

♦ **State SHIP programs**
These are free programs for seniors, utilizing volunteer insurance counselors, under direction of a federal program. Find your local program by calling Medicare (information in the following section) or your state's office on aging (Appendix C), or the Eldercare Locator number listed above.

Medicare

♦ **Medicare website**
www.medicare.gov
The Medicare website has many publications that can be easily downloaded and printed out. It is a great place to get your questions on Medicare answered. For more information, you can also call 1-800-633-4227 (1-800-MEDICARE).

♦ **Original Medicare or Medicare Managed-Care Plan**
To find out if you are in original Medicare or a Medicare managed-care plan, call your local Social Security Administration (SSA) office, or call SSA at 1-800-772-1213.

Medicaid

♦ **CMS (Centers for Medicare and Medicaid Services)**
www.cms.gov/medicaid/
Formerly known as Health-Care Financing Administration.

♦ **Elder Answers**
www.elderlawanswers.com
This well-done site provides easy-to-understand information on Medicaid and other issues of concern to seniors and their families.

- ◆ **NAELA (The National Academy of Elder Law Attorneys)**
  1604 North Country Club Road
  Tuscon, AZ 85716-3195
  520-881-4005
  www.naela.org

- ◆ **State Medicaid Offices**
  For state Medicaid office information, please see Appendix B.

Companies That Rate Insurances

Most public libraries have access to ratings services. Insurance agents can give you copies of ratings, also. You can find these popular ratings services on the Internet:

- ◆ A.M. Best Company
  www.ambest.com/index.htm

- ◆ Standard & Poor's
  www.standardandpoors.com/RatingsActions/RatingsLists/Insurance/index.html

- ◆ Moody's
  www.moodys.com

Reverse Mortgages

- ◆ National Reverse Mortgage Lenders Association (NRMLA)
  1625 Massachusetts Avenue NW #601
  Washington, DC 20036
  202-939-1741
  www.reversemortgage.org
  The National Reverse Mortgage Lenders Association is a national nonprofit trade association for financial services companies that originate, service, and invest in reverse mortgages, both in the United States and Canada. At their website you can find lenders in your state who do reverse mortgages.

- ◆ AARP
  www.aarp.com
  AARP is the leading membership organization in the country for people age 50+. At their website, they have extensive information on reverse mortgages (as well as many other topics). At the site is also have a calculator to help you see what a reverse mortgage might pay you.

Miscellaneous

- **l Security**
  1-800-772-1213
  www.ssa.gov
  Learn all about Social Security at this site. In addition to reading information, you can apply for Social Security benefits online, request your earnings report and benefit estimates, and even check if you're eligible for Social Security benefits.

- **Settlements and Viaticals**
  The Viatical and Life Settlement Association of America
  800 Mayfair Circle
  Orlando, FL 32803
  1-800-842-9811
  www.viatical.org
  The Viatical & Life Settlement Association of America is a nonprofit trade association. Consumers can learn more about life settlements and viaticals at their website.

- **Living Benefits Financial Services, L.L.C.**
  www.livingbenefitsllc.com
  Although this website is for the use of insurance agents and other financial advisors, there is information that consumers will find helpful here.

- *The Medicaid Planning Handbook*, by Alexander A. Bove Jr., Little, Brown and Company (1996).

Glossary

accelerated death benefit   An optional benefit on many life insurance policies. It lets the insured get the insurance death benefit before he or she dies. In order to get this benefit, you must meet the terms of the contract. For example, the contract may require that you are expected to live less than six months, or that you are permanently confined to a nursing home.

adverse selection   Describes the fact that people who are at the highest risk for an event are more likely to apply for insurance protection.

assets   Any property of value. An asset may be tangible, which means that it has a physical form, such as a home. Or an asset may be intangible, such as an annuity contract or a savings account. In order to qualify for many government-provided long-term care services, you must have very few assets.

assisted living facility   A place that combines the best aspects of apartment-style living with prepared meals, housekeeping, and personal care services often desired and needed by seniors.

beneficiary   In long-term care planning beneficiary has two different definitions. (1) A Medicare beneficiary is someone who is covered by Medicare. (2) The beneficiary of a life insurance policy or of an annuity is someone who is named by the contract owner to receive payment when the insured or annuitant dies.

benefit trigger   Defines how someone qualifies for benefit under an insurance policy. For example, dying is the benefit trigger for a life insurance policy.

bequest   An asset, such as money, left to a person or other entity in a will.

care coordinators   People, often with a nursing or social worker background, who help families with all aspects of long-term care. In addition to accessing the situation and recommending services, they can monitor and help the family if and when the need for care changes, or if something goes wrong.

caregiving circles   Consist of a group of people who agree to take care of each other.

community spouse   The spouse who is not living in the nursing home and is living in the community. Sometimes called the "healthy spouse."

countable assets   Assets that count in terms of qualifying for Medicaid. Countable assets must be spent-down before you can qualify for Medicaid from an asset point of view.

custodial care   Consists of nonmedical long-term care. Custodial care includes activities such as transferring someone from a bed to a chair, or helping them get dressed or take a bath. Caregivers can be family members, friends or licensed professionals such as home health aides.

death benefit   The amount of that the insurance company pays the beneficiary when the person covered by a life insurance policy dies.

elder law attorney   A lawyer who specializes in legal matters for seniors, such as applying for Medicaid and Medicaid planning. Some elder law attorneys also do planning for disabled children and adults.

elimination period (EP)   Sometimes called the "waiting period," it is the number of days that you must first receive care before your policy benefit can start. Like a deductible, most policies require that you pay for care for a day to count toward your EP.

full-pay policies   Stand-alone insurance policies on which you pay premiums until care is needed. While you are collecting a benefit on claim, with most policies, premiums are no longer due.

geriatric care manager (GCM)   A care coordinator.

guaranteed renewable   As long as you pay your premium, your policy is in force. Premiums are not guaranteed to remain level. Only a noncancelable policy means that premiums are guaranteed to never increase.

home equity   The value of your house that is truly yours. Take the amount that your house could be sold for and subtract the amount of any mortgages or loans against the house. In the early years of a mortgage, the home equity can be very low. Most seniors have no mortgage and their homes have appreciated, giving them a lot of home equity.

illiquid assets   Assets that are difficult and costly to sell. Two examples are homes and fine jewelry. The most liquid asset is cash, which can be used immediately.

life settlement   A life settlement is when a senior citizen with a life expectancy of 12 years or fewer sells his or her life insurance. This sale of a life insurance policy is different than a viatical settlement, because the insured does not need to be terminally ill.

limited pay policies   Insurance policies where you pay premiums for a limited number of years, but the insurance coverage continues for the rest of your life. You pay a higher premium to pre-pay for a lifetime of insurance. At the end of the premium-paying period, you may be susceptible—or not—to having to pay additional premiums if the insurance company has a rate increase approved.

long-term care   Ongoing assistance that allows someone with a chronic health condition or functional limitation to maintain their abilities and quality of life. This help can include skilled medical care, as well as custodial care. Anyone at any age can require long-term care, either due to physical limitations or a cognitive impairment. Most long-term care is not medical or skilled care; it's custodial care.

look-back periods   Refers to how long the government looks back to see if you have made transfers to individuals or trusts. Most transfers within look-back periods trigger a period of Medicaid ineligibility.

means-tested   A program which looks at an applicant's financial situation in order to either approve or disapprove his or her benefit application. For example, to qualify for Medicaid, you must be poor, so Medicaid is a means-tested program.

Medicaid recipient   Someone receiving a benefit from the Medicaid program.

medically underwritten annuity   An annuity that pays out a highly regular (such as monthly) payout to those applicants whose health is impaired. A traditional annuity bases the payout on the applicant's age, not health.

Medicare beneficiary   Someone covered by the federal Medicare health insurance program.

Minimum Monthly Maintenance Needs Allowance, or MMMNA   The amount of the nursing home spouse's (Medicaid recipient) income that the community spouse/healthy spouse can keep to live on.

morbidity risk   The phrase that insurers use to describe the chance that an individual will become disabled.

mortality risk   The phrase that insurers use to describe an individual's chances of dying.

noncountable assets   Sometimes called excludable assets, these do not count towards your Medicaid eligibility. However, these assets may be subject to estate recovery.

nursing home spouse   The spouse on Medicaid (Medicaid recipient) who lives in the nursing home.

patient-paid amount   Income paid to the nursing home each month by someone on Medicaid. This amount is usually equal to all their income, less certain deductions such as medical insurance premiums, a personal-needs allowance, and, if married, the Minimum Monthly Maintenance Needs Allowance (income reserved for the healthy spouse).

personal-needs allowance   The amount of money that someone on Medicaid is allowed to keep each month for personal use.

policy forms   Different contracts for the same type of insurance which may be offered by the same insurance company. For example, one long-term care insurance policy form may include a reasonable and customary benefit limitation while another, offered by the same insurance company, does not.

private-paying   For long-term care means paying with either your own money or long-term care insurance.

recovery (or estate recovery)   The name of and the process that your state government goes through when you pass away after having been on Medicaid. Mandated to do so by the federal government, during recovery, the state government tries to recover from your estate the cost of what was paid for your care.

respite care   Temporary care to allow a caregiver to have a break, such as a vacation. Many facilities, such as assisted living facilities, have rooms dedicated to temporary respite stays. Many LTC insurance policies have a benefit for respite care.

risk management   Deciding what financial risks that you are willing to keep on your own shoulders, and which risks that you will transfer to an insurance company by purchasing insurance.

skilled care   Medically necessary care given by licensed medical professionals under a doctor's orders. This care is paid for by health insurance or Medicare.

spend-down   Selling assets and spending the proceeds on your care (or other allowable expenditures) until your assets are low enough to qualify for Medicaid.

surrendering   To give up, or cancel, an insurance policy (or annuity contract), such as a life insurance policy. Any surrender value would then be sent to the policy owner, and no future benefits paid.

term insurance   Life insurance designed to provide life insurance for a specific number of years. It is pure protection only, and does not build up cash value. It's very inexpensive, unless you want to maintain it longer than it was designed for. You can buy term insurance that locks in the same flat premium for 20 or even 30 years.

terminally ill   Means that someone is expected to die within a specified time period, usually less than two years in insurance policy definitions. When someone is described as terminally ill, it means that a doctor has determined that there is no hope of recovery.

underwriting   Underwriting usually refers to medical underwriting, which is the process of looking at someone's health and making a decision about issuing insurance. When you apply for long-term care insurance, the insurance company tries to evaluate your health in terms of your likely risk of needing long-term care.

uninsurable   Someone who is not able to purchase insurance due to health reasons.

Index

I–J–K

L

Check Out These
Best-Selling
COMPLETE IDIOT'S GUIDES®

Understanding Catholicism — SECOND EDITION
Bob O'Gorman, Ph.D. and Mary Faulkner, M.A.
1-59257-085-2
$18.95

Learning Spanish — THIRD EDITION
Gail Stein
0-02-864451-4
$18.95

The Bible — SECOND EDITION
James S. Bell Jr. and Stan Campbell
0-02-864382-8
$18.95

Being a Groom — SECOND EDITION
Jennifer Lata Rung and Mark Rung
0-02-864456-5
$9.95

Grammar and Style — SECOND EDITION
Laurie E. Rozakis, Ph.D.
1-59257-115-8
$16.95

Playing the Guitar — SECOND EDITION
Frederick Noad
0-02-864244-9
$21.95 w/CD

Personal Finance in Your 20s & 30s — SECOND EDITION
Sarah Young Fisher and Susan Shelly
0-02-864374-7
$19.95

Knitting and Crocheting — SECOND EDITION — Illustrated
Barbara Breiter and Gail Diven
1-59257-089-5
$16.95

The Perfect Resume — THIRD EDITION
Susan Ireland
0-02-864440-9
$14.95

Buying and Selling a Home — FOURTH EDITION
Shelley O'Hara and Nancy D. Lewis
1-59257-120-4
$18.95

Low-Carb Meals
Lucy Beale and Sandy G. Couvillon, M.S., L.D.N., R.D.
1-59257-180-8
$18.95

Calculus
W. Michael Kelley
0-02-864365-8
$18.95

More than *450 titles* in *30 different categories*
Available at booksellers everywhere

ALPHA